Individualist Feminism of the Nineteenth Century

To Queen Silver, who taught me to respect
feminism of all stripes, individualist or socialist

Individualist Feminism of the Nineteenth Century

Collected Writings and Biographical Profiles

by
WENDY MCELROY

McFarland & Company, Inc., Publishers
Jefferson, North Carolina, and London

ALSO BY WENDY MCELROY

Sexual Correctness: The Gender-Feminist Attack on Women
(McFarland, 1996)

EDITED BY CARL WATNER *WITH* WENDY MCELROY

*Dissenting Electorate: Those Who Refuse to Vote
and the Legitimacy of Their Opposition*
(McFarland, 2001)

Library of Congress Cataloguing-in-Publication Data

McElroy, Wendy.
    Individualist feminism of the nineteenth century :
collected writings and biographical profiles / by
Wendy McElroy.
        p.   cm.
    Includes index.
    ISBN 0-7864-0775-1 (softcover : 50# alkaline paper) ∞
    1. Feminists—United States—Biography.   2. Male
feminists—United States—Biography.   3. Feminism—
United States.   4. Individualism—United States.   I. Title.
HQ1412.M26   2001
305.42—dc21   00-67619

British Library cataloguing data are available

Manufactured in the United States of America

*McFarland & Company, Inc., Publishers
    Box 611, Jefferson, North Carolina 28640
    www.mcfarlandpub.com*

Acknowledgments

There are many people whose influence upon me over the years enabled this book to appear. Murray N. Rothbard's work *Man, Economy, and State* converted me to anarchism, and it was from Murray that I first heard of nineteenth-century radical individualism. Ken Gregg once casually suggested that I index Benjamin Tucker's *Liberty*—which I did, thus beginning my fascination with the early radical periodicals. The Center for Libertarian Studies provided the grant that enabled the index. In particular, I am indebted for the grant to the generosity of Joseph Peden. I thank Michael Coughlin for originally publishing the index. I thank Alan Koontz at the Internet site "The Memory Hole" for republishing it and other material from the nineteenth-century individualist anarchist periodicals.

Several prominent individualist feminists have shaped my own thoughts on the tradition, either through their work or through personal contact. Joan Kennedy Taylor is paramount among them, not only through her book *Reclaiming the Mainstream* but also through her activism with the Association of Libertarian Feminists. In several books, Ellen Frankel Paul, a professor at Bowling Green State University, has provided a brilliant economic analysis of various feminist issues: I use them as touchstones. Andrea Millen Rich of Laissez Faire Books has given unstinting support, not only to me, but also to other individualist feminists.

Carl Watner of *The Voluntaryist* provided me with the microfilm run of *The Word* that I used in researching this book. John Zube not only provided a microfiche set of *Liberty*, he is also responsible for preserving that periodical and many other political classics for posterity. For the microfilm-microfiche reader itself, I am indebted to Prof. Jack High.

I have drawn upon too many sources in researching radical individualism to credit them all. But I cannot neglect to mention the invaluable work of James J. Martin, who rescued an entire tradition from the dustbin. The title of his book, *Men Against the State*, may seem to fly in the face of feminism, but he established the framework for *all* subsequent research into radical individualism, including my own.

As a last word, I am indebted to my husband, Bradford Rodriguez, for considering my passion to stare at old newspapers on microfilm to be an endearing eccentricity.

Contents

Acknowledgments   v

Introduction   1

Section I: *The Word: A Monthly Journal of Reform* (1872–1890, 1892–1893)

1. Agela Fiducia Tilton Heywood: In the Shadow of a Man   19
2. Women of *The Word*: A Biographical Dictionary of the
   Day-to-Day Radicals   48

Section II: *Lucifer, the Light Bearer* (1883–1907)

3. Moses Harman: The Paradigm of a Male Feminist   89
4. Edwin Cox Walker and Lillian Harman:
   A Feminist Couple   125

Section III: *Liberty: Not the Daughter But the Mother of Order* (1881–1908)

5. Sarah Elizabeth Holmes: The Study of a
   Silenced Woman   135
6. Gertrude B. Kelly: A Disillusioned Woman   164

Notes   191
Select Bibliography   199
Index   201

Introduction

Contemporary feminism in the United States has forgotten its roots and has taken what I believe to be a disastrous turn away from the true interest of women: namely, absolute equality under just law, without privileges or sanctions based on gender. The vision of such an equality is to be found in the rich and distinctly American tradition of individualist feminism which flourished in the nineteenth century.[1]

Individualist feminism is based on natural law theory and on the derivative belief that all human beings are sovereign, or self-owners. That is, every human being has a jurisdiction over his or her own body which no other human being can rightfully violate. Individualist feminism demands equal respect for the natural rights of *all* individuals. In short, the law should neither grant privileges nor impose restrictions that are based on a secondary characteristic such as race, gender, or religion. The law should treat everyone equally on the basis of their primary characteristic: their humanity.[2]

Throughout most of American history, the government has denied equality to women by relegating them to second-class status under the law. For example, entry into various professions was restricted, married women routinely lost the right to their own property including wages, and women were denied access to knowledge about their own bodies (birth control information).

Because the legal oppression of women was based on gender, it became necessary for women to organize along gender lines to demand the rights being denied to them as a sex. These organizing efforts evolved into a feminist movement, which found expression within various preexisting traditions, including individualism. Individualist feminism advocated equal treatment of all human beings under natural law. As a movement, it demanded that the law be blind to the secondary characteristic of sex and treat women according to their primary characteristic of being human, on the same level as men. Thus, in a letter (1837), the individualist feminist Angelina Grimke wrote, "... I recognize no

1

rights but *human* rights—I know nothing of men's rights and women's rights."[3]

In the last few decades, the greatest threat to genuine equality between the sexes has not come from legal restrictions imposed upon women but from legal privileges granted to women based upon gender. Examples of these legal privileges include affirmative action or sexual harassment laws. For any class of people to seek or to accept legal privileges is unjust, because the privileges must come at the expense of another class. Granting privileges to women not only damages men, it also damages women who depend upon the paternalistic protection of the government rather than upon their own efforts.[4]

Thus, the ultimate goal of individualist feminism is a society that reflects equal respect for the natural rights of all individuals, male or female. The greatest enemy is government, which has historically legislated privileges or restrictions based on gender. Indeed, without the vehicle of government and law, men could not have oppressed women historically except on an individual basis.

The Foundation of Natural Law

What is "natural law?" The simplest of the two words to define is "law," which is not used in a legal sense. It is not a synonym for legislation. Rather the word "law" refers to a principle, or a governing rule, much as one might speak of the laws of physics, or of the law of gravity.

The meaning of the word "natural" is a more complicated matter, and it has occasioned a great deal of debate within the natural law tradition itself. One school of natural law views the concepts of right and wrong as types of fact: That is, this school claims that certain actions are objectively right while other actions are objectively wrong. Individualist feminism tends to use a much more flexible interpretation of natural law, arguing that human values should be grounded in or based upon fact, and that the concepts of right or wrong should be discovered through a process of reasoning. It examines human nature and human interaction in order to evolve a reasonable concept of right and wrong.

According to this interpretation, natural law is nothing more than an attempt to ground human values in the facts of reality and in human nature. It asks the question: Given what we know about reality and what we know about human nature, is it possible to reason out a universal code of behavior to maximize the happiness and safety of human beings?

The answer offered by many individualist traditions, including individualist feminism, is the concept of "natural rights." The idea of rights as an answer to a question, or as a problem-solving device, was proposed by the nineteenth-century individualist Benjamin R. Tucker. Tucker believed that all ideas arose and persisted within society because they served a need, they answered a question.[5]

Tucker used this problem-solving approach in analyzing the concept of property. He asked, "What is it about the nature of reality and the nature of human beings which gives rise to the concept of property in the first place?" He concluded that property arose as a means of solving conflicts caused by scarcity. In our universe, almost all goods are scarce, and this leads to an inevitable competition or conflict among human beings for their use. Since the same chair could not be used in the same manner at the same time by two individuals, it was necessary to determine who should use the chair. The concept of property resolved this social problem. The owner of the chair should determine its use. "If it were possible," wrote Tucker, "and if it had always been possible, for an unlimited number of individuals to use to an unlimited extent and in an unlimited number of places the same concrete thing at the same time, there would never have been any such thing as the institution of property."[6]

Individualist feminism derived its concept of rights in a similar manner. When analyzing the issue of slavery (circa 1830), abolitionist feminists considered another scarce resource—the bodies and labor of human beings. The catalyst for their question was the institution of slavery. They asked, "who has the rightful use of the scarce resource of black labor?" They answered, "A human being's labor and actions must belong to the man or woman who *is* that human being." With the concept of self-ownership, abolitionist feminists attacked slavery in America. They used it to address the problem of women's inequality as well.

What Is Feminism?

Consider the statement: Women are, and should be treated as, the equals of men.

For many, the foregoing sentiment constitutes the core of feminist theory and policy. But feminism is not a monolith, and agreement tends to disintegrate quickly. There is substantial disagreement within feminism over the proper meaning of the term "equality." Does it mean equality under existing laws? Or, equality under laws that express more justice than the existing ones? Does it mean an economic equality that requires the government to rearrange economic relationships to ensure a system of distributive justice? Or is it captured by cultural equality—a society in which women are, by law, accorded the same social status and respect that men enjoy, and not merely the same legal status?

Throughout most of the nineteenth century, the mainstream of American feminism defined "equality" as equal treatment with men under existing laws, and equal representation within existing institutions. For example, the cry of the National American Woman's Suffrage Association—which became the League of Women Voters after the passage of the Nineteenth Amendment—was not one of revolution; it was a cry for reform. These women wanted to be included in the existing political process through which the State was constituted. As such, the mainstream of nineteenth-century American feminism aimed at reform, not revolution.[7]

The more radical feminists of the day disagreed. They argued that the existing laws and institutions—in short, the political system itself—were the source of injustice toward women. The system was inherently corrupt and, as such, could not be reformed. The political structure needed to be entirely replaced before women's rights could be secured. In her book *Anarchist Women*, the historian Margaret S. Marsh writes of the more radical feminists, who fell outside the mainstream framework: "They believed that if women truly intended to be equal, their first step must be a declaration of economic, psychological, and sexual independence from men and from male-dominated institutions, beginning with marriage."[8]

In simplistic terms, the two voices of this more revolutionary feminism were socialist feminism, from which contemporary radical feminism draws heavily, and individualist feminism, which is sometimes called libertarian feminism. These two traditions establish the extreme ideological boundaries of feminism. In many ways, the traditions are ideological mirror images of each other.

Ideological Differences

One of the key ideological differences between socialist and individualist feminism resides in the concept of "class." A class is nothing more than an arbitrary grouping of people who share a common characteristic, and the characteristic chosen depends entirely upon the purposes of the person defining the class. For example, a researcher studying drug addiction may break society into classes of drug-using and non–drug-using people. Classes can be defined by almost any characteristic, such as income, hair color, age, nationality, or sexual habits. Again, this depends entirely on the purpose of the definer.

To radical feminists today, gender is the characteristic that defines a class. Society and the political structure are broken down into two basic classes of people—men and women. Men share not only a similar biology, but also political interests which are maintained through the institution of patriarchy: That is, they are maintained through white male culture and male economics, or capitalism. The interests of men are necessarily in conflict with the interests of women. The pioneering gender theorist Adrienne Rich defined patriarchy in her book *Of Woman Born*: "... the power of the fathers: a familial—social, ideological, political system in which men—by force, direct pressure or through ritual, tradition, law, language, customs, etiquette, education, and the division of labor ... in which the female is everywhere subsumed under the male."[9]

Viewed through this political lens, maleness ceases to be a biological trait and becomes a cultural or ideological one. Men not only share a biological identity, they also share specific political interests that are based upon their male identity. The foremost interest of men is to keep women, as a class, under their control. Thus, the concept of gender as a class becomes a causative factor in society: It predicts and determines how men will behave toward women.

To free women, it is necessary to destroy maleness itself. In *Toward a Feminist Theory of the State*, Catharine MacKinnon insists, "Male is a social and political concept, not a biological attribute."[10] In *Our Blood*, Andrea Dworkin states, "In order to stop ... systematic abuses against us, we must destroy these very definitions of masculinity and femininity, of men and women...."[11]

To individualist feminism, class has no necessary connection to gender. The political characteristic that determines the class to which an individual belongs is *his or her* relationship to the use of force in society. There are two basic classes: (1) the criminal or political class that uses force, including legislation, to acquire wealth and power; and (2) the economic class that acquires wealth and power through voluntary exchange. The political class is at war with the economic class, upon which it preys. But each class can and does contain both men and women, and individuals change their class affiliations at will.[12]

To restate this point: Individualist feminists define class in terms of an individual's relationship to the institution of State power (or other use of force). An individual is either one of the rulers or one of the ruled. Both classes contain both men and women who can cross class lines by altering their behavior.

This last point is key. In the radical feminist view, one's class affiliation is static because it is based on gender: A person is born into a class and stays there. In the individualist feminist view, class is fluid: Men and women can and do change their class affiliation constantly and by choice. Thus, for individualist feminists, there is no *necessary* conflict between

men and women. This one factor alone may explain why the individualist tradition and history contains as many prominent male figures as female
ones, and why gender attacks on men tend to be rare within it. When an
individualist feminist says "Women are, and should be treated as, the
equals of men," there is a recognition of the logical corollary, "Men are,
and should be treated as, the equals of women."

Predictably, the two traditions also define "equality" in differing ways.
To socialist feminists, equality is a socioeconomic term. Women can be
the equals of men only after patriarchy—a combination of capitalism,
white male culture, and the family structure—is eliminated. By contrast,
to individualist feminists equality refers to equal treatment under laws
that protect natural rights. When such laws are applied impartially to both
men and women, equality has been achieved. Individualist feminism
makes no reference to women being economically or socially equal, only
to equal treatment under just laws.[13]

The differing approach to equality involves another profound ideological difference: It is contained in the question, "what constitutes justice?" Since radical feminism advocates socioeconomic equality, its
approach to justice is ends-oriented. That is, it defines justice in terms of
a specific social condition. Radical feminism provides a detailed blueprint
of what social and economic arrangements constitute a just society. A just
society is one without white male culture or capitalism, in which women
are the political, legal, economic, and cultural equals of men. In other
words, justice is an end state. Justice is the point at which society embod-
ies certain explicit economic, political and cultural arrangements. When
women arrive at this end state, they can say, "We are there, this is just."

By contrast, individualist feminism insists only upon equal treatment
for women under laws that protect the freely chosen actions of individuals. As it is impossible to predict the economic or cultural choices people
will make, it is not possible to define justice as a particular end state.
Thus, the individualist feminist concept of justice is means-oriented: That
is, justice refers to a method of social functioning, not to a specific social
end state. Whatever results from the voluntary interactions of everyone
involved is by definition politically just, because justice refers to the
process by which an end state is achieved.

Another question immediately arises: What if one does not personally approve of a social arrangement, even though it is voluntary? For
example, what if a privately funded medical college refuses to admit
women? The solution for radical feminists is clear: They can use the force
of law to institute their version of justice. Within the context of radical
feminist ideology, using the force of law makes sense. After all, the ideal

of socioeconomic justice *can* be established through legislation. A specific economic arrangement can be imposed upon society, albeit at a huge cost to personal freedom. But the individualist feminist ideal of a voluntary society cannot be created by force. Choice cannot be nurtured at the point of a gun. Indeed, the only role force plays in a voluntary society is defensive: Force can be used to defend the peaceful choices of individuals, including the right to discriminate.

When confronted with voluntary situations that are immoral—assuming here that discrimination is immoral—individualist feminists cannot find recourse through the law. If they wish to change the situation, they must fall back on the persuasive strategies that have been used successfully by reform movements for centuries, e.g., education, protest, picketing, boycott, noncooperation, moral suasion.

In short, radical and individualist feminists disagree on the proper role of law in society. Radical feminists advocate using the force of law to impose a standard of proper behavior on voluntary exchanges—that is, to impose a politically/sexually correct form of virtue. Individualist feminists believe that the only proper function of law is to protect the voluntary nature of the exchange—that is, to prevent violence. Virtue must be left to the conscience of the consenting individuals involved.

The individualist feminist rejection of law as a means to impose virtue did not spring from indifference to social problems. Consider the nineteenth-century individualist feminist Dr. Gertrude B. Kelly. Kelly worked as a medical doctor with women in New Jersey tenement houses who had been forced into prostitution by poverty. As a result, she became a determined labor activist, demanding the elimination of legal barriers that shackled women from competing in the workplace. Kelly spent her entire life working to remedy the social evils created by poverty, yet she remained firmly committed to the political principle of individual choice.

Thus, when individualist feminists joined the nineteenth-century social purity campaigns, e.g., temperance, they did not advocate enforcing purity through legislation. Instead, they used voluntary measures, such as persuading people toward abstinence and circulating public oaths to that effect. The demand for voluntary participation was not merely an ideological stand, but also a pragmatic one. The writings of early individualist feminists reflect the belief that wrong choices cannot be legislated out of existence. As with the use of drugs in the present society, the abuse of alcohol in the nineteenth century could be countered only by changing the hearts and minds of people who made the choice to abuse substances. Laws that attempted to impose virtue only made a bad situation worse.

The Lost Women

To the extent that nineteenth-century individualist feminists have received attention, they have generally been miscategorized. In *Anarchist Women*, Marsh makes what I believe to be an error in analyzing the "anarchist feminists." She writes: "Anarchist-feminism, an ideology created and elaborated during the last third of the nineteenth century, developed directly from the cornerstone of anarchist philosophy: the primacy of complete personal liberty over all else. Although the factions within the movement disputed endlessly and vehemently about the proper methods for attaining such freedom, they all agreed on its fundamental importance."[14]

Even if it is true that anarchist feminists agreed on the "primacy of personal liberty," that statement is no more enlightening than the previous definition of feminism as "men and women should be equal." Just as different traditions of feminism define equality in contradictory manners, so too do they approach the concept of "personal liberty."

The confusion is understandable. Without a clear sense of the ideology of individualist feminism, it is easy to view figures within this tradition as being inconsistent socialists.[15] Again, consider Dr. Gertrude B. Kelly. As well as being a medical doctor who worked with tenement women, she was Secretary of the Newark Liberal League and a frequent contributor to anarchist periodicals, including the prominent *Liberty*. As an Irish immigrant who had been involved in the Irish No Rent movement, Kelly brought from Ireland a hatred of rent, interest, or "landlordism" in the language of her time. She also railed against capitalism and capitalistic practices, e.g., government-issued currency, all of which were considered to be "usury."

In an article on the subject of prostitution published by *Liberty*, Kelly expressed two themes which were common to her analysis of poverty and of women. First, Kelly argued that women had been oppressed by the cultural stereotypes dominating society. Second, she contended that charity organizations and "the rich" were hypocritical in their attitudes and behavior toward the poor.[16] She particularly ridiculed the philanthropic groups popular in her day in which working "… girls are given lessons in embroidery, art, science, etc., and are incidentally told of the evils of trade-unions, the immorality of strikes, and of the necessity of being 'satisfied with the condition to which it has pleased God to call them.'"

The foregoing sounds like the words of an intelligent and politically sensitive socialist feminist. But consider another article by Kelly entitled "State Aid to Science," which is a transcript of a speech that Dr. Kelly delivered to the New York Women's Medical College.[17] There, she argued against the College soliciting or accepting any government funds. Again, she addressed two themes. In Kelly's own words, "first, that progress in science is lessened, and ultimately destroyed, by state interference; and, secondly, that even if, through state aid, progress in science could be promoted, the promotion would be at too great an expense of the best interests of the race."

Kelly claimed it was impossible for government to promote knowledge: "It seems to be generally forgotten by those who favor state aid to science that aid so given is not and cannot be aid to Science, but to particular doctrines or dogmas, and that, where this aid is given, it requires almost a revolution to introduce a new idea." She claimed that an arrangement of government patronage creates "a great many big idle queens at the expense of the workers." In other words, Kelly argued *against* what is considered to be a standard nineteenth- and twentieth-century feminist position—namely, that government should use subsidies or law to open the doors of professions that were otherwise closed to women.

In the presence of both articles, how would a researcher evaluate Kelly? Into what established category of feminism would she be placed? And, when Kelly did not fit neatly into an established category, would the adequacy of the categories be questioned, or would Kelly's second article be dismissed as an odd inconsistency?

The fact is that both articles are consistent with each other and with nineteenth-century individualist feminism. Like most individualists of her day, Kelly viewed capitalism as the major cause of poverty. Yet she rejected any governmental remedy to social problems, including economic ills. Although it may sound bizarre to modern ears, Kelly considered the free market to be the natural remedy for capitalism.

To understand Kelly's position, it is necessary to appreciate the nineteenth-century definition of capitalism within the individualist movement. Kelly considered capitalism to be an alliance between business and government in which the latter guaranteed special privileges to the former through the vehicle of law. To break this alliance, it was necessary to break the power of government for, in Kelly's words, "... all the laws have no other object than to perpetrate injustice, to support at any price the monopolists in their plunder."[18]

Capitalism and government laws were to be fought vigorously, but with peaceful means, for, as Kelly wrote, "You cannot shoot down or blow up an economic system, but you can destroy it by ceasing to support it, as soon as you understand where its evils lie."[19] Some of the specific evils she sought to destroy were restricted bargaining, protectionist tariffs, and government created monopolies (e.g., currency). The solutions offered were free banking, free trade, and open competition—in short, the free market.[20]

The radical individualist movement of the nineteenth-century, of which individualist feminism was a subset, repeatedly advocated the free market and the abolition of government privilege as the means to destroy capitalism. The nineteenth-century anarchist periodical *Lucifer, the Light Bearer* (1883–1907), which was also the main vehicle for individualist feminism, answered the question of whether it advocated socialism with the words, "We have never advocated the abolition of private property."[21]

The prominent free love and free labor periodical, *The Word* (1872–1890, 1892–1893) served as a voice for the New England Labor Reform League.[22] The purpose of the League was described as follows: "Free contracts, free money, free markets, free transit, and free land—by discussion, petition, remonstrance, and the ballot, to establish these articles of faith as a common need, and a common right, we avail ourselves of the advantages of associate effort...."[23]

Without the category of individualist feminism, it is difficult or impossible to make sense of a woman such as Kelly. This difficulty may partially explain why such women are generally excluded from standard feminist histories such as the three-volume biographical dictionary, *Notable American Women*, issued by Harvard University Press. Indeed, most of the women discussed in this book do not appear in that dictionary.

To appreciate the context of individualist feminist women, it is necessary to understand that individualist feminism is not merely a contrarian position on issues such as affirmative action. It is a comprehensive, integrated system of beliefs concerning women's relationship to society. It has a deep rich history that significantly impacted the status of women in the nineteenth century. It embraces a large body of literature—novels, political tracts, poetry, diaries, speeches—and it involves a distinctive historical interpretation of events such as the Industrial Revolution.

The richness of this tradition is not surprising when you realize that the roots of American feminism were profoundly individualistic.

Synopsis of Nineteenth-Century Individualist Feminist History

As an organized and self-conscious movement, American feminism arose during the 1830s.[24] Although courageous figures advanced the status of women prior to this period—women such as Anne Hutchinson and Francis Wright—they spoke out as individuals rather than as members of a self-conscious organization dedicated to women's rights.

As mentioned previously, American feminism grew from the ranks of abolitionism—a movement that demanded the immediate cessation of slavery on the grounds that every human being is a self-owner. Moreover, many abolitionists were Quakers, with a tradition of female ministry that led the women abolitionists to speak out. Inevitably, these women asked: "Is it only black male slaves who are self-owners? Do not we own ourselves as well?"

Gradually, abolitionist women began to apply the principle of self-ownership to themselves. The historian, Aileen S. Kraditor, wrote in her book, *Up from the Pedestal*: "A few women in the abolitionist movement in the 1830s ... found their religiously inspired work for the slave impeded by prejudices against public activity by women. They and many others began to ponder the parallels between women's status and the Negro's status, and to notice that white men usually applied the principles of natural rights and the ideology of individualism only to themselves."[25]

This was the birth of American feminism, and it was individualistic in content. Individualist feminism was expressed largely through lectures, pamphlets, and articles which appeared in periodicals, especially *The Liberator* (Boston, 1831–1865).[26] Soon, another tradition provided a vehicle for individualistic women: transcendentalism, which is most often associated with Ralph Waldo Emerson and Henry David Thoreau. This philosophy was rooted in natural law and a belief in the perfectibility of human beings.

The Civil War (1861–1865) led most feminists to put aside their own concerns in order to work for the war effort. Afterwards, the majority of feminists joined a mainstream campaign to embed the rights of women in the U.S. Constitution (the Fourteenth and Fifteenth Amendments). Their efforts failed, due to a lack of support from men. Women felt betrayed. In the *History of Woman Suffrage*, Susan B. Anthony wrote, "We repudiated man's counsels forever." Perhaps this was the beginning of the emotional backlash against men which some believe characterizes contemporary feminism. Thereafter, the drive for women's suffrage began to dominate feminism.

As an ideological voice, individualist feminism tended to find expression in radical periodicals, especially those that championed free love, free thought, and individualist anarchism. Of these three movements, free love was the most important vehicle for feminism. In his book, *The Sex Radicals*, the historian Hal D. Sears observed, "'The doctrine of free love,' wrote an early-twentieth-century family sociologist, 'was bound to develop as an ethical counterpart of laissez-faire economics; both are anarchism; both were stimulated by the spacious freedom of the new world.'"[27]

Free love declared all sexual matters to be the province of the adult individuals involved, not of government. Free lovers advocated marriage reforms that ensured women's equality and free access to birth control information. As a movement, freethought insisted on the separation of church and state, leaving all spiritual matters to the conscience of individuals.[28] Individualist anarchism argued for a voluntary society, which was called "society by contract."

Three periodicals in particular expressed the theory and voices of individualist feminism. The most important free love periodical was *Lucifer, the Light Bearer*, edited by Moses Harman.[29] The anarchistic *The Word*, subtitled *A Monthly Journal of Reform* and edited by Ezra Heywood, began as a labor paper but soon focused more on free-love issues such as birth control. The prime individualist anarchist periodical *Liberty*, subtitled *Not the Daughter But the Mother of Order* and edited by Benjamin R. Tucker, provided another forum for women. Its contributors were a virtual honor list of individualist feminists: Gertrude Kelly, Bertha Marvin, Lillian Harman, Clara Dixon Davidson, Ellen Battelle Dietrick, Kate Field, Emma Schumm, Juliet Severance, Charlotte Perkins Stetson, Josephine Tilton, Helen Tufts, and Lois Waisbrooker.

This book offers a glimpse into the rich history of nineteenth-century individualist feminism by presenting commentary on and reprints from such feminists—both male and female—who published within these three periodicals.

Synopsis of Contents

The individualist feminists in this book were selected to provide a representative overview of the nineteenth-century tradition in America as it was expressed through *The Word*, *Lucifer, the Light Bearer*, and *Liberty*. Each chapter offers a prototype.

Chapter One

Angela Fiducia Tilton Heywood: In the Shadow of a Man.

Angela Heywood was a tireless and prominent activist for women's rights and labor reform, but history has permitted her to linger as a footnote to her husband and partner in radicalism, Ezra H. Heywood. Ezra and his contribution to American radicalism have been subjects of recent interest to scholars, and deservedly so. Angela's voice was more radical and consistent on women's issues, but Ezra's persecution under the Comstock law for circulating birth control information has given him enduring prominence. The persecution of Ezra Heywood galvanized the radical community.[30] Meanwhile, Angela performed the essential task of holding together the various radical organizations that the two of them had created under the umbrella of *The Word*.

"In the Shadow of a Man" presents a biographical sketch of this remarkable woman and offers reprints of some of her articles, which are a strange blend of flowery and sexually graphic language.

Chapter Two

Women of *The Word*: A Biographical Dictionary of the Day-to-Day Radicals.

It is a well-known phenomenon: Women are responsible for the daily operation of ideologies and movements—from planning church potlucks to handling the phones for radical civil liberties organizations. Men commonly assume the center stage, while women perform the less-visible tasks, without which the organizations could not function. This phenomenon was even more pronounced in the nineteenth century than it is today, when women enjoy far greater equality.

"The Day-to-Day Radicals" is a biographical dictionary of the women who worked in the background of *The Word* and of the organizations that surrounded it. For many of these women, even those significant in their own day, the biographical dictionary is the first visibility they have received since their names originally appeared in *The Word*.

Chapter Three

Moses Harman: The Paradigm of a Male Feminist.

Giving a voice to silenced women is a commendable goal of modern feminism. It has an unfortunate consequence, however. Contemporary feminism tends to ignore or downplay the role of men who have made substantial contributions to the freedom and dignity of women—men such as Moses Harman. In her autobiography, *Living My Life*, Emma Goldman credited Harman with pioneering the public discussion of sexual issues that allowed her and Margaret Sanger to advance birth control decades later. The absence from feminist history of such vigorous champions as Harman impoverishes it.

"The Paradigm of a Male Feminist" provides a biographical sketch of Moses Harman along with reprints from *Lucifer, the Light Bearer* in order to provide a sense of his philosophy and the extent of his activism. It is a glimpse into the invaluable contributions that many men have unselfishly made to feminism.

Chapter Four

Edwin Cox Walker and Lillian Harman: A Feminist Couple.

In the nineteenth century, women relinquished many, if not most, of their rights upon marriage. For example, married women often lost the right to their own earnings, the custody of their own children, and it was de facto impossible to convict a man of raping his wife no matter how brutally he had acted. In this atmosphere, several couples came forth to oppose the legal oppression of women within marriage. Usually their challenge to the system revolved around a refusal to seek church or state sanction for their sexual union. Instead, the couples signed purely private contracts that acknowledged the full equality of both partners within the union. The impact of these "free marriages" and of the persecution endured by couples who entered them has not been adequately explored by feminist scholarship.

"A Feminist Couple" briefly sketches the non-State, non-church marriage of Edwin Cox Walker and Lillian Harman, as well as their resulting imprisonment.

Chapter Five

Sarah Elizabeth Holmes: The Study of a Silenced Women.

For every woman such as Gertrude Kelly with a will strong enough to court public controversy, there were numerous others who shied away from a contentious limelight. The men who shared their views and published in the same periodicals could have encouraged them. Too often, such men did precisely the opposite, and the discouraged women fell silent. One such woman was Sarah E. Holmes, who performed a valuable service as a publisher and translator of feminist and other radical works. Holmes strayed onto the center stage of *Liberty* with her own work only fleetingly, however. The core of her intellectual foray was an exchange with Victor Yarros, the associate editor of *Liberty*. It became a classic work within individualist anarchist and individualist feminist literature. The disrespect which Holmes was accorded, however, also signaled her departure as a contributor of original material to the periodical.

"The Study of a Silenced Woman" chronicles the unfortunate interaction between Holmes and *Liberty* that seemed to be what impelled her to return to a less-visible role. The chapter also reprints some of Holmes's original work.

Chapter Six

Gertrude B. Kelly: A Disillusioned Woman.

Unlike *The Word* or *Lucifer*, *Liberty* was not particularly respectful of women or "the woman question," as feminist issues were often labeled in the late nineteenth century. The men who formed the intellectual circle surrounding *Liberty* behaved toward their women counterparts, such as the brilliant Gertrude Kelly, in a manner that probably typified the behavior of most radical men of the day. The women were treated as nominal equals, but the men's air of courtesy often dissolved into condescension. Kelly is a good example of the price that periodicals such as *Liberty* paid for being unenlightened, if not boorish, toward its women contributors. They left its pages.

"A Disillusioned Woman" presents a biographical sketch of Gertrude B. Kelly which emphasizes her relationship with *Liberty*, as well as reprinting several articles by her from that periodical.

Since the purpose of this book is to make a neglected tradition within feminism more visible, my commentaries often defer to contemporary voices by offering their observations of people and events.

Section I

The Word: A Monthly Journal of Reform (1872–1890, 1892–1893)

Editor: Ezra H. Heywood

Prospectus:

"THE WORD favors the abolition of speculative income, of woman's slavery, and war government; regards all claims to property not founded on a labor title as morally void, and asserts the free use of land to be the inalienable privilege of every human being—on having the right to own or sell only his service impressed upon it. Not by restrictive methods, but through freedom and reciprocity, THE WORD seeks the extinction of interest, rent, dividends, and profit, except as they represent work done; the abolition of railway, telegraphic, banking, trades-union and other corporations charging more than actual cost for values furnished, and the repudiation of all so-called debts the principal whereof has been paid in the form of interest" (May 1872, p. 1).

Although THE WORD began as an organ to express the views of the American Labor Reform League and the New England Labor Reform League, the periodical soon began to focus more upon free love and feminist issues.

1

Angela Fiducia Tilton Heywood: In the Shadow of a Man

Like many women married to prominent men, Angela T. Heywood was an equal partner in life and love with her husband Ezra H. Heywood. Nevertheless, she has been virtually ignored even while her husband's profile in America's radical history has become more prominent through recent research. Yet, in her day, Angela was the subject of much attention and speculation. Many of those associated with the Heywoods' labor-reform and free-love periodical *The Word* (1872–1890, 1892–1893) considered Angela to be far more radical than Ezra.

Ezra Heywood became notorious for refusing to accept the restrictions that the Comstock law imposed on the circulation of sexual information, especially birth control information. His rebellion against censorship led to years of legal persecution and imprisonment, much of which sprang from the distribution of his pamphlet, *Cupid's Yokes*, in which he advocated placing sexual urges under the control of reason rather than "animalism." Perhaps no other work was as influential as *Cupid's Yokes* in opening nineteenth-century America to a discussion of free love and birth control.[1]

When Angela Heywood married Ezra in 1865, she became an equal partner in his work, but her contributions rarely received equal credit. For example, one of Ezra's best known works, *Uncivil Liberty*, was acknowledged to have been written with her "aid."[2] The extent of the aid rendered by Angela was never delineated or properly credited. She did seem to receive a full measure of blame, however, for the problems that beset *The Word*. For example, Angela was regularly blamed for the periodical's "plain-speech policy" by which sexual issues were bluntly discussed, e.g., the sexual organs were correctly identified without euphemism. The September 1892 issue of *The Word* reprinted a letter to Angela from reader Laura C. Eldridge who expressed a common sentiment:

… You foul mouthed, disgusting thing! You ought to be tied to a whip-
ping post until you promised to use decent language. Your demented old
idiot of a husband isn't half-so much to blame as you are; I think he
would be half decent if it wasn't for you…. Of course Heywood will go
to prison where he ought to go, only you ought to be there too—and put
in close confinement—where you couldn't contaminate the rest of the
felons with your dirty tongue. You nasty brute! You vilest *thing* in the
country!… Your children ought to be taken away from you and very likely
will be….[3]

Others deeply admired the "plain-speech policy" for which Angela
seemed responsible. Yet the policy made Angela the subject of much speculation. What other radical woman of the day insisted on publicly pro-
nouncing words such as "penis" from the podium, while privately
maintaining a personal life that was beyond reproach? She was a devoted
mother who advocated abstinence as a form of birth control. She was a
legally married woman who decried the intervention of clergy or magis-
trates into sexual relations and called marriage "the auction-block of primitive sale and slavery of woman to man…."[4] What other birth control
advocate lamented the fact that someone else (Ezra) was arrested by
Anthony Comstock when she so clearly deserved the honor more?

In pursuit of the paradox that was Angela, a contributor to the popular radical newspaper *Boston Investigator* did some journalistic investigation. Under the pen name "Tourist," he questioned the Heywoods'
neighbors in Princeton, Massachusetts, and reported back the words of
one of them:

"I don't know what to think of them," said an old Farmer, "they find fault
with everything; all society, law, government, and religion, are, in their
estimation, out of joint and in disorder." "Well, aside from their theories,
what do you think of their character as shown by their conduct? Do they
do wrong?" I asked. "No," said he, "so far as behavior goes they are jest as
good as anybody. Nobody round here ain't more obliging then they be.
They're no more free-lovers in their conduct than I am. I believe they are
as true to each other as any married couple in the world ever was."[5]

Not knowing what to think of Angela's policy of "unrestrained reference to sexual distinctions"—a policy of which he clearly disapproved—
the nosy journalist finally contented himself with denouncing her for not
accepting the expediency of respecting society's prudishness.

Angela bewildered even those who were familiar with the radical
politics and attitudes expressed by *The Word*. L.V.P.—probably Lucien V.
Pinney, editor of the *Winsted Press*—speculated at length about the osten-
sibly contradictory spirit of Angela:

Mrs. Heywood, the Woman of Princeton, is a mystery beyond my depth—but I claim no profound depth in the study of woman. I feel that a totally wrong idea of her prevails among those who have not the pleasure of her acquaintance. If anybody supposes that she is coarse or masculine he is mistaken. If anybody says that she is lewd or lascivious he lies. She is a power acknowledged here and consulted on all occasions, and the commotion of thought raised by *The Word* is as much due to her as to anybody. To leave her out of an account in this Princeton drama would be like leaving Joan of Arc out of the history of France, yet I can hope to do her only fragmentary justice in this brief space. She is light in complexion, fine in texture, joyous in disposition, 50 years old, and mother of four children, all living. While Mr. Heywood is methodical and moderate in his thought, arriving at his conclusions by the toil of intellect, she is quick and impulsive, arriving at her conclusions by the flash of intuition. She has vision, hears voices, and dreams, and she is at times a whirlwind of words, delivered with startling effect.[6] She is naturally musical and instinctively dramatic, loves the lights, colors and rhythmic sounds of the theatre, loves Art in action hanging draperies over stark Utility, but she is in nothing frivolous, and she dwells with rare fortitude in the "cellar basement" of experience—a hard working housewife, doing as an artist the work of a "scrub." She is volatile in expression and frets under the inexorable and necessary editorial condensation of Mr. Heywood which she rightly feels is fatal to flexible and melodious expression. He is the sententious writer of resolutions butchering her beautifies of song to expose the bare bones of an idea. She is a fine colloquist, a quick-witted and appreciative listener, brim full of good humor, a woman of tact and nice discrimination, and with strong moral self-reliance and courage combines tender solicitude for the wronged and oppressed. She has the same infatuation for the human race that leads her husband through the fires of persecution to ideal Liberty, but she has a more attractive and vivacious way of expression, and is as sunny and winsome in her various notions as he is solid and sedate. If anything is to be known of a woman by appearances she is the most loyal of wives and loving of mothers. Mr. Heywood's confidence in her is implicit, and the trustful reliance by which she holds her children to herself in close companionship (I speak of little Psyche and Angelo of whom I see most, Vesta and Hermes being at school in Providence) is evidence of her mother love.[7] She takes good care of her very large house and sometimes very large family (guests) and like many a labor reformer believes in eight hours and works sixteen.

"The situation" without Mrs. Heywood would be no situation at all or worse. She is the light, the life, and I am tempted to say the motive power of the establishment. She believes that Mr. Heywood is right, that with him she has a serious life work to perform and that she should do her full share of the labor cheerfully, suffering any sort of deprivation necessary to help him develop new ideals. Her intelligence, breadth and clearness of vision are shown in her leaflet literature, where on the difficult and intricate subject of sex she has said some of the best things that have yet appeared in print, without saying any of the worst. She is voluble but it is a volubility weighted with good thoughts on every subject. About her house with her children she is a laughing joyous girl; she is also a tender, sympathetic and compassionate woman; she delves in the earth with her hands and touches the skies with her thought; in impromptu expression she is amazing, in all things she is feminine, and the courage and fortitude she displays under the trying conditions of her life must win admiration from all who are acquainted with the facts....[8]

Let us ask the same question that occupied the attention of nineteenth-century radicals: Who is Angela?

Angela Fiducia Tilton Heywood was born in Deerfield, New Hampshire, to Daniel and Lucy Tilton.[9] The farm couple appropriately named their daughter Angela Fiducia—the "angel of fidelity." On her maternal side, she was descended from the bloodline of the English philosopher John Locke. On her paternal side, she traced her roots to the Scotish Thomsons, Shaws, and Crosses. At ten years of age, Angela was forced to leave home to earn a living by taking care of children and doing housework as a domestic. Eventually, she passed in and out of a variety of factory and sweat-shop jobs. The jobs she later listed as part of her life experience included dressmaker, barn cleaner, writer, cook, public library attendant, milking cows, convention organizer, and lecturer. Even while she was occupied by jobs that involved little manual labor, e.g., lecturing, Angela worked tirelessly at running the boarding houses that provided an income for her family. Without question, a lifetime of hard physical labor at low-paying employment led Angela to become an ardent advocate of labor reform for working girls.

She also became an early voice calling for women to be compensated for performing housework. A report of the New England Labor Reform League (NELRL) Convention held on May 25 and 26, 1873, stated, "Mrs. A. T. Heywood presented this: *Resolved*, That the labor of girls in housework is better performed than present compensation deserves it should be; if it is uneducated and unreliable, it is because it is underpaid and regarded as disreputable; when bread making and house cleaning are justly rewarded and honored as all true labor should be, and the idleness of so-called ladies is alone deemed vulgar, the vexed question of 'our help' will virtually be settled."[10]

Although Angela became deeply critical of traditional religion, this stance evolved through experience as well. At the age of eighteen, she had a religious experience that led her to join the church, where she taught Sunday School. During this period, she also attended lectures by such radical thinkers as William Lloyd Garrison, Wendell Phillips, and Ralph Waldo Emerson. Such teachers led her to question the political and religious world about her, but Angela maintained that her most valuable life lessons came from her association with common people, especially from women. She declared, "[W]ashers, stitchers, cooks, farmers, ditchers, hodcarriers were my immediate teachers ... I have been & am known & loved by many noble women, always counting two women among my intimate friends to one man knowing me."[11]

Angela inherited the tendency to trust common sense and common people from her mother, who considered book-learning to be virtually a waste of time when compared with the richness of experience. As Angela explained, "Mother Tilton admonished us children & others she taught ... never to defer to doctors, lawyers, clergymen but meet them simply as persons; never to bow lower or courtesy quicker to 'educated' than to unbookish people."[12]

Accordingly Angela did not defer to her more-prominent and better-educated husband on radical matters. In the early years of *The Word* and of the several reform organizations that revolved around the periodical, Ezra certainly took the more visible role.[13] For example, he often assumed leadership of the NELRL and was responsible for conducting meetings. This did not prevent Angela from standing up in the audience to call him publicly to task. For example, at one NELRL meeting in 1873, Ezra presented what he must have thought to be a safe resolution: "*Resolved*, That since the assumed right of men to govern wives, mothers and sisters without their consent is an odious relic of savage power, we favor the removal of the word 'male' from the voting lists and the immediate abolition of the financial and social subjection in which men now think it best to keep women."[14]

One can only imagine Ezra's surprise when—as the report of the meeting went on to state—"Mrs Heywood objected to her husband's shameful resolution on the woman question, because in its opening it made no reference to women who have no male relatives. Such women are at the mercy of their employers, if the employers know their circumstances. Has my husband, said Mrs. Heywood, any more right to be a rascal towards a friendless girl than he would like the supreme rascal that can be found to be toward our daughter? If a new system of government is to be formed, 'us girls' mustn't be left out."[15]

Little wonder that Angela was among those who met on December 1873 to form an American Woman's Emancipation Society.

One of Angela's first contributions of material to *The Word* was a letter on prostitution in which she upbraided the free love advocate Moses Hull, "the Editor of *Hull's Crucible* of Jan. 15." Hull had expressed the sentiment: "It would be better for that woman [a married woman who could not bear her husband's touch] if her husband could be prevailed upon to go to a regular prostitute for gratification rather than to so frequently require of her what her soul and body loathe."[16]

Again, Angela took extreme exception to a man's analysis of a woman's issue. She claimed that any woman who married a man whose touch she could not bear—or who stayed married to him after physical loathing had developed—had no business calling another woman a prostitute. Taking offense from Hull's remarks, Angela was not above making the attack on his position into a personal one. She asked, "Is Mr. Hull's sister, mother, wife, or daughter the regular prostitute to whom he refers, or is it some other less fortunate woman who he so coolly damns to the lecherous uses of his brother man?... Prostitute! The word is man-coined and man-preserved to fit the victims of a man-ordained and man-upheld *industrial servitude* which Mr. Hull has yet found no place, in his 'Crucible' to condemn."[17]

Angela was beginning to find her voice. Meanwhile, she continued in a role that was no less vital to the health and well-being of *The Word*. She was largely responsible for making the money upon which the family and the periodical depended. The *Cambridge Press* commented, "While in Princeton, the other day a large good-looking edifice was pointed out to us as a summer boarding house kept by Mr. E. H. Heywood, the somewhat famous labor reformer...." To his credit, Ezra corrected the newspaper, saying that the house was owned and run by Angela through which she earned "*our* board and clothes" (emphasis added).[18]

Angela worked literally from dawn 'til dusk to provide an income for the family, and she remained the emotional mortar that held it together throughout Ezra's long imprisonments. But she also assumed a new and more intellectually active role. With Ezra, she formed the Co-operative Publishing Company in order to issue Ezra's pamphlets along with other radical tracts. In the innovative manner typical of Angela, the Co-operative Publishing Company sought to turn a profit through the use of Lady Agents. These were saleswomen who toured New England, the Midwest, and as far north as Canada to visit factories or the other places where working people gathered. Once they had found their audience, the Lady Agents spoke on subjects such as labor reform and birth control, then offered their pamphlets for sale to the workingmen and women. Among the most prominent Lady Agents were Angela's sisters, J. Flora Tilton and Josephine Tilton.[19]

Although many articles in *The Word* were published without identifying the author, Angela's hand was clearly the one behind a series of letters on "Book Canvassing." These letters offered practical advice to the young Lady Agents who, in their travels, would encounter a great many males with lascivious intentions. One letter stressed that the women should study the books they were attempting to sell as a means of protecting themselves against male advances. Angela explained, "A man likes to play 'hide and seek' with a girl's thought and easily becomes 'personally interested to know her more intimately'; but you are to call his idle curiosity and rising heats to order, fix his attention by the serious sincerity of your manner... "[20]—in other words, talk on an intellectual rather than a personal level.

In dealing with how the two sexes interacted, Angela's letters to Lady Agents hinted at the arena in which she would find her true voice: the advocacy of free love.[21] In this arena, and especially with the inauguration of the New England Free Love League (NEFLL), Angela came to the forefront.

One attendee of a NEFLL meeting commented, "Our idea of order was better enforced by the well-chosen words and impressive appeals of Mrs. Angela T. Heywood, who is a coming teacher of wild boys and infuriated husbands in Free Love conventions."[22] *The Word* also announced that Angela was now co-lecturing with Ezra in several venues throughout Massachusetts. The subject was "Love and Marriage."[23] Subsequent reports made it clear that it was Angela, and not her husband, who most impressed the audiences. Her popularity might be partially ascribed to the novelty of a woman speaking out plainly about sexual issues. The novelty, or notoriety, might also explain some of the unruly mobs which greeted the lecturing couple.

At the same time, Angela began to receive more credit and attention for the material she contributed to *The Word*. The "credit" was not always positive in nature. For example, when Benjamin Tucker announced his departure from his role as co-editor of *The Word*, he explicitly blamed his disillusionment upon the periodical's new stress on free love. The shift was largely due to Angela's influence—a fact of which Tucker took explicit note.

Ezra felt impelled to defend his wife: "For this timely and beneficent issue [of *The Word*] the public is indebted, not to us, but to Angela T. Heywood. The part of her speech which raised a commotion in Boston last May was where she painted the processes by which, out of profits derived from the less-paid labor of women, a man acquires the money and the effrontery to offer five hundred dollars for the virginity of a girl. A.T.H.'s articles since printed in *The Word* ... have the same purpose— *the liberation of woman from the special financial thralldom* in which she is now held *by man*, and by which, as compared with man's wages, she is defrauded of fifty per cent of her rightful earnings...."[24]

Over and over again, Angela was elected as an officer of NEFLL, and her stance on woman's rights became increasingly more radical—or, perhaps, her views were merely more freely expressed than before. She wrote, "... Women are not bound to obey existing laws, for they have no voice in making them; these laws are only the registered opinions of men."[25] Meanwhile, Angela and Ezra began to hold classes in Socialism in Nassau Hall, Boston, under the auspices of the NEFLL.[26] In the wake of these classes, the Rev. Joseph Cook publicly described Angela as, "A brazen woman who stands up to call herself the wife of one man, and in leprous language with profanity before a mixed audience proclaims her perfect freedom to do as she pleases.... They [Angela and Ezra] do not comprehend how the deeper heart of the community is against them...."[27]

If the couple did not comprehend the extent of societal resistance to their ideas, enlightenment was soon in coming. On November 3, 1877, Ezra was arrested for sending *Cupid's Yokes* through the mail in violation of the Comstock law. The February 1878 issue of *The Word* described how, upon being sentenced, Ezra had sent for Angela and their children so that he could see them once more before being imprisoned under terms that included extremely limited visitation privileges.

In Ezra's absence, Angela continued to work on *The Word* and to serve as the acting manager of an upcoming NEFLL Convention. She herself did not escape harassment by the authorities, as was reported in *The Word*: "An officer of the law came in and forbid her taking fees at the door because she had not a license!... A.T.H. promptly refused to recognize the official terrorism as law, dismissed the convention and will assert the right of the people to assemble and her right to speak without a 'license' at an early day in Boston."[28]

A series of protest meetings in support of the incarcerated editor were held in Boston. From prison, Ezra wrote a report that gave the flavor of one such meeting, the details of which were most probably related to him by Angela. He wrote,

> Benj. R. Tucker, A. E. Giles, Esq., and Rev. Jesse H. Johnes greatly served Truth and Liberty by their presence and attitude in Comstock's Boston meeting, May 28th. Alluding to us [Ezra and Angela] as "a most infamous publisher who only awaits sentence," adding of A.T.H. "His wife is at the door with an insult on her lips and a curse for me as I entered," (which latter is false since Mrs. H. only looked at and designated him to a friend) he referred to Mr. Tucker as one present "who had followed him in many places and shown his scornful face as the cause had been argued" and pointed him out to excited Christians who shouted, "Where is he?" "Show him up"; whereupon Mr. Tucker rose, saying he "was not afraid or ashamed to be seen" and declared Comstock "a liar."[29]

Meanwhile, the imprisoned editor wrote fondly to Angela, "From June 5th 1865 to June 25th, last,—thirteen years and nineteen days,—we had lived together doing our chosen work, and rejoicing in the pledges of love given us...."[30]

Ezra may have been writing love letters to Angela from jail, but public opinion tended to be harsher in its attitude toward her. People blamed her—and the plain-speech policy she championed—for her husband's imprisonment.[31] In *The Word*, Ezra commented at length on the swelling backlash against his wife:

> Mr. Waite elsewhere gives one main "reason why" we got two years in Dedham Jail, viz: because "the woman in the case" [Angela] spoke plainly, in Boston, Worcester and elsewhere, on "the bodily relations of the sexes even in a state of nudity"; A.T.H. was fiercely assailed by court officers, religio-political magnates—and "cultured" exponents of propriety; quoted by Comstock before Congressional Committees, and in an affidavit letter to President Hayes,—all to show first that *we must be imprisoned* and afterwards that we MUST NOT *be released*, lest we might again hold Free Love Conventions in which "Mrs. Heywood" was the "provoking" but always popularly interesting and instructive speaker. She "still lives" and "The Classes in Socialism," which her telling addresses did much to make effective, self-supporting and honorably famous, have a future as well as a past....[32]

Criticism of her plain-speech policy seemed only to spur Angela on to more flowery and explicit language in her demand for woman's autonomy and for men's respect. Readers of *The Word* soon divided into two camps: those who praised Angela's graphic style and bravery; and, those who decried her frankness as a foolishness that jeopardized the cause of sexual freedom, as well as other important related issues such as labor reform. Since the debate was aired in a forum controlled by and sympathetic to the Heywoods—namely, *The Word*—the defenders of Angela were the loudest and most eloquent voices. One of them was J. H. Swain who believed that society's prudishness was a veil drawn across the sexual abuse of working girls at the hands of "respectable" men. He wrote:

> Mrs. Heywood ... has had an experience that probably not one of her critics know aught of. How the working girl is defrauded; how her honor is assailed; how she is tempted, and if she yields how her virtue is bought with that which is her rightful due, product of her toil.... Of the gentle men and women upstairs that her class served, some were ignorant, others indifferent,—to all it was distasteful, shocking to even think about such a subject....The working girl already overworked could do not more; she [Angela] must at least save them and the innocent children.... She would begin by stating the case: even this was no easy task.[33]

Another admirer, the anarchist Dyer D. Lum, was inspired to write a poem to immortalize the term that Angela used when she referred to marriage—that is, "The Penis Trust."

> To Angela President of the Penis Trust
>
> Of all the Trusts that men have framed
>   From yellow gold
>   To charld dust
>   Within the fold
>   Of legal "must,"
> There is no older can be named
> Than licensed Love—the Penis Trust.
>
> The rampant bull, salacious goat,
>   And rooting boar,
>   In passion's gust
>   Like many more,
>   Get rid of rust
> Without a Comstock taking note
> To curb their freedom in a Trust!
>
> They, like the farmer moving West
>   Their flagstaff raise:
>   "Pike's Peak or Bust!"
>   Then once more graze
>   Though Nancies cussed
> That they should think their own way best
> Than joining in a Diddling Trust!
>
> Though Comstock rave and Nancies wail
>   In legal lore
>   Is it more just
>   Behind the door
>   Than open lust?
> Tho' you thereby escape the jail,
> E'en if you're in a Penis Trust!
>
> Whate'eve Miss Nancy morals doubt,
>   'Tis Nature's freak,
>   And there's no "must"
>   To hide and seek,
>   Nor term it lust,
> Because some priest with shirt without
> Has failed to bless your Penis Trust![34]

Yet, as bluntly and persistently as Angela spoke out, it was Ezra who continued to bear the brunt of legal persecution.[35] In October 1882 he was again arrested on obscenity charges and taken to Boston where he was detained briefly. Then, he was released to await trial. Ezra persistently defended his wife whom he declared to be a victim of the Comstock law even though she was spared arrest. He wrote,

> ... Since she, from platform & in print, has proclaimed Woman's Natural Right, *in all respects to be mistress of her own person*, three men—Anthony Comstock, Samuel R. Heywood & Joseph Cook have virulently assailed A.T.H....[36] In singling her out for assault persecution is logical; for INSURGENT WOMAN is the rising power destined to put down sex-knowledge monopolists, male supremacy, imprudent obscenists. The trial to come one, after March 20th, brings Woman to the front; whatever is its result, I herald revolt against further effort to manipulate, legislate, church or court maul women into male subjection; citizens, people, persons, equals,—women....[37]

Others agreed: Angela was as much a target of the law as Ezra through whom Comstock sought to punish her. Regarding a subsequent arrest and imprisonment of the editor, the *Foote's Health Monthly* observed, "Sending Mr. Heywood to the penitentiary a few years was not a fair deal; but the real object was to punish indirectly Mrs. Heywood for a dreadful speech which she made in Boston, which the authorities had not the courage to deal directly with her for. So now it would appear that again the authorities have attempted to punish Mrs. Heywood who is really the guilty person, by arresting her husband."[38]

Not entirely sympathetic to what it called Angela's "nasty" tongue, *Foote's Health Monthly* had candidly observed in an earlier article, "If the Vice Society is disposed to proceed against Mrs. Heywood herself on the charge of insanity, and can make out a good case, perhaps they might succeed in putting her into the madhouse, but we would pity Comstock ... if she lived to get out."[39]

Such extreme and often contradictory reactions to Angela Heywood makes any biographer return again and again to the question posed near the beginning of this essay: Who was she?

Perhaps the most interesting portrait of Angela came from the pen of the individualist anarchist and fellow free-love advocate, Stephen Pearl Andrews. He wrote:

> Mr. & Mrs. Heywood are the occupants, under some embarrassments & encumbrance, of one called Mountain Home, which was in prosperous operation under their management, until its success was much disturbed by the scare of Mr. Heywood's repeated arrests; since the first of these its fortunes have varied. Their house has been confessedly a model institution. Mrs. Heywood is the model housekeeper and manager, even

among a group of women distinguished in the same way. They are about the most industrious couple I ever knew, laborious & devoted to the last degree. Unfortunately, however, for their worldly success, they have ideas, convictions and purposes outside the ordinary routine. They were both reared in the outspoken, audacious school of the radical Abolitionists; when they grew to have new views with regard to the sex question & the rearing of children, they carried their *Abolitionistic* boldness of speech into that subject....

To Andrews, Ezra would have been a familiar figure, not only personally but as a "type." He would have encountered Ezra's stern and prim New England nature at countless labor-reform and free-love meetings. Angela's nature was more unique. Andrews commented,

Mrs. Heywood is a far more difficult character to analyze [than Ezra] ... To some extent I think I do understand her.... This revolt against the literary and "cultured" classes was inherited by Mrs. Heywood and intensified and extended to other wrongs by her experience as a shop girl. Also deprived of the opportunity of a literary education adequate to the classic expression of the thoughts with which her observant and active brain was teeming, she was noted & marked as a distinctive and representative girl, well known in the old antislavery ranks, courted and sought for, for her bright, original, daring manifestations of genius, in certain aristocratic quarters, where, however, her whole soul revolted against the superciliousness and pretension of superiority by the rich and "cultured" over the skilled workers, who knew more, it might be, in a day, of real useful knowledge, than they would know in a life-time. Harassed, insulted, worried,—not so much on her own account as on behalf of the class she represents, her whole life settled down into a devoted championship, first of the skilled labor class as a whole; secondly, of the women, especially of that class; finally, & especially, of the working-girl. Being herself of that class, not of the grim order, but lively, jovial & entertaining, she could venture on saying what she thought with the most unconventional audacity; her bold denunciations of the snobbery around her only served to increase her attractiveness and power within the two circles of life which she served, in a manner, to connect. But she always identified herself absolutely with the working-girls, & refused to be accepted among the wealthy on any other terms. Under the circumstances of her life, with her quick observation & dead-in-earnestness of her character, notwithstanding the laugh on her lips, she could not fail to see that society was composed of two worlds, in another sense. She & others of her order were constantly approached & tempted or insulted by men of the so-called superior classes, whose private language and lives, as she came to know them, were utterly corrupt, but who were delicate and refined to the last degree in their public manifestations.... She found that this organized hypocrisy was as characteristic of the women of society as of the men. Her natural and inherited revolt against a pretended sanctity, propriety & culture on the part of the polished hypocrites, men and women, thus urged to its utmost, has culminated in her determination that folks shall hear openly talked about what in secret they dwell on as the staple of their lives; that the hypocrisy shall be exposed; that the inflated pretense of virtue which does not exist shall be punctured and collapsed. This at least seems to be part, but not the whole, of the *rationale* of Mrs. Heywood's peculiar use of the English language.

Andrews went on to say that her marriage to Ezra undoubtedly had confirmed her in a radical course, as had Comstock's dogged persecution of the couple. Andrews continued,

> She is ... utterly destitute of the sense of fear. She laughs and rollicks over what seems to the on-looker the edge of a fearful precipice. She would sooner see her beautiful home ruthlessly sacked, her children scattered, herself driven, as a drudge, into somebody's else [sic] kitchen, than she would back down an inch from her full claim to the right to say her full thought in her own words. Louise Michel is no more heroic than she is. She is vexed & annoyed to the last degree that it is Mr. H. who is attacked and not herself.... He and she are far more comrades in a common cause, where he annoys her by being in the front, than they are the ordinary husband & wife. She threatens that if he gets in prison this time, she will never so much as visit him there, as she will not have it understood that she is a mere wife, following the fate of her husband, instead of a free individual fighting her own battles. It is not all, however, that she courts or even believes in martyrdom, but simply that she is willing to take the consequences of her own acts. Folks must not mistake Mrs. Heywood for any weakling; womanly ladylike, prepossessing and eminently domestic, she is yet hard as a flint when her rights, or the rights of those whom she represents, are invaded.... She provides elegant parlor accommodations for her boarders, for the reformers, for other lady visitors, yet keeps herself secluded in the basement, doing more work than three ordinary women, and training her children in the most laborious, painstaking, housewifely artistic way. At the same time, her children excel all the children in town in learning, in demeanor, and in a certain reserved and distinguished bearing. They are welcome guests at all the neighboring houses, but seldom go. Mrs. Heywood herself is far less excluded from the society of the ladies of Princeton.... She is a riddle to them. They cite her beautiful household, her children at the head in the schools and public exhibitions, their deportment, the chasteness & elegance of their dress, &c; some of them have the logic to quote the old book, that "we do not gather grapes from thorns nor figs from thistles," and to conclude that Mrs. Heywood can be no other, after all, than a very good woman. Still she says such awful things; she is understood frankly and openly to teach her children all about those processes of nature which other parents conceal and religiously lie about.

Andrews concluded that Ezra was better liked by neighbors than Angela, with "... the people, especially the women, strongly inclining to lay all the blame on Mrs. H., against whom, notwithstanding the favorable points, there is as yet a strong current of condemnation...."[40]

* * * *

The following reprints of articles by Angela T. Heywood from *The Word* will allow readers to judge more accurately for themselves, "Who is Angela T. Heywood?"

"Woman's Love: Its Relations to Man and Society"

July 1876, p. 1

The most genial and natural garden is woman's womb; men realize its existence, but do not appreciate its value. It is the planting-ground of all human society, wherein Nature readjusts herself, in her most subtle deficiencies, unless coerced by the physical-force plan of men. Earth is abnormal to us; society begins with a he and she, with individual approach, with "How do you do?" That is, how do you behave? what is your power for excellence?...

We hear of "the man of the house," as though the woman was one of the children, the daughter of her husband. Men's philosophy has speculatively reckoned money a greater matter than human identity; made it the groundwork of foul play towards each other, of stealthy exchange greatly to the detriment of their soul and sense. How can men think straight, when they take things as they have arranged them to be the real facts of Nature?

The natural product of man's and woman's work is a child ... Baby's first lesson is to be social, have good manners, not bite mamma's breast. Can we talk intelligently of art, science, and culture, unless we are first introduced to ourselves and know who, what, and whence we are? Man has suppressed woman because she has different genitive organs from him; though she is an innate natural personage on earth, he has dwindled her to asking him for a cent, to a breeder, a drudge, a prostitute,—*leaving her nothing but her person to trade in.* Difference in pay turns on difference in sexuality, on difference in reproductive organs: you hire a boy and a girl to fill a wood-box; each brings in the same quantity of wood; yet you pay the boy twenty cents, the girl ten cents, and ask her to take sexual intercourse for the balance due. Paying a girl less than a boy, keeping her wages so low that she must "marry for a home" or for a night to secure food and clothes is the monster dragon of to-day, a devouring usurpation of man over woman. This makes it possible for a man to consider himself irresponsible for sexual intercourse for which he *is* responsible, and should be held to be so in the estimate of his mother and sisters; for as they are willing that men should deal unto others, so shall men deal unto them. Honesty is the only levee which can breast out the ocean of wrong. Men have been learning from opportunity, and women from *in*opportunity; their lessons are therefore different. What will be the final result? Revelries in sin, however, demand a more active and regenerative capacity, and it is to you, boys and girls of the present and rising generations, that we look for the sequel of better life.

We are all at home at least nine months in our mother's womb, and no distinctions of sex prevail before birth. Why, after birth, should a girl's person be pawned "for a home" more than a boy's? A good woman is a person who has ability to discern what is right, and lives it as against opposing influences. But virtue is below par, and money is plus; there is no value to well-doing as against successful ill-doing; to be poor and virtuous has no weight of excellence as against being handsome and rich, as things are accepted to-day. How shall I portray to you the ingrained deference to wealth, to the fact of wealth, irrespective of how it is acquired? Why are not virtue and labor recognized on their own merits? Why are shop-girls, mill-girls, and house-girls regarded below par in social life simply because they work and have not means accumulated from others' earnings? This is a question of great importance, because the fact of inequitably-acquired wealth is a great barrier between girls and their rightful opportunities in forming association, choosing their mates, and becoming mothers. These crippling customs destroy the genial travel of love from woman to man and from man to woman, make havoc of magnetisms, and render heart-sickening all filial affections and social friendships. It is the duty of every man, woman, boy, and girl, to thoughtfully study these matter-of-fact issues which we find intertwined in life and lurking about us for a true adjustment. Men of to-day cannot longer be held irresponsible for light and trivial treatment of the love question, and it is just at this point that we wish to induce them to make a rational study of their own love natures as related to woman. The power of poor pay to force girls into the physical embrace of men is a stupendous and appalling fact. Girls' lives are not matters of choice, but of persuasion and compulsion. The girl question has come home to men's thought as well as the girl to their personal embrace, and they must attend to it with the sincerity of true fathers and noble brothers. The tone of their demeanor towards her reflects their real characters. Married men are desperately in love with unmarried women, deception being the railroad on which love passes to and fro. Man loves woman enough, but recklessly and selfishly; he should not only feel, but think,—consider responsibility, not gratification merely, drawing his heart up through his intellect as a bucket from a well. How can you take woman's best nature, drag it out, and leave it a nude skeleton before the world? It tries girls mortally to say "No I thank you" to warm, attractive men. Often have I cried to think that, for self-preservation, I must fight men.

As Patrick Henry said to the Colonial insurgents, "We must fight," but we will fight to redeem, not to destroy, each other. Men's wars are grotesque and bloody; but wars between men's and women's eyes and ideas will become unique and renovating and the unsheathed, two-edged sword will be the human tongue. Religion will repent of the subjection it has imposed on women; learning will confess its ignorance of us; books (simply because they are *he* books) will move forward from their alcove-shelves and come down ashamed longer to be books; and male science will dissolve itself to escape from the infamy of its rude and savage treatment of us. The impression that man can do as he likes without being responsible therefore is base folly, and arises largely from the great selfishness which grows out of his unnatural ascendancy over woman through property usurpations and the subtle relations of physical force to her as his mater in primitive stages of growth, as from the animal to the human animal. Having arrived at a human identity, we wish to be recognized as a part of the collective identity, and, once escaping animalism, we do not wish to become the victims of manism. We want a social order which will bespeak the welfare of both, that we may, in candor, face each other eye to eye and ask "Who are you, what are you, and how do you earn your living?" These questions are all potent and significant of genuine or false character, and, in true society, must be of imperative importance. In the process of events the great institutions of the world will come under terse review, and woman will take her rightful place in religion, literature, art, and philosophy. After this play of masculine force down through the centuries, which has hitherto ruled and depraved life, the social, religious, and moral world, by natural law and necessity, must change in its vital essence and aspects. Dealing by suggestion rather than by argument, going below evil to purify the sources of life, with the dissecting knife of thought we will cleave through unnatural hindrances, take account of the ebb and flow of circumstances, and stir people with words of fire and power, in order to get a true analysis of life as we find it. And here comes in equality, the glad spectacle of men and women working together, impelled by love, not compulsion; for, to achieve renovating power, the feminine principle must be hereafter accepted as an imperative condition of growth.

* * * *

"Men's Laws and Love's Laws"

September, 1876, p. 1

The ceremony of legal marriage by a third person—a clergyman or magistrate—who represents society, debars us from personal responsibility, invades personal liberty, and exhibits the weakness of accepting conventional force rather than essential right as the arbiter of love relations. The religious law of the Church conflicts with the civil law of the State; the Church marries, saying "What God hath joined, let not man put asunder"; the State, divorcing any two for cause, "puts asunder" whom it pleases. Discarding the authority of both Church and State, lovers should feel themselves bound never to be less than just to each other and their offspring in making or dissolving their social contracts. In human relationship there is the law of consanguinity and the law of affinity; the centrifugal force to go and to get. Under the consanguinity law I love my father, brothers, uncles, nephews, cousins, grandfather, and great-grand-father; under the law of affinity my father kisses me "good-by," and I go over to the world of affinity to love a stranger.

Accumulation and possession have a special right of way from the fact that we are born naked and need clothes; with a stomach and need food; with fatigue and need sleep and shelter; receptive and need love. This drives us into a most thorough and complete analysis of the proper right of accumulating, by work and gift-taking; and the consumption thereof, by spending and gift-giving. Especially should this analysis be searching and accurate because it involves that decisive rule of right, justice, and equality which exists between the law of consanguinity and the law of affinity in the conflicting claims of property, which cause family feuds, high wrangling, and low dealing. In examining love and free love we have two great and general departments, each equally vital unto our life and happiness. How shall we behave under blood ties, and how under attraction or ties of affinity? This is a question of *art*, of the physical adjustment and play of our senses though our individual bodies and deeds towards one another. I kiss my father and I kiss my lover. Is there a difference, and what is the ground of that difference? One walks closely with the tie of consanguinity, and the other with the tie of affinity; both are pure good, and inspired as by Fate. My father kisses me under the jurisdiction of one law, and sends me forth to be caught and kissed by a stranger under the equally legitimate jurisdiction of another law. Again art asks, "How do you abide the law of touching one another, which still more deeply involves the aptitudes and play of all our senses?" There is something so kind and wonderfully inviting from the souls of good and noble persons! It quickens one to new expressions of love and inspiration, better thoughts, happier dreaming, and tinges life's cool and shady road of experiences with delicate hues of sentiment, appreciation, and thoughtfulness towards one another as we breathe out the warm, genial love of mate and friendship! How truly inspiring the human identity through the body form! Shall we ever become gentle enough in this world to know and realize the value of physical and soul love? To this accumulation of eye glances, sweet breath, warm kisses, hand pressures, and deep, rapturous sense and desire of loving, art still addresses her question, "How are you to deal with your possessions and adjust the somber claims of consanguinity love with the aesthetic claims and the persuasive invitations of affinity love?"

To suppose that love can be regulated by statute marriage laws is an absurdity; statute law to secure good behavior is a failure; all existing laws are but the registered opinions of men, one-half the people, the women never having been consulted in the enactment of these opinions, called "laws," that we are commanded to "obey!" Your "public servant" is the most dangerous wolf in sheep's clothing that now travels up and down the earth to devour submissive and unthinking women. We have crouched in subjection too long, and must now rise in behalf of reason and equality. In touching my person a man touches *me*, and must seriously study the right and duty, the use and responsibility, of that act. Jesus perceived that by a woman's touching the hem of his garment "virtue had gone of out him." Dr. Wm. F. Channing says that the law of touch is a world yet unknown. All know the power of magnetism; when lightning strikes one in a row of cattle, it kills a dozen as easily as one; a flash of electricity collects its own, and is gone! Some do not believe in magnetism, do not see good in it, think nothing but evil comes of it; yet it is an imperative power. How far can one meet a man and not be enslaved by his magnetic control? In seeking my chosen mate I asked, "Do I wish the blood of this man to flow in the veins of my children?" The broadcloth deference and arrogance, the compound of silks, insinuation, laces, and mincing called society, neither knows nor observes the deepest laws of its life.

How shall the sexes meet and help, but not harm, each other? We must learn the equitable method of affectional exchange, the cost principle in love as well as in grain and money. One of the essential modes of expression with lovers deeply attracted to each other is through the sense of touch; before marriage they like to be much alone, kissing and caressing each other; after marriage sense is not so imperative, because the opposite poles of magnetic attraction have met and love deepens thought and action. Attentive to agriculture and other pursuits in earth, sky, and sea, men have not run their trains of thought into the depot of internal life, being more interested in a kernel of corn than in the face of a babe. Either because they did not know, or had not courage, or were not destined to do it, men have left the realm of sexuality for women to explore; and impelled by love (which is greater than justice and includes it), she will beckon mind down to renovate the basement stories of the body. It is generally supposed that free love means reckless sexual intercourse, but it is the beginning of discretion and sobriety, the law of mine and thine applied to the subtlest relations of life. Seeing a silk dress in a shop window, I want it, but have no money to buy it, and cannot thrust my hand in and take it; if the handsome merchant says he will give it to me, his offer is the greatest barrier of the three to my having it, for he may expect such pay as will hurt and disgrace me. The question between me, the man, and the silk dress is not one to be settled by "religion," a magistrate, society, or the State, but by me and the man, subject only to essential right. We must take no step and assume no relation to each other which we cannot be responsible for the results of. When people ask what is right as well as what is pleasing, sexuality will come under the jurisdiction of intelligence and good sense, love will be free, honor reign, and calamity cease.

"Love and Labor"

October 1876, p. 1

My mother was compelled by poverty to send me and my sisters out into the world as a flock of chickens to pick our way. Starting with birth and naked requirements, which render it a prime necessity to labor, it should not only be highly respectable to work, but blameworthy not to work. As the result of work, people should have pay, money, which will bring them food, clothing, shelter, and culture—means and training for business and refinement. Work will then be a glory, not a shame; and those who labor not, instead of being the fashionable dolls of the day, will be condemned as useless idlers. People who are industrious and properly rewarded are those who will constitute civilized and befitting society. Having this education, women are fitted for varied service, not the least of which is companionship and maternity. What better guarantees of civilization than intelligence and capacity? Using, not words, but incisive thought and clear speech, at home, on street corners, wherever two, three, or more meet together, we must talk over the social problem, turning the light of all we know or can learn upon its dark and entangling mysteries. The life of girls has much to do, for good or ill, with home and the national welfare; however lightly it has been considered hitherto, such depreciation cannot continue without serious impoverishment to the race. Hence it behooves us to make a study of this sad problem, and realize the fact that girls are now berated through literature as *prostitutes*, your daughters or perhaps mine. Fast-living America has seemed to enjoy the sweets of prostrate girl forms; but we must stop and ask what it costs, where tends it, and whether its ravishing reflex will not finally blast the very home thought of civilized life? So fast have we lived that it becomes almost an evil to live. The existence of prostitutes is the most damaging act, the most accusing evil, in human society. However must we may love him, the devastating power is man … however complex or disagreeable it may be, the force of woman's tongue will erelong be considered an active means of calling men to more worthy and sincere dealing, as though every man was the father of every other man's child; the phrase "our girls" will mean *all girls* and "brotherhood" signify at least social honesty. We must bless man by putting coals of fire on his head,—that is, our love will be inflamed by warm words calling him to order with himself and woman.

There are mental, moral, and social divisions of life. In the mental we find an immediate monopoly of scholarship, of the brain over skill in the hands, so classified, drilled, and directed as to make labor ignoble and subject to false aristocracy. It is not innate good sense, but arrogant class usurpation, which cripples us; it is the tyranny of cunning brain over the honest hand, of one part of the body over another,—members of the body at war with each other. Hence my mother Tilton cursed scholarship and wished colleges were tipped into the sea; but mother Heywood would have her pet boys educated and finished off for ministers. The moral division relates to our bodies as they are related one to another and to their mutual dealings. The social relates to things as the result of mental and moral forces, of the relations not of one to another merely, but of each to all and all to each; this requires close consideration of what is true and choice, of equity and exchange. Thought must be active and penetrating, must walk through business as a needle plies through cloth, impelled by the sewing machine treadle....

Why not consider the temptations of girls as well as those of men? When hungry I have passed a baker's shop, and made half a dinner on the sweet scent of bread which came up from the smoking loaves below. Did it cost me nothing to resist the warm, rich, employing baker, who would have taken me to his arms and given me of his abundance? Though she have the honesty of toil in her nerve and habit, yet, shut into the dark alcove in inopportunity, is it strange that a girl goes to the winning person of man, when his eye, with the blaze of a light-house lamp, is turned on her in her dismal chances? Born to labor and to love, capable of all that is serviceable and enjoyable in life, Solomon, speaking for "religion," says, "Her feet go down to death, her steps take hold on hell"; "literature" crucifies her as a "prostitute"; "science" turns on her path the lecherous hounds of "supply and demand"; and the rotten respectability of society regards her with virtuous horror! Yet to her as the High Priestess of Love and Labor, the most potent divinities of civilization and progress, must the oracles of religion, literature, science and art come to learn deeper lessons of life than they yet know. Moved by the cold, calculating impulses of business, many men now marry for money, and many women for a home, with inevitable disaster to both; but lovers, arriving unto each other, not for money, but for themselves and truth, suggest unused forces which will redeem and adorn life, now desolated by marriage tyranny and property robbery. A chance to love wisely and serve honestly and prosperously is the inestimable boon which Labor Reformers and Free Lovers offer to those cursed by enforced poverty, and to the more pitiable idlers who are savage enough to be willing to live by usury or other speculative profits.

✳ ✳ ✳ ✳

"The Ethics of Sexuality"

April 1881, p. 3

The mind and matter of us; our distinct personalities yet, confluent desires and needs; the affections, actions, destinies apparent in different bodily structures, disclose the rights, duties and laws of Sexed Being. If Persons are not *in*visibly related to each other seldom can there be an *ex*ternal, visible union of durable strength; spiritual precedes material association; Mind proposes to Matter. But Mind must appear in worthy salutation or remain outside waiting to be housed: for Matter yields only when its equality of merit and dignity of position are recognized. Man and woman, you and I meet, embrace, melt away in each other, only to reappear as Persons with new vigor, again and again in everlasting frolic, if the meeting is well-done in clear knowledge of the way to, from and with each other. When Love inspires Association the meeting is so complete, ecstatic that comparison is sacrilege; "Competition in Love" is as impossible as the rude idea is unnatural; real Association does not flourish on such wily, irresponsible ground. Love, biding its time, by its own inherent life, transcends rivalry in companionship; the very self-essence of power, it does not come or go, because some one wishes to appropriate it, but it is *there* self-existent, indestructible, irresistible. One is not a Free Lover because she cohabits with one or more men, or with none at all, but rather by the import and tone of Association; mutual impulse and mating tendencies crave expression, relish grace in its bestowal, rest in its acceptance. Sexuality is a divine ordinance, elegantly natural from eye-glance to the vital action of penis and womb, in personal exhilaration or for reproductive uses. Free Love calls for sincere thought and true action; it is the advent of Health and Order amid disease and chaos; centrally entrenched in and fully imbued with royal attention, jealous care and discreet regard for *others welfare* in their separate, united, active and passive accounts, we are joyfully held to mutual choice and duty in the ceaseless round of Change. May I have a child and by whom? Voiced in Nature, rising from the depths of the heart of Being this question admits of no equivocal answer; desire for offspring, Integrity of parents and Rights of the Child *forbid insincerity*. Arrived in this earth-realm of animated action our child has to recognize its own existence without blush or shame; Existence recognizes the child, calling for a father, a mother,—who are there without calling, unless inhuman habits forbid. Love outwits intrusion; Lady Nature can put Madame Intellect behind the door, further than you can think while she revels with a man to her heart's content; but Temperance is the imperative Law: Mr. A. is drunk with soberness; Mr. C. is sober in drunkenness; neither knows the equitable, *balanced* use of persons. The Cost Principle is vividly apparent in coition; when a man *uses* only what he can pay for there will be no prostitutes. *Until woman has equal pay for equal work with man* she cannot prove her natural independence; without Liberty and Sex-Equity Love is impossible. Whether it is God smoking a cigar in heaven, Grantism here or stealthy usurpations in commercial and domestic life, invasive Heism stifles us; but Ethics assure equality, free and intelligent Mutualism.

The "marriage institution," the fruit of irrational intrusion and heistic folly, is but a fly-speck on the great fact of Social Destiny. It is the auction-block of primitive sale and slavery of woman to man, as *un*reliable and *ill*binding as such forsaken-fidelity to personal Integrity could permit; its legitimate fruits are prostitution, abortions, infanticide and thousands of skulking fathers. The Ethics of Sex do not admit of any regime of action, whereby Human Beings can possibly be *abused* into "prostitutes," be they male or female. "Houses of Ill-fame" which "statistics" declare "are mainly supported by married men," and young *un*married men too, are simply relics of *heistic usurpation and sheistic-slave disease.*

We, man and woman, boy and girl are *here* with desires, needs, uses, hopes,—with all our capacities for Work to transcend tragic evil in ecstatic good.

The spirit of Culture does not exist.
Where thought of Service does not persist.

Standing with her hands upon his arm, with steady look into his eyes he meets her gaze intoned with a thought of profound nearness to him; in tremulous vibrations thrilling her being he knows how densely she understands his electric sway, invoicing her every sense to participate in a united welcome use and enjoyment of their birthright Powers for ingenious blendment and judicious Creation. When a man given his Passion to a woman she feels he *must* love her, else he *could* not yield it to her; for *his passion*, to her, is the divine in human semblance; as she adores *it* she deems that *he* equally holds it in honor unto himself. Hence she feels safe, for he has given her rest and trust through his bestowal of Love. He blesses her through his *retained* Passion. Has she not already counted the cost, and does he not compute its exactness unto her, as well as unto himself, and bless her with Love from his centre-self, while yet he retain a fruitful expression of his Passion? Can he be otherwise than dear to her? Does she not know her own and feel secure that as nature yields its own through Gravity giving, it also yields its own through Levity's acceptance thereof? If she, as woman, duly gives to man who cometh in unto her, as freely, as equally, as well as he gives her, how shall she be abashed or ashamed of the innermost? This meeting is not abortive but fruitful, the Over Soul, Reason transcending Force in realized Society! Both are glad; satisfaction accomplished, yet is ever deeply in store for them; as free and equal Persons they experience good; still, as Artists they may create better, best in form, activities and destinies of new Human Beings. Art illustrated in flesh and blood; Mind, (mathematics), and Matter, (mechanics), conspiring to produce quick souls in sound bodies,—this is Life! To grow a handsome, capable child under our heart, and born that child from between our limbs is finer work than aesthetic words from the mouth, or hand-wit with brush or chisel. Sedate in airy, yearning, jaunty, throbbing Faith woman waits; in royal form with first step man comes; the Outer and Inner of the two are *one* to welcome chosen Trinity.

The tendencies of Sexual Freedom to personal health and social strength no intelligent, honest observer of the Free Love movement questions. False modesty born of timid ignorance has had its day; let Truth now speak; we like men because they *are* men; being women we born babes not from our eyes or lips but from our wombs. Man as a physical ruler of the household, like the imperialism of bulls in the barnyard, is not a Lover but a beast, seeing in woman a breeder, or food for insatiable appetites; any alliance with him that limits Choice I detest; but the word wife never, in the three or four hundred years I have lived, seemed irrational to me; it expressed a relationship of the most candid order, twixt a woman and a man; as husband words the masculine side, wife words the feminine side of plural unity. I had no idea that the word wife in its true meaning implied *servitude*; I accepted it and the relationship as announcing equality with man in the realm of Service; never did I feel demeaned by so accepting the term wife, or the fact wifehood. Still, I hear the word means something awful; a serfdom, at first forced on woman, but by long endurance and custom agreed to, overlooked, forgotten, yet ever still expressed in the woman slave held by man as king of brutes, her "generous" lord and "protector" of course! To some wifehood may seem slavish, not self-adjusted service; but such bondage is foreign to my girl and woman ideas; while Serving I always felt to be royally worthy. I used to think Passion was something *bad*, and was taught, by those who did not know, that Lust is the opposite of Love; I was mistaken, for the antithesis of Love is *hate*; while Lust means full, glowing, healthy animal heat. Passion is a fruitful source of beneficent power. A man may love me yet have no passion for me; so one may have a passion for me, but not love me. Man does not "fall in love" with woman, for love is Essential; he may have a rise of heat, a magnetic, fervent attraction for her. Yet, whatever their views and feelings, the sexes can never escape Moral Responsibility for their actions to and with each other; the whole person, from crown to foot must obey Reason. Women have no respect for men who excuse "indiscretions" on the ground of mental or physical weakness; who say a man is "innocent" because he is "insane," "overpersuaded"; or, worst of all, "virtuous" because he is impotent, attempting to hide behind the inability of his penis to have an erection! Woman may pretend "she does not want anything of men," but her lady-nature knows it is the very great *everything* she wants to do *with* man; it is useless to deny Nature's functionary powers because, as yet, we know not how to appropriate them in Use, that Beauty may follow and Misery be dissolved. Intrusive power can *never* answer to the validity of *Integrity*, vested in, and called for, from the personal-resident I Am of each other. Personal Responsibility has been *ill*regarded, set back, put to blush, by third-party, arrogant intermeddlement, of the physical force code of domestic, commercial, educational, church-and-state *heisms*. Evasion, intrigue thwart spiritual concord; repression is as great a physical and mental crime as aggression; mothers who attempt to *act for* their daughters; over-officious "friends," finesse, however bland in purpose or robed in the imitations of culture—all vicarious intrusion between Souls violates Nature. We are related sexually; let us face the glad fact with all its ineffable joys, its fruitful Power, its invigorating Science and consequent responsibilities. Thought-exchange, mental Articulation has its twin-mate in magnetic mutuality, physical Vibration. The Penis and Womb, the Outer and Inner are sublimely worthy peers in body faculty; their attentions, purposes, capacities, demands, supplies, —moved by Brain and Heart are the pith and glory of Being. As "the corruption of the best is the worst" so abuse or neglect of sexuality makes Society impossible; but knowledge of ourselves and mutual discretion in unity light the vestal fire of Soul-Worship on every hearth-stone. As Sex is the profoundest relation of Life, generation is its ceaseless business; Generation so well-done as to require no *re*generation. Thought moved by impulse discovers and incarnates Spiritual Forces, wed Use to Beauty, creates attractive Persons who find in Reason Religion, and in Love Law.

✳ ✳ ✳ ✳

"The Woman's View of It—No. 1"[41]

January 1883, pp. 2–3 [Some material has been edited out of the following series of articles for space reasons.]

... It is so strange that human life could have throbbed on thousands, if not millions of years without intelligent, serious consideration of our body-sexed selves, of the pregnant issues involved in personal, blended Being; so strange that, because if intent attention is given, here in Princeton, to the Sex Question, United States officers should, again & again, burst in upon us, seize, carry off the sire of my children & cage him with so-called criminals! Yet not strange, for, while Comstock incarnates the intermeddling tendencies of ignorant, invasive Individualism and Collectivism, of the hell-bound purpose of vindictive ecclesiasticism, Mr. Heywood stands for Natural Liberty, Personal Sobriety, Intuitive Enterprise. The demand for the repeal of Comstock's "law" originated here Jan. 1876, in the first edition of Cupid's Yokes & had been persistently urged ever since;... Mr. Heywood said "Either Comstockism or this book will go under." The combat deepens; invasive heism, arbitrary repressive ecclesiasticism which hitherto have *subjected* woman to man's desires now find her insurgent. Woman's Rights, declared by Mrs. Stanton, Lucretia Mott & others at Seneca Falls, N.Y., 1848, now seconded by the Massachusetts Democracy led by Gen. Butler, are realized in woman's growing impulse to be *mistress of her own Person*; in the arrival of Natural Equality of the sexes in social relations.

Before, "the Heywood case" meant the right of private judgment in morals; Cupid's Yokes transcended vindictive repression on that line. Now, not books merely, but a Syringe [a birth control device] is in the fight; *the will of man to impose vs. the Right of Woman to prevent conception is the issue.* The giddy, evasive ways, in which the sexes have, hitherto, met must turn to serious facing of facts. Does not Nature give *to* woman & install *in* her the right of way to & from her own womb? Shall Heism continue to be imperatively absolute in coition? Should not Sheism have her say also? Shall we submit to the loathsome impertinence which makes Anthony Comstock inspector and supervisor of American women's wombs? This womb-syringe question is to the North what the negro question was to the South; as Mr. Heywood stood beside the slave demanding his liberation, so now he voices the emancipation of woman from sensual thraldom. Clergymen tell us we must "bear the cross," that is the penis; Congressmen vote our persons sluice-ways for irresponsible indulgence, empower Comstock to search bureaus and closets,... As well might woman vote that man shall flow semen only when she says; that he must keep his penis tied up with "continent" twine; that he shall constantly have, near by, specified strings to assure "virtue."—the which, if he is found without, he shall be liable, on conviction by twelve women, to ten years imprisonment and $5000 fine; that a feminine Comstock shall go about to examine men's penises and drag them to jail if they dare disobey the semen-twine "law"!

The savage assault on Citizen Right, the rude exposé of woman's person, which would again put Mr. Heywood in prison uniform, is fruitful in many thoughts that I publish as ways and means allow. The barbarous insolence of this blow at Domestic Sanctity, the ineffably sacred realism of Sexuality, who can voice them! No other function is endowed with such befitting elegance as is the persuasive teasing power of the penis and the womb, of the eye and hand. This subject of Sex is so innately nice, so full of wisdom, that it will bear all the investigation and conversation persons or Race may desire.... We must thank ourselves, our day and age that we are to do somewhat of the steady work required to lift the *sex fact* out of the slough it has so long been submerged in, filling the world full of irresponsible, clandestine life and intense evil,—all of which must be wrought off and out from among us as a race by the power of the mind to dissolve misery and *balance* animal Feeling with Electric Thought, finding in Use and Beauty, Temperance. There is almost as grave a fight going on relative to J. F. Pickering (standing as he does, a genuinely-impelled man with a highly endowed moral nature, an instinctively legal cast of mind, personizing Ethics in court utterances, innate Law and order) as there is against Mr. Heywood in the realm of intuitive and promulgative analysis, *outside* of the courts. Many years Mr. Pickering has been an intelligent, devoted, persistent defender of the legal rights of Girls and Women; timely, efficient, royal Service to women defrauded of their Labor, Property Rights, by stealthy Heism, *selects*, Ordains Mr. Pickering to speak, by inspiration, now when all that is sacred in Sexuality is meanly, murderously assailed. Some say "Mr. Heywood should plead his own case": that might do for Theodore Parker's time when the physical negro, body-form, the matter-man was enslaved; but present issues are integral, *essential*; we travel toward the center of things; Mr. Heywood stands for physical, mental, spiritual, social, industrial, financial Liberation; for the New Order, for Mutualism, in all of its transcendent manifestations....

"The Woman's View of It—No. 2"

February 1883, pp. 2–3

It is not Mr. Heywood that lifts the Syringe Question to public view, but the U.S. Government, by ill-luck of allowing itself to become basely subservient to ecclesiastic, church Intrusion; the wily, sinister, bigoted exponent of perverse churchism, Anthony Comstock makes these States the cat's paw of ecclesiastic ferocity to pull its lucrative chestnuts out of the fire of social evil which the church, by subjecting Woman to male supremacy, by forbidding Liberty & Knowledge, perpetuates. By Nature & all legislation, previous to Comstockism, woman's womb is her own private property; Republican Congresses & Courts ... now empower one man not merely to search houses as they do in Russia, but to enter bed-chambers to look for semen in woman's person! Because he resents this unmitigated, ineffable outrage Mr. Heywood is now held for trial! As the fugitive slave bill made all humane Northerners friendly to its fleeing victims so the revolting, devilish purpose of Comstock statutes calls Intelligence to Woman's side asserting her Natural Right to ownership & control of her person....

Because Free Lovers, by grace of self-knowledge & control have no special use for artificial means of preventing conception does Fate bid them now defend a syringe, forbidden to women by statute as a means of saying "No" to unwelcome male advances....

They [the newspapers] say "Mr. Heywood is the pink of perfection in physical-self, culture, books, wit, wisdom; but for the saying of his wife," which means *me*, "he is a pattern of propriety & fidelity." ... Nature ordered just such a man as he to stand, by his own choice with a woman impelled to be & do like me.

"The Woman's View of It—No. 3"

March 1883, pp. 2–3
... In the arena of Mechanics, Socket & Pivot are the law, the fact of action; the socket is soft, receptive iron, the pivot hard; projective; through realms of metals this analysis takes us into vegetable kingdoms where we find stamen & pistil, pollen & ovule with all their prolific uses & destinies. Why not make voyages of discovery into our body-selves, study attractive, fruitful lessons in Moral, Sexual Physiology? Why blush or be shamefaced in Stirpiculture more than in Agriculture ... Are not the Penis & Womb as native, handsome & worthy in use as pivot & socket, pistil & stamen, pollen & ovule? What rioting debauchery, what rotting disease, what stroke of moral-death or stark idiocy is upon men that they are less intelligent, respectful & orderly with their own body-selves than with metal, wooden or vegetable manifestations of form and power.

"The Woman's View of It—No. 4"

April 1883, pp. 2–3
Love is the one Law which pervades Being; illustrated by Thought allied to Reason, Love inspires Logic, brain power with renovating health; the very essence of Conscience, its seat in the bosom of nature, its voice the harmony of Life, Love is the soul of Rectitude....

Vital feeling, pulsation, expecting tendencies clasp persons; superstitious unreason, "pure" ignorance, idiotic "virtue," unable Girls to speak of the beauty, fullness, exhilarating & creative value of the Penis; but they are tongue-tied only at the expense (self-consuming wealth) of an overcharged, vibrating Womb unduly craving the natural offices of our Savior, the Penis. Yet in a deep, continent sense, women save men from delirious excesses & deadly results by affording healthful, redeeming association. In nothing is the devilish stupidity of men more apparent than in decreeing sexual knowledge "obscene"; no man every more fatally wordshot himself than did Dis't Att'y Sanger when he said "Mr. Heywood is a bad man" because he insists that Thought, Truth must mediate between the sexes. A beautiful girl, caught up in tidal waves of poverty, ignorance & destitution, accepts the warm embraces of a genial-faced, Boston "gentleman"; believing him good & true as father, brother, or Lover she admits him to utter intimacy; next day with richly-dressed wife and daughter & gold-head cane he passes her on the street without recognition! Amazed, indignant, yet strong in real power, she says, "Well, you have him *to-day*, but I have him *to-night*." Why should she not clutch, appropriate him, in turn, since he, taking all that makes life dear, abandons her to be common prey & rot unburied as a "prostitute?"...

[T]he *pivotal* question of to-day is ... what degree of association is justifiable this side of impregnation....

"The Woman's View of It—No. 5"

May 1883, p. 2

The verdict, "Not Guilty," closes one act in this play, though the It of personality & adjustment, in the great drama of Love & Labor, remains, is really what constitutes Religion, while the *absence* of Love is the presence of dissolute irresponsibility....

Relative to personized Love what "the woman" does or does not do— that is strictly my affair. It was surprising with what impetuous abruptness & nonchalant grace persons picked up the *inside* action of themselves towards me.... I was made to feel, to my heart's core, how my almost every word or thought, touching the Sex Question, was *by them* held to be "a real vulgarism, unwomanly & unfit for *their* ears."...

Many a thrust which I was "fated" to suffer pierced me to the heart, while other expressions or non-expressions were simply laughable; *then* I dwelt inside myself & alone. But *now* I cannot well be made to be so crisp before any man's or woman's pressure of thought, look, word or deed towards me, but find myself able to work with ease & pleasure at dissecting, analyzing, classifying & recording, in the most central sense, the right & purpose of way, the actions & reactions of the Penis & Womb.... Some may despise me intently, others love me devotedly; the social or unsocial wave may run high towards us, or otherwise, as did like waves run & surge before....

2

Women of The Word: *A Biographical Dictionary of the Day-to-Day Radicals*

Some of the most passionate women radicals America has produced have been lost in the dusty pages of nineteenth-century periodicals, such as *The Word.* The following biographical dictionary is an attempt to pull away a corner of the veil that hides them from historical view by providing a listing of the women who contributed to *The Word* or who were mentioned within its pages in some significant context.

The Dictionary is merely a starting point for continued research: It is not presented as a definitive statement of women's involvement with *The Word.* For example, for reasons of space, I generally omitted women whose names appeared only once or tangentially during the periodical's run.

Moreover, I cannot claim certainty as to spelling of some of the names, since *The Word* often used different spellings from issue to issue to identify the same woman. I have used the most commonly rendered version and noted alternate spellings. Another difficulty in compiling the Dictionary lay in the fact that women were sometimes identified as "Mrs.," and it is far from clear whether the initials that followed that designation belonged to the woman or to her husband. Moreover, the dates which indicate when a particular woman was associated with any organization in no way suggests she was not so affiliated at other times as well.

The locations, when indicated, refer to the places from which letters to the editor were posted. They are included in the hope of further identifying the woman in question, also to provide researchers with one more clue of where to profitably look for more information.

For reasons of space, the following abbreviations have been employed:
ADL: Anti-Death League
ALRL: American Labor Reform League

ATH: Angela T. Heywood
ATL: Anti-Tax League
AUS: Anti-Usury Society
CY: *Cupid's Yokes*
EHH: Ezra H. Heywood
FLB: Free Love Bureau
NDA: National Defense Association
NEFLL: New England Free Love League
NELRL: New England Labor Reform League
NLL: National Liberal League
TW: *The Word*
URL: Union Reform League
W&CW: *Woodhull and Claflin Weekly*

Angela T. Heywood explained the differences between the four key organizations associated with *The Word* as follows: "[T]he Labor Reform League deals with industrial and financial interests; the Free Love League with affectional societal life; the Anti-Death League with religion, and the Anti-Tax reform with government: labor, love, religion, and the State,—four worlds we are born into, must explore and conquer to know the true conduct of life."[1]

Biographical Dictionary

Lizzie Adams, Kansas City, Mo. Admirer of *CY*. Wrote to *TW* describing death of Charles Fowler. (January 1890, pp. 2–3)

Mrs. Mary E. B. Albertson, Boston, Mass, then Vt. Advocate of prison reform. Elected 1874, 1875 as officer of NELRL. Elected 1881 as officer of ADL. Elected 1882 as officer of ATL.

Sarah S. Allen, Dress Reformer. Wrote to *TW*, "... I have traveled in 22 of the states during the past 15 years, wearing the bloomer & New Order costume, in my diet confining myself to the plant world...." (June 1885, p. 3)

C. Fannie Allyn, Attended NEFLL meetings. A Signatory on the Call for a Woman's National Labor Convention (1876).

Lucia True Ames Brief review of her work "Memoirs of a Millionaire" (December 1889, p. 3).

Mary D. Andrews. Elected 1880 as officer of ATL and ADL.

Mrs. Atwell. Elected 1881 as officer of NELRL.

Sadie [Sada] Bailey [later Fowler] Philadelphia, Pa. A frequent contributor of small sums to *TW* and EHH. Among those announced as organizing an American Woman's Emancipation Society on December 7, 1873.

Supported *TW*'s plain-speech policy.[2] Her book "Irene, or the Road to Freedom" briefly reviewed as "... a book which marriagists and libertarians should own and lend" (October 1886, p. 3).

TW later reported, "The latest outrage on the freedom of the press is the assault on Mrs. Fowler's 'Irene'; Dist-Atty. Graham told her husband, Dr. Fowler, that on his demand the Lippincott's gave up $10,000 worth of books and plates to be destroyed by the N.Y. Vice Society, and said Irene & its plate must also be sacrificed to appease Comstock's 'pure' wrath. But Mrs. F. sent a firm refusal, advertised Irene by large posters, put the books at the front door of her residence & and sells them to all comers! Rejoicing in her resolute assertion of citizens' right to select their own books, the Co-operative Publishing Co. advertises it on the 4th page, & will send it, prepaid, on receipt of price, $1.00. Brick Pomeroy booms Irene in his 'Advance Thought' & sells it openly...." (January 1889, p. 2).

Addie L. Ballou. Among those announced as organizing an American Woman's Emancipation Society on December 7, 1873.

Mrs. P. A. Beaman. Defended EHH against Comstock laws. *TW* reported, "The citizen's petition to drop the case [EHH's prosecution], drawn by Stephen Pearl Andrews, [is] headed by Mr. & Mrs. P. A. Beaman...." (July 1884, p. 2).

Mrs. E. M. Beckwith, Long Island City, N.Y., then New York City. Free-love advocate. Wrote to *TW*, "A right sexual establishment I believe to be the only foundation upon which permanent co-operation can exist ... I have seen Mr. Andrews [Stephen Pearl Andrews] often, and learned much from him; many new ideas develop within myself by coming into communion with him and others who are with him. If I should remain in N.Y. to hold meetings, I shall take your books and paper to sell in spare moment" (March 1876, p. 3).

Informed EHH, "I think your book 'Cupid's Yokes' has a well-balanced power which all reasoning people cannot fail to see and appreciate. Hope I shall do some more general work by next Fall, and, if so, shall be very glad of your aid.... All men who wish to be worthy of the name Free Lover should be sure that they never propose nor even accept a relations with any woman that they would not be willing to recommend to their daughter of sister or mother in relations to some other man. If our political swell throughout the country and *some* of our wise men would practice with truth and candor the above rule, the yawning abyss of prostitution would be in waiting for every unguarded woman and even the little girls of our nation."

Aided in conduct of 1878 Free Love Convention in Boston.

Mrs. Beecher Hooker. *TW* mentioned she received permission from Charles Sumner to substitute the word "sex" for "color" in all his speeches in order to promote woman's suffrage (May 1874, p. 3). She also arranged for the Heywoods to address the 1877 annual Convention of the Connecticut Woman's Suffrage Society. *TW* briefly reviewed her work "The Constitutional Rights of the Women of the United States" (February 1889, p. 3).

Annie Besant. *TW* briefly reviewed her book, "Marriage As It Was, As It Is, And As It Should Be" (November 1879, p. 4). It reported on an Australian editor W. W. Collins (ed. *Freedom*) being convicted of obscenity for selling Besant's "Law of Population," then released upon appeal. Her work "Law of Population" was advertised in various issues of *TW*.

Catherine H. Birney. TW briefly reviewed her book, "The Grimke Sisters" (December 1885, p. 3).

Lydia Eve Blackstone, Chester, N.H. Frequent supportive letters to the editor, e.g. praising *CY*. Supported plain-speech policy.

Mrs. Ellen M. Bolles, Providence R.I. Attended 1876, 1877, 1879, 1881 NELRL Convention. Addressed 1878 URL Convention; elected 1879, 1880 as officer. Elected 1878, 1879, 1880 as officer of ALRL. Elected 1878, 1879, 1880, 1882 as officer of NEFLL. Elected 1880, 1882 as officer of ADL.

TW advertised her as a lecturer. She spoke at an "indignation meeting" held to protest the sentencing of EHH on obscenity charges. Frequent supportive letters to the editor, including letters endorsing spiritualism.

Mary Bolton, Charlotte, Mich. Wrote to *TW*, "'Uncivil Liberty' is the best thing of that nature I ever read. We will try to get up a club for The Word here" (April 1873, p. 3).

Mrs. Annie W. Bowdrie [alt. spelling Bodrie] Addressed 1879, 1881, 1883 NEFLL Convention. Addressed 1880 NELRL Convention Addressed 1881 ADL Convention. Supportive letters to editor.

Mrs. Nahum Brigham Addressed 1880 NELRL Conv.

Mrs. Brinkerhoff Addressed 1878 NEFLL Conv.

Etta Bullock Attended 1875 Social Freedom Convention at Paine Memorial Hall.

Maria L. Buxton, Milford, Mass. Elected 1882 as officer NEFLL.

Letters to the editor, commenting upon the status of women. For example, one letter praised "Uncivil Liberty." "Who ever heard of a man being called a prostitute, no matter how excessive he may have been in his relations with women? But if a woman is seduced by a man whom she loves with her whole soul, he and society will crush her...." (March 1876, pp. 3–4).

Another letter commented, "I wish you would talk a little about the naughty men that capture women to destroy them. It will be a long time before man and women (especially men) will be good enough to live up to the teachings of your book—*Cupid's Yokes*. We like the book, but we think it will be a long time before it will be appreciated and understood as you intend it to be" (May 1876, p. 3).

She helped organize 1876 Love and Labor meetings addressed by Heywoods in Malboror and Milford, Mass. In turn, when she spoke at a 1876 NEFLL Convention, *TW* reprinted extracts of the speech which was reprinted in full in the *Boston Herald* of May 22: It was entitled "Natural Law vs. Marriage Law" (July 1876, p. 3).

Mrs. Mona Caird. *TW* quoted from her article in *Westminster Review* of November 1888 in which she argues for free love. Also quoted her from *Westminster Review* on women in marriage.

Mrs. A. F. Campbell, Providence, R.I. Wrote to *TW*, "Cupid has been dipped in Passion until he is soaked through; I would now have the elements necessary for immersion composed of Passion united with Reason, which, rightly proportioned, give the perfection of Love. I think I could sell many of your new (?) 'yokes.' The subject of the relation of the sexes has always had absorbing interest for me. The less Law, the *better* for us humans...." (March 1876, p. 3).

Rachel Campbell, Grass Valley, California, then Manchester, New Hampshire. Elected 1877, 1878, 1879, 1880, 1881, 1882 as officer of NEFLL. Elected 1878 as officer of ALRL. Elected 1882 as officer of URL.

TW briefly reviewed her pamphlet: "'The Prodigal Daughter, an Essay' read before the N.E. Free-Love League in Boston, Feb. 1881, by Rachel Campbell, is a clear, cogent statement of the Free Love views, well-suited to inform those obtuse enough to think marriage defensible" (June 1885, p. 3). *TW* also extracted an article entitled "Marriage Savagery," first delivered at the NEFLL (August 1885, p. 1).

Supportive letters to the editor, relating personal experiences. For example, "I had been for several years an operative in a cotton mill. My health was beginning to fail, and I had not money enough to rest three months if my life depended on it. I felt that I could not much longer keep up, and looked about for some kind of labor that would, perhaps, be as remunerative and less exhausting. Telling my plans to a friends, we agreed to go to Boston and seek some lighter employment.... I finally told one man, who seemed quite anxious to have us work for him, that we could not live on the wages he offered. 'Why!' said he, 'the girls do live, you can see, our girls dress nicely, and don't overwork; we keep help enough so they can have a holiday whenever they desire it.' ... 'Oh!' said he, with a sly wink, at the same time tapping me under the chin, '*I will introduce a gentleman who will pay your board*'" (November 1877, pp. 3–4).

In a later letter, she seemed to be taking after ATH in terms of plain speech style, e.g. "The electric thrill lovers experience in clasping hands, kissing etc. is of the same nature as the sexual orgasm. The embrace, the kiss, the caress or glance of love lit eyes all radiate the sex power and are as surely sexual intercourse as actual coition" (May 1881, p. 4).

Nevertheless, she concluded that EHH had been arrested largely due to his wife's use of plain language: "Does she want to send you there again? It is cowardly to court danger & defy law when the suffering falls on another. I am out of all patience with her; if she wants so much to say words that offend decent people, let her go to a brothel & say them over and over until she is satisfied" (May 1887, p. 3).

TW announced her demise: "Rachel Campbell, recently risen, was many years a factory operative; quiet, thoughtful, attractive, her tongue & pen instructed many people; her 'Prodigal Daughter,' the lecture first delivered by her before the Free Love League in Boston, lives a classic in reform literature" (November 1892, p. 2).

Mrs. Lucinda B. Chandler, Vineland, N.J., then from Boston. Supportive letters to the editor.

Mrs. H. Dean Chapman. Addressed 1880 NELRL Convention.

Mrs. S. L. Chappelle. Addressed 1879, 1881 NEFLL Convention. Addressed 1879 ADL Convention. Addressed 1880 NELRL Convention. Addressed 1880 URL Convention.

Josephine Chase. Dress reformer.

TW reported, "Seward Mitchell and Josephine Chase are in jail in Norridgewock, Maine, 60 days for the crime of living together as they think right, rather than as scandal-begetting ministers and bribe-taking statesmen command...." (July 1878, p. 2).

TW announced her death, identifying her as the devoted companion of Seward Mitchell. On March 1881, an obituary notice written by Seward Mitchell appeared, "On the eve of Nov. 2, 1873, we, sitting alone in Bangor, Me., agreed to live together as long as we could live happily, and she went with me to my home the next day. Losing our home in 1874, we went to several places, but finally were offered a home by a dear friend, and then commenced the persecutions that led to our imprisonment in 1878. To that dear friend's house I had been a hundred times at least with a legally married *wife*, and no one interfered, but when, by invitation of the owner of the place, I went there with a *free woman*, then the lower regions of the people's vile hearts were moved. First by mob violence which failed, then by arrest for 'fornication.' We were taken before a trial justice, tried, convicted, and condemned to imprisonment for 60 days in 'separate cells.' When the judge pronounced those words 'separate cells,' the low rabble in attendance gave signs of great satisfaction. We were committed the same day. During our imprisonment, not one word of complaint ever came from Mrs. Chase.... One other thing I must say, that her wearing a neat, healthy Reform dress, Josie received a great many sneers, and in almost every case from her own sex" (p. 4).

Mrs. Dr. Sarah [Sara] B. Chase, New York. *TW* reported she "... was arrested by Comstock, May 9th, on the charge of selling articles designed to procure abortion; a woman of ability, culture and character. Mrs. Chase is a graduate of Cleveland Medical College has lectured widely West, and much during the last three years in New York and Brooklyn. When she first came East she attended a Convention of the Labor Reform League and won the respect and esteem of all present by an intelligent, womanly address. Justifying her business as right, necessary and humane she said to Comstock, '...I am doing God's work by preventing poor families from being burdened with children whom they cannot support'" (June 1878, p. 2).

TW later corrected the account: "Misled by the Tribune's lying report of Mrs. Chase's arrest we wrote in last Word supposing she had sold instruments to procure abortion; they were only vaginal syringes; unanimously refusing to find a bill against her the Grand Jury advised her to prosecute Comstock for damages. Her tenants fled in dismay, her lectures were broken up and her practice well-nigh ruined. We hope all friends who can will aid her..." (July 1878, p. 2).

Three years later, *TW* enthused, "Thanks to the timely action of friends, Chase's Physiologist, *Foote's Health Monthly*, & *Kingets Health Journal*, all are now admitted to the mails without restriction! The U.S. Government has retreated from its untenable position. Comstock's savage effort to so far confirm traditional subjection of woman to man that she shall not even know how to resist male use of her person by preventing conception is illustrated in his base assaults on citizens for selling syringes. Provoked to good works Sarah Case invented one for this very purpose; he arrested her, but she escaped" (July 1881, p. 2).

TW offered to send a syringe to anyone upon receipt of $10. EHH was arrested. As for Chase, "Dr. Sara B. Chase ... held for alleged malpractice, has retained Mr. Pentecost for defense...." (March 1893, p. 2).

Mrs. A. C. (Etta) Cheney, Mass. Helped organize 1877 NEFLL Convention. In 1890 bailed out Dr. Sims, imprisoned for obscenity. She reported, "[I] ... went to North Adams, thence to the County Jail in Pittsfield, bailed Dr. Sims & brought him home to his delighted family. Seize a man, imprison him 10 days, subject him, his family & friends to all sorts of costs, then concede there is not case vs. him & let him go,— such is obscene law in Mass'tts!" (April 1890, p. 2).

Mrs. Cordelia Cheney, Boston. Elected 1882 as officer of NEFLL. Elected 1884 as officer of NELRL. Attended 1883 NELRL, 1885 URL, and 1888 ADL Conventions. Attended Heywood's 1883 trial. And she was "registered in the FLB; attractive, personally she is a woman of positive power in many servicable ways" (May 1883, p. 2).[3]

Tennie Claflin. Free Love advocate. Co-publisher of *W&CW*, which advertised in *TW* and was often quoted in early issues. Later moved to England and claimed never to have advocated free love. *TW* quoted the *N.Y. Sun*, "Very soon one of the wealthiest men in England, & titled, will marry Miss Tennie C. Claflin..." (August 1885, p. 2).

Lucy N. Colman [alt. spelling Coleman], Syracuse, N.Y. Attended 1880 ALRL Convention. Elected 1880 as officer of AUS. Attended an 1880 NLL meeting. Addressed 1881 ADL Convention. Attended Heywood's second hearing and trial under Comstock laws.

TW reprinted her from *The Truth Seeker*. One article argued for education on sexual matters. Another commented on Lucy Parsons, wife of the Haymarket martyr Albert Parsons. Colman wrote, "She is a splendid woman, a mulatto; only think of it—one of a race who, a few years ago, were held in such absolute bondage by government that some of us jeoparded [sic] our lives by saying, 'Down with the government!'... Shall such a woman be made a widow & her children orphans because Mr. Parsons dared to speak his honest thought?" (November 1886, p. 3).

TW quotes her as saying, "The remedy for economic troubles is cooperation, & free trade, with all the word implies" (August 1889, p. 1).

Jennie Collins. Attended NELRL meetings. She founded and managed "Boffin's Bower" in Boston at which she served free meals to poor girls and women. Anna Fales and Mrs. McGee assisted her. *TW* described Boffin's Bower as "one of the institutions born of Labor Reform Conventions, illustrating what the wit and energy of one woman may achieve for her sex; the native genius of Girls, their relations to Labor, to unsocial evil, what Woman's nature requires as a safeguard against pecuniary want and unnatural association with Man, are inquiries started by this well-written and very suggestive tract" (March 1879, p. 2).

In reviewing Boffin's Bower Annual Report, *TW* declared it to be "... a skillful piece of pen-work giving, in quick, throbbing Facts, impressive views of Life in Boston, as it is, does and suffers in *working!* Girls and

Women. A natural orator, 'the most eloquent woman in New England' Col. Wm. B. Greene used to say, Miss Collins years ago, stepped from the platform into close fellowship with her needy sisters to share with them the struggle for Liberty and Life, often tragic, yet always fruitful in suggestive experience. The dark problem of poverty whose mysterious labyrinths are filled with toiling, suffering, trusting inmates; the mute appeal of those who have not, to those who have; demand and supply incarnate in every worker; the stupendous issue of Justice to Labor now overshadowing all other questions.... What an intuitive, sympathetic, alert woman can do is told in many incidents of Miss Collins' notable career...." (January 1885, p. 3).

Julia Cowles. Elected 1883 as officer of ALRL.

Amanda Curtis. Spoke at the Sexual Science Association Meeting. Also addressed 1876 NELRL meeting and ADL Convention.

Mary A. Cutler. *TW* called her a "former co-worker" and an "effective supporter" of Labor and love reforms who was "in the field again" (May 1877, p. 2).

Mrs. Dr. Abbie E. Cutter. Addressed 1876 NEFLL meeting. She wrote, "I am a wife of twenty-seven years, a mother twenty-five years, a physician twenty-four, and this free-love question—I judge from experience—is the foundation of all reforms. We must have freedom before we can have love and love-children. Those Spiritualists who say they will not discuss these questions are just as bigoted as the church people ever have been. It is our business to seek out the best way to improve the race, and the proper way is to begin with intelligent generation" (March 1875, p. 4).

Mrs. E. L. [L. J.] Daniels, Kansas. Addressed NELRL meeting at which she "took the platform and said she was an orphan at four years of age and never had cause to blush for the treatment of any man of her orphanage. She believed in men, and said they were oppressed by women, as much as women are oppressed by them. But she did not intend to speak on the women question, and she went on to address herself to the general question. She argued that most of the debts of the world were no better than gambling debts, and should be no better protected by law; and that the accumulation of wealth should be limited by law to a fixed amount. She did not mean to say that all capitalists are oppressors, or that all workingmen are gods" (December 1873, p. 4).

In February 1879 she wrote to congratulate EHH on his release from prison. March 1893 issue announced, "... active in Spiritualist & labor Reform twenty years ago, [she] died recently in N.Y...."

Sarah M. Day. Among those announced as organizing an American Woman's Emancipation Society on December 7, 1873.

Voltairine de Cleyre. Brief review of work "Sex Slavery ... is a vigorous arraignment of marriage showing it guilty of many crimes meriting death, in order that women and men may begin to truly live; a Free Contract." (November 1892, p. 3)

Mrs. Elizabeth M. F. Denton, Wellesley, Mass. Elected 1880 as officer of NEFLL, though she explained she could not hear nor speak in public and, therefore, could not attend meetings. Elected 1881 as officer of NELRL. Elected 1882 as officer of ATL. Elected 1885 as officer of URL.

She wrote, "The impoverishment and degradation of labor are too evident to be denied; but where is the cause, and what is it? It would seem not to be in what is termed 'wages slavery'; for wages is an acknowledgment that equity should prevail between employer and employed; an attempt to actualize the condition which justice demands" (January 1873, p. 3). Expanded this theme in an article entitled "Property in Land, and Other Raw Materials, Robbery. The State an Intrusion" (May 1874, p. 4), in which she argued that labor alone gives rightful claim.

Her focus was broader than economics. She greatly admired *CY*, and wrote of prostitution, "The conflict today is not between purity and prostitution, but between *prostitution under sanction of the marriage system*, and prostitution without that sanction" (May 1878, p. 3).

Her frequent supportive letters initially praised the plain-speech policy and sale of the Comstock syringe. Letter to editor (March 1883) decried the lack of support EHH received from the liberal community for his second arrest. "... Subordination to Authority as a condition of societal existence is an idea that has been burned into our very beings from ages so remote that but very few of us *dare to even think* in opposition to the behests of whoever or whatsoever we may have invested therewith; hence every investigation that tends to unsettle the faith of the millions in the infallibility of accepted authority, sends a thrill of horror through all the nerves of society. It is to this fact, Mr. Heywood, that you are indebted for the indifference & the utter lack of such a general uprising among so-called Liberals as should triumphantly compel these legal robbers of your rights & ours to stay their hands..." (March 1883, p. 3). April 1883 *TW* quoted Denton from *The Boston investigator* trying to rally liberals to Heywood's defense.

TW stated, she "... is one of the Jury of sixteen women Mr. H. quoted in Court, to show that the syringe, at least, as 'a war measure' ... should be vindicated against vice-society heism. A born lady, and a thoroughly domestic woman, Mrs. Denton's pen is a power for Right whenever and wherever persons are invaded" (June 1883 p. 3).

She became critical of the plain-speech policy. She wrote, "The honesty of your [ATH's] intentions, I never question; the purity of your motives, I never doubt; but the wisdom of your methods, is not always apparent to me. In one particular, at least, I must regard them as a positive injury, if not ruinous both to yourselves and to the cause you especially advocate.... The words [c---, c---, and f---] ... are in no way worthy of the price that must be paid for their redemption" (March 1887, p. 3).

Nevertheless, Denton was one of the people who met EHH at the door of the State Prison upon his release on May 13, 1892.

Alvira DePuy. A Signatory on the 1876 Call for a Woman's National Labor Convention.

Etta DePuy. A Signatory on the 1876 Call for a Woman's National Labor Convention.

Mrs. Fannie C. Dexter, Providence, R.I. Attended meetings of NELRL and NEFLL.

Anna E. Dickenson [alt. spelling Dickinson]. Lecturer. *TW* commented, "The press praise Anna Dickenson's new lecture on 'The Social Evil'"; but, though 'eloquent' enough, it shows the 'plentiful lack' of thought which characterizes all of Miss Dickenson's efforts...." (April 1875, p. 3). December 1883 *TW* indicated she had joined the Knights of Labor.

Mrs. Abbie [alt spelling Abby] C. Dike [Lee], Boston, then Texas. Elected 1881 as officer of NELRL and the ADL. Elected 1882 as officer of NELRL. Arrested April 4, 1878, for selling *CY* and "The Fruits of Philosophy." Released after jury split 6 to 6. *TW* September 1883, declared, "Abby Dike served here [Mountain House] until the suitor, John Lee, took her to Boston where they have lived happily together several years...."

Mary S. Dike. Elected 1880, 1881 as officer of URL. Elected 1882 as officer of NEFLL. *TW* announced, "A. D. Wheeler ... & his mate Mary Dike have a fine boy; he first met her here [Mountain House], in house and type work, under the banner of Union-Reform...." (September 1883, p. 2).

Mattie Dike, South Westminster, Mass. *TW* commented, "... another of these attractive and capable sisters, Mattie Dike, South Westminster, Mass., has also done well here in Mountain Home; if some one of the able men of the F.L.B. engages her attention, she too may be come prosperously Cupids-Yoked" (September 1883, p. 2).

Mrs. Dillingham. Attended NEFLL meetings and the 1888 Annual ADL Convention. *TW* announced, "Mrs. D. is studying elocution and hope that, erelong, her well-informed mind will voice itself in public conventions...." (April, 1877, p. 2).

Mrs. Mary Dingwell, Fall River. Attended 1877 Convention of NELRL. Spoke at 1877 NEFLL Convention.

Mrs. Jennie A. Doane, Vineland, N.J., then Grahamville, Fla. Frequent supportive letters to editor regarding plain-speech policy. For example, "'The three words are certainly of unmistakable meaning,' I thought so when I ardently favored their use but have learned that they are mistakable & surely the characters of many who use them are mistaken; so I come to the conclusion that sexual scientists need new words unmistakable in meaning.... I am weary of being 'compelled to take the ground that there can be no such thing as obscenity' for I believe there is & can be obscenity & profanity.... I have not gone back on myself for if I must use the word 'coition' or 'a worse one' I will take the 'worse one.' I simply want new words independent of the prudes and slums" (October 1888, p. 3).

TW of December 1889 thanked her for a photo of her in "reform dress." In the same issue, she stated "My present dresses come a little below the knees in length. My pants fit in my button shoes; some of them are gathers & put in a band; some are plaited, other are plain, with biases taken in them so as to somewhat closely fit my legs from the shoe-top to the garter-line. I am not opposed to *loose garters*; so at the elastic line I put elastic in my pants which keeps them looking neat & beautiful & saves wearing any on the stockings.... Celia B. Whitehead wears a costume similar to mine" (p. 3).

Mrs. Amie Eaton, New Hampshire. Elected 1887 as officer of NEFLL. Staunch supporter of "Hull's Crucible" (Boston). *TW* called her "an unflinching exponent of Social Freedom" (July 1876, p. 3).

Mrs. Minnie [Mina?] Maria Egli. Supportive letter to editor re: EHH's imprisonment. A member of the FLB (1883).[4] Attended 1884 URL Convention and was described: "... an educated & highly accomplished Swiss lady, recently of Dakota, opened the evening session by a sensible & cogent statement of Free Love views...." (August 1884, p. 2). Addressed 1885 ALRL Convention.

Fanny Fairbanks. Elected officer at 1881 NELRL Annual Convention.

Kate Field. *TW* quoted George MacDonald in *Freethought* as saying "Kate Field, the lecturer, is fighting the Prohibitionists on the ground, among other things, that the Bible opposes prohibition...." (April 1889, p. 3). Also quoted, *Worcester Telegram*, "Kate Field is to edit a paper at Washington. She announced in her prospectus that she believes in free trade. It is quite natural that she should. Kate is an old maid. She doesn't believe in helping along the infant industries" (December 1889, p. 2).

Susie [Susan] Willis Fletcher. Speaker at 1876 Annual Meeting of the Sexual Science Association.

Marie C. Fisher. Brief review of her work "Ought Women to be Punished for Having Too Many Children?" (February 1893, p. 3).

Maria L. Follett, Le Claire, Iowa. Advocated sexual freedom. Elected 1880 as officer of NEFLL. Elected 1880, 1881 as officer of ALRL.

TW announced, "*The Le Claire Pilot*, Iowa, has the following relative to the scandalous persecution of Maria L. Follett by the religious secular numskulls of that bat-blind town:—

"The little book called *Cupid's Yokes* about which there has been such a furore [sic] and commotion during the past two weeks was ... consumed by fire at the parsonage of the M. E. Church, Mrs. Follett herself consigning it to the flames, saying as she did so: 'Michael Servetus was burned; and John Brown was hung; but the truth goes marching on. So in like manner, the truth contained in that little book will live when its oppressors, and the evils its author seeks to eradicate from society shall have passed away and been swept from the earth.' Mrs. F. declares the book to be the axe laid at the root of the tree of a terrible evil which has for thousands of years defied legislation of church and state, and still defies them" (July 1879, p. 3).

Follett had loaned the book to a male "friend" who took it to the local clergyman who threatened her with circulating obscene material. Because two small children depended upon her, she chose to burn the book.

TW announced her novel, *Libra Dawn, or Dawn of Liberty, A Sequel to* Cupid's Yokes, which appeared serially in the *Le Claire Pilot* (Iowa). Follett was termed a "resolute and Talented Free Lover...." (March 1880, p. 2).

H. L. Barter, the publisher of the *Le Claire Pilot* was arrested for printing *Libra Dawn*. *TW* reprinted a Barter-Defense Fund appeal from *The Truth Seeker*. "This time it is a woman who writes a prosecuted story.... Mrs. Follett is a true, gentle, genuine woman, a citizen of Le Claire from her youth up, a trifle over forty years of age, owns her own house and grounds, having her young daughter and aged mother with her, who also owns a farm adjoining the village and is a substantial citizen. She has been twice married, and has reared a family of children, some of whom also are married.... She suffered much in her two marriages, and knew of outrages among her friends and acquaintances worse than any experiences of her own. So she sat down and told all these stories in a book. She calls it a novel, but there is very little imagination in it. The story is only a thin clothes-line on which to hang out her foul marriage linen to air and dry and disinfect itself. It is too fearfully realistic to be pleasant reading, but it is true; and can't we men stand anything women choose to say on this subject? Can't we survive without imprisoning publishers?..." (November 1880, p. 3).

Follett reciprocated the admiration. She wrote, "To me The Word is the leading journal of free thought, progress & reform; I cannot afford to miss a copy" (June 1881, p. 3).

Abbie K. Foster, Worcester, Mass. Published letter written jointly with Stephen S. Foster condemning taxation. She refused to pay taxes because she was denied the right to vote (June 1876, p. 2).

Helen H. Gardner. Brief review of her work, "Is This Your Son, My Lord?": "... a well-told story, showing the real and moral obligation are inseparable from Love, and binding alike on both sexes" (*TW* October 1892, p. 3). Brief review of her work "Pray You Sir, Whose Daughter?": "... portrays the financial & social conditions environing girls & women, but fails to show that they are crucified between two thieves, Usury & Marriage" (February 1893, p. 3).

Emma Goldman. *TW* quoted *Boston Advertiser*, "Emma Goldman [sic] is a blonde, German woman of medium stature, has a fine figure and an intelligent and rather pretty face, with large, clear, blue eyes. Miss Goldman was asked what she knew of Bergman and said: 'I have known Bergman for a long time and lived with him for the last two years. He is a quiet, studious, courageous fellow, who hates capitalists and tyrants.' 'Did you know that he was going to kill Frick?' asked our reporter; 'I did not, Bergman is a man who, having once made up his mind to do a thing, does it without saying a word to anybody.' 'Was it right to shoot Mr. Frick?' She replied, 'I think that all men who are tyrants ought to be put down, but not in that way" (August 1892, p. 2).

Bessie Greene. Daughter of Col. Wm. B. and Anne Shaw Greene. A close friend of Josiah Warren, she was a member of NELRL and the French Section of the International Working People's Association of Boston. Killed in a shipwreck on May 7th, 1875.

Mrs. Ida Gregg, La. Elected 1885 as officer of ALRL.

S. Mira Hall, New York. Among those who called for a Woman's National Labor Convention to meet in NYC in December 1876. Addressed 1878, 1879 ALRL Convention. Attended Bennett's 1879 court trial. Elected 1880, 1882, 1884 as officer of ALRL. Letter to editor: "The marriage institution belongs to the barbaric ages, the era of brute force, the condition of master and slave" (August 1881, p. 3). Attended 1883 URL Convention.

Mrs. L. Myra Hall [probably the same person as above]. Elected 1885 as officer of ALRL. Death on April 15, 1886, announced.

Orpha Hammond, Fredonia, New York. Brief review of her work, "Love Versus Fascination": "... traces the subtle play of physical and psychological forces, showing how Intrigue blasts hope & brings tragic unrest while Love assures beneficent growth & ecstatic peace..." (April 1881, p. 3).

Dr. Ellen Beard Harman [alt. spelling Harmon], Ancora, N.J. In 1879 spoke at URL Conference, ADL, and a Temperance Convention in Princeton. *TW* advertised her lecture on Health and Dress Reform. Elected 1880 as officer of URL.

Lillian Harman.[5] *TW* quoted her. It also commented and reported sympathetically upon her imprisonment at age sixteen along with E. C. Walker for violating marriage statutes. Printed her appeal for support to keep *Lucifer* publishing. ATH defended Lillian and Walker in article entitled "Sex Rights" (October 1886, p. 3).

TW commented on the Court's refusal to accept bail: "While many hearts yearn to open those jail doors by paying costs, the ins have the logic of it *vs* the outs, & each hour's restrainment of their liberty brands Kansas with every burning blackening infamy. A girl of seventeen, Lillian Harman, in electric self-possession, intuitive wisdom, unconscious courage surpasses most living womanhood, & ... may be so attractive in history that all human kind will feel related to her..." (March 1887, p. 2).

When Moses Harman was arrested, *TW* reprinted one of her letters: "Papa suffers more than I do, & I feel so sorry for him. It was hard to decide whether it was my duty to go with him or stay here, but I decided that the fine should not be paid. I have chosen my course, & shall not depart from it. But my conscience troubles me when I look through the bars and see his eyes filling with tears as he talks to me" (March 1887, p. 3).

"Walker & Harman were released Apr. 4th on payment of $113.80 costs...." (May 1887, p. 2). They paid the fine in order to keep *Lucifer* running. *TW* commented, "Now, we understand Edwin & Lillian are in something of a quandary as to what to do. The court has pronounced them legally arrived, yet they dare not live together as husband & wife, for their enemies are ready to pounce upon them again" (Ibid. 3).

The July 1888 issue announced the periodical *Fair Play* published by Walker & Lillian. She attended the celebration that followed EHH's May 1892 release from prison.

Mary H. Henck. Among those announced as organizing an American Woman's Emancipation Society on December 7, 1873.

Eliza Hewes, Boston, Mass. *TW* quoted, "To the Liberal League, an earnest body of workers for the uplifting of Humanity I must unreservedly accord all praise, for their generous, and well planned method of bringing that persecuted, but I think *God appointed* woman, Victoria Woodhull, to public hearing in Boston, after the suppression of her speech by the stupidity, ignorance and bigotry, of municipal authority" (May 1873, p. 3).

Angela T. Heywood. See Section I, chapter 1, of this book.

Vesta Vernon Heywood. Daughter of EHH and ATH. Elected 1880 as officer of URL.

Her comments quoted in *TW.* For example, "When there were no men or women, in either world, who made the man and the woman?" (July 1873, p. 3). "Mamma, what is property? Is it what is mine, or is it something which somebody has got away from someone else?" (January 1874, p. 3). Or, "I suppose, Mamma, the most happy and satisfactory expression of my life would be to accomplish my work well" (June 1876, p. 3).

Annie E. Higby. Among those announced as organizing an American Woman's Emancipation Society on December 7, 1873.

Mrs. Dorcas Roper Hoar, Princeton, Mass. Mother of EHH. Quoted, "When Labor Reform ideas come in fashion, I shall be one of the first women of society" (February 1873, p. 3).

Mrs. Clara Hoffmann. *TW* quoted from address to the International Council arguing that inequality within marriage leads to, among other evils, prostitution (June 1889, p. 1).

Sallie Holley, Va. Elected 1878, 1879 as officer of ALRL.

Mrs. Sarah Elizabeth Holmes, London, England. Letter to ATH after EHH's arrest: "You are in great trouble again; I am, *we* are always loving you & want very much to help you. Tell us if there is any way in which we can do anything. Some day there will come special comfort and peace into your heart that could not have been but for to-day's pain; there will come to the world great gain, through all this loss & suffering, on your part; I know your perfect faith in Right & your knowledge of how wrong oppose & crushes it. But some share in the final replacing of evil with good I want to reach, as great healing & peace, deep into your own true woman heart. When I heard this news I felt so sorry & so afraid that my silence might have let you feel that I was dropping away from you; but you are always close & dear in my heart. Let us hear from you; we want to know & help; believe that always. We shall be in England this winter" (January 1883, p. 3).

Zadie E. Holmes [Same as Sarah E. Holmes?], Boston. Attended URL meetings.

Mrs. E. T. Housch. Editor of *Women at Work,* a monthly periodical devoted to Labor Reform, which *TW* endorsed.

Elizabeth Hughes, San Francisco. A passionate and lengthy letter to the editor about labor reform (March 1875, p. 3).

Elvira Hull. Among those announced as organizing an American Woman's Emancipation Society on December 7, 1873. Defended Moses Hull. *TW* quoted her from *Hull's Crucible*: "We continued to cohabit until I being physically the weaker of the two, found my health was rapidly giving way. Moses did not separate himself from me. I claim all the honor, if honor it be, of the step that finally separated us sexually. We both believed that sexual communion where there is not sexual desire and satisfaction is adultery, *yes, prostitution. I* do *not* desire to be a prostitute. *I will not*, if I know it, prostitute myself, either sexually, socially, financially, or in any other way. Consequently I said to Moses, 'We must be consistent; we profess to despise prostitution, yet we are living it every time we are together. We must stop it, or cease preaching.' Moses was *grieved* that the time had come. It was I who was inexorable. The time had come when the move must be made or we would stand before the world branded, truthfully branded, as hypocrites. It was for me to take the step. I did not do it rashly or thoughtlessly: on the contrary, it cost me a struggle such as I hope may never fall to my lot again" (November 1876, p. 1).

Mary Florence Hull. Daughter of Moses Hull. *TW* stated she "has formed a matrimonial copartnership…. The parties have signed a written contract, promising that they will try to control each other only by advice or persuasion" (February 1877, p. 2).

Mattie Hull. See Mattie Sawyer.

Ann Ellsworth Hunt, Sharonville, Hamilton Co., Ohio. Letter to editor, February 1876, lamenting current economic status of women within marriage.

Hannah J. Hunt. Mother of Lillie D. White, Lizzie M. Holmes, C. F. Hunt, and S. A. Hunt. Died December 11, 1903, at the age of 78 at the home of her daughter, Mrs. Holmes, in La Veta, Colo.

Helen Hunt. Reprinted a poem by Hunt published by the *Independent*, "On Charlotte Cushman" (June 1876, p. 4).

Mrs. Lydia Hutchinson, Milford, N.H. Elected 1880 as officer of NELRL.

Mrs. Olive H. F. Ingalls, Glenora, N.Y. Attended 1879 courtroom trial of D. M. Bennett for selling *CY*. *TW* January 1880 reprinted her letter to the *New York Sun*, attacking that newspaper for criticizing Hayes's pardoning of EHH. Her summer resort advertised in *TW*.

Josephine Jackson. Brief review of her work "What's the Matter?": "[It] attacks corsets tight shoes, skirts and other unnatural enemies of woman's health, freedom and prosperous activity…." (December 1880, p. 3).

Mrs. L. K. Joslin. Attended 1876 NELRL Convention. Death announced: "… is affectionately remembered by many friends who knew her personal worth; spiritualist in faith, she was a liberal, active worker in all fields of growth; the hospitable welcome which she, Mr. Joslin & the children always gave to reformers makes their house historic in progressive enterprise" (January 1884, p. 2).

Mrs. Abbie Joslyn. Elected 1882 as officer of ADL.

Mrs. A. P. Joyce, Westvale, Concord, Mass. Attended 1875 Social Freedom Convention. Spoke at 1877, 1879, 1880 NEFLL Convention. Aided in conducting 1878 NEFLL Convention in Boston. Spoke at 1879 NELRL Convention. Elected 1880 as officer of ADL. Letter to editor supporting EHH in his 1883 imprisonment.

Laura Kendrick, San Francisco, Ca., then Boston. Lecturer. Spiritualist. Elected 1878, 1879 as officer of NELRL. Elected 1878 as an officer of NEFLL.

TW advertised her lecturers. For example, "[She] has drawn good audiences in Boston, lectures in New Bedford, during February. A very eloquent speaker, she is an intelligent exponent of living thought and feeling sincerely reliable in word and deed" (February 1878, p. 3).

September 1878 issue described her speech at Faneuil Hall on behalf of the imprisoned Heywood. The Defense Association (for EHH) delegated her to take a petition to Washington to ask Pres. Hayes to pardon him. A pardon ensued. Elected 1878 as officer of the new NDA to defend persons prosecuted by Comstock.

February 1882 issue announced her death on January 11.

Mrs. Kimball. Elected 1881 as officer of ADL.

Martha C. Kingman, Cummington, Mass. Supportive letter to EHH in his fight against Comstock. "... I well remember you way back in the old Antislavery Reform, when you came to Cummington with Garrison, Phillips, and a host of other grand old heroes...." (February 1885, p. 3).

Mrs. Dr. Abbie Knapp, Dowagiac, Mich. Several supportive letters to *TW*, backing plain-speech policy.

Mrs. H. S. Lake, Clinton, Iowa, then Milwaukee, Wisc. Supportive letters to *TW*, for example congratulating EHH on selling the Comstock syringe.

Anna M. Lant, New York City. Wife of imprisoned John Lant. Letter to editor in *TW* February 1876.

Ann Lee. Elected 1880 as officer of ADL.

Mrs. Mary A. Leland, N.Y. Elected 1874 as officer of ALRL. Spoke at 1876 NEFLL Convention. Supported EHH in his 1879 imprisonment. Attended 1880 NDA meeting. Elected 1880 as officer of URL. July 1892 issue mentioned her dying during *TW*'s two-year suspension.

Mrs. S. J. Lenont, Northfield, Minn. Elected 1885 as officer to URL Convention. Supportive letters to the editor, especially concerning EHH's imprisonment.

Mrs. Cynthia Leonard, N.Y. Addressed 1886, 1887 ALRL. President of the Science of Life Club, which aims to "improve the human race through a better understanding of the laws of hereditary transmission" (May 1885, p. 2). Quoted her as saying, "... there is nothing about our government to be proud of so long as a single person must sleep on the benches in the parks unprovided with a home...." (September 1886, p. 1). Brief review of her work "Pen Pictures": "[It] gives her opinions of men, women & things in clear, cogent style, having much matter to quicken thought...." (January 1889, p. 3).

Helen M. Lewis. A Signatory on the 1876 Call for a Woman's National Labor Convention.

Jennie Leys. Among those announced as organizing an American Woman's Emancipation Society on December 7, 1873. *TW* carried her statement, "I stand alone, having pledged myself two years ago to do the work assigned me to do, and to know neither father nor mother, sister nor brother, husband nor home in this life forever. While I walk the earth I will have neither touch, nor look for word of love from living man, not because I do not respect and honor true men, but because I must stand apart, and do my work without let or hindrance" (December 1874, p. 3).

Mrs. Elmer Lincoln. Attended 1883 trial of EHH.

Eleanor L. Lindsay. Among those announced as organizing an American Woman's Emancipation Society on December 7, 1873.

Mrs. Mary C. Livermore. Quoted on several occasions. Most notably, March 1890 issue quoted an article from *N.A. Review* in which she criticized man-made laws of marriage and divorce.

Ann Lohman (Madam Restell). *TW* announced, "... Comstock broke into her house under a false name and by deliberate lying caused the death of a woman [Lohman] by suicide...." (May 1878, p. 3).

Mrs. J. S. [J. E.?] Longley. Attended 1884 URL Conference. Supportive letter to editor 1892.

Mrs. A. C. Macdonald [McDonald]. Elected 1883, 1885, 1888 as officer of ALRL. Addressed 1886, 1887 ALRL Convention.

Frances Rose Mackinley. Among those announced as organizing an American Woman's Emancipation Society on December 7, 1873.

Harriet Martineau. Brief review of her work, "The Lover" (March 1888, p. 3).

Josephine McCarty. December 1873 issue carried her article, "Working Girls."

Mrs. Dolly A. Melvin. Attended 1884 and 1885 URL Convention.

Mrs. E. A. Meriwether, Memphis, Tenn. Letters to editor. *TW* declared her "speech to the Democracy at St. Louis was brave, able & timely...." (July 1888, p. 2). *TW* quoted the *New York Sun* as saying, "... the distinguished woman who had the pluck to appear before the National Convention at St. Louis & demand a hearing, deserves the highest honors of her sex. It was a tremendous thing for a woman to do. Mrs. Meriwether's pluck stands out all the more boldly because her companion Mr. Minor has not sufficient courage to mount the platform & face the multitude. Mrs. Meriwether's speech will doubtless be framed in letters of gold, as it deserves to be and hung up among the archives of the Woman's Suffrage League. All honor to the little lady who thanked the assembled Democracy for giving her ten minutes in behalf of thirty millions of women & it would leave each the most infinitesimal fraction of a second—not enough to wink even of to put out her tongue. Mrs. Meriwether has stormed the parapet, got clean over the walls, but she leads what may yet be by no means a forlorn hope. The party through whose instrumentality the women of America may be enfranchised will find itself a round thirty million votes the better" (July 1888, p. 3).

Mrs. Minnie Merton, Riverhead Jail, Long Island, N.Y. Letter to editor: "I am in a jail, through the false oath of a fraudulent medium ... who is trying to swindle me, and has laid claim to my goods as her own. I am worn out & feeble, and no one to give bonds which are $100. I have no money to help myself with. Cannot a sum be raised for me, or must I die because I am a woman? They accuse me of Communism, Nihilism, Spiritualism, & a thousand crimes" (October 1882, p. 3).

Louise Michel. November, 1886, issue quoted her on revolution.

Mrs. Anna M. Middlebrook, M.D., Bridgeport, Conn. Frequent supportive letters to editor. Among those announced as organizing an American Woman's Emancipation Society on December 7, 1873. Spoke at 1878 ALRL Convention. Elected 1879, 1881 as officer of ALRL. Elected 1879, 1880 as officer of URL. Elected 1881 as officer of ADL.

Letter to 1878 NEFLL Convention. "... Our religion has given the woman to the man, from the very beginning, or ever since the Almighty tried the *rib* experiment.... [O]f her, He said, 'In sorrow shalt thou bring forth children, and thy desire shalt be to thy husband and he shall rule over thee.' The masses governed by superstition instead of by a true social science have taken this as infallible law, and under its dictates have condemned woman to a miserable subjection, making marriage a cloak to cover (in many cases) a beastly prostitution, legalized by legislation and made sacred by religion, while *illegitimacy* is only reserved for *divine persons* like Jesus!!!" (July 1878, p. 4).

Supportive of plain speech policy. December 1873 issue quoted her on Social Freedom.

Married to H. V. Twiss, a N.H. merchant, apparently adopting his name. Defended herself in *TW* for marrying. "When women can have a voice in law-making, some of these wrongs will be redressed. At present, however, I believe she is more justly treated under its protection than outside of it" (November 1880, p. 4).

Mrs. Lula Mulliken. Elected 1875, 1877, 1878 as officer of NELRL. Acted as part of the NELRL financial committee (1876). Assisted Heywoods in the 1876 NELRL Convention.

Helen Nash. Among those announced as organizing an American Woman's Emancipation Society on December 7, 1873.

Emma A. Newton, Worcester, Mass. *TW* Advertised her essay, "Pre-Natal Culture; Suggestions to Parents Relative to Systematic Methods of Molding the Tendencies of Offspring before Birth."

Mary Overton. Among those announced as organizing an American Woman's Emancipation Society on December 7, 1873.

Mrs. E. L. [L. J.] Palmer, S.C. Elected 1888 as officer of ALRL.

Fanny H. Parmelee. A Signatory on the 1876 Call for a Woman's National Labor Convention.

Mrs. Lucy Parsons. Wife of Haymarket martyr Albert Parsons. Quoted her as praising the red flag of revolution. February 1888 issue appealed to readers to send her $1 for pamphlet "Anarchism" advertised therein.

Mrs. L. M. Patterson, Alleghany, Pa. Labor reformer. Letter to editor: "The large force of women and girls in our cotton mills go to their work an hour earlier and stay in an hour later than most workingmen, in other employments. If women are weaker than the other sex (as some men say) why should more labor at less price, be exacted of them and their vitality be taxed to fill the bottomless pockets of greedy monopolists? Is slavery abolished?

"Mrs. Woodhull may be a martyr to the cause of social freedom, and her witnesses be bribed into silence. But in the destiny of things *truth will out* first or last. Ten years ago my daughter, then sixteen, from whom for fundamental reasons, I had always concealed my sentiments, said to me, 'Social freedom, in an under current, obtains everywhere; and it is nearly to the surface, for it keeps bubbling up here and there, and the day is not far distant when it will burst out like a volcano.' Is not her prophecy being fulfilled? It is not probable that the case in hand will be decided impartially, for the very men who try the case are as guilty as Beecher has been pronounced (if guilt it be). I honor Mrs. Woodhull for her bravery: may God and Angels sustain and bless her" (January 1873, p. 3).

In another letter to editor, she wrote, "The time is near when the millionaire will be glad to handout his ill gotten gains to save his life. Men will not stand supinely by and let their families starve. One man at Burlington, in a meeting of the strikers, got up and said, 'Gentlemen, I have worked for this railroad for 11 years, and half the time I have not had enough to eat. I have five children and have had a good deal of sickness, in my family, and my expenses have been too much for my income, which is now reduced to $1.10 a day. Look in my dinner bucket and you will see only bread and a little cheap meat. I cannot afford butter, nor anything that I can relish" (November 1877, p. 3).

May [Mary?] Peterson, South Hanover. Attended 1879 URL Convention. Elected officer of URL in 1882, 1885, 1886. Elected 1880, 1882 as officer of ADL. Elected 1881 and 1882 as officer of NEFLL.

Eliza W. Philbrooke [Philbrook]. Elected 1881, 1882, 1884 as officer of NELRL.

Mrs. M. H. Plunkett. Published the *Christian Science Magazine*. Elected 1875 as officer of NELRL. *TW* quoted article about her in Brick Pomeroy's *Advance Thought*, accusing her of defrauding men of money. *TW* mildly defended her (September 1889, p. 2).

Mrs. Chappel Polley. Spoke at 1876 Sexual Science Association Meeting. Attended 1876 NEFLL meeting. Spoke at 1877 ATL Conv.

Mrs. L. M. R. Poole [Pool], Vemillion, then Swanton, Ohio. Among those announced as organizing an American Woman's Emancipation Society on December 7, 1873. Elected 1874, 1878, 1880, 1881 as officer of ALRL.

Frequent letters to editor, expressing sentiments such as: "What right has government to sanction the servility of woman, and educate and compel every man, whether he is the best man alive, or the lowest drunken vagabond and fiend incarnate, to support he may justly have full possession of one woman during her natural life, thereby depriving seven eighths of all women of the power to give to the world anything but misery, disease and death?" (October 1872, p. 3).

"Those who think prostitution is doing, ever has or ever can do anything for humanity can have plenty of it; I should advise them to drink deep & fill themselves of the damnable thing while it lasts, for as sure as woman ever has the opportunity to vote & help make the laws, marriage & its twin devil prostitution, will get themselves down & out. Unmitigated, selfish heism, stalks abroad, rides rampant over every weak thing...." (November 1882, p. 3).

TW referred to her as "a veteran Socialist of The Word school...." (January 1884, p. 2). She supported the plain-speech policy.

Emeline A. Prescott, No. Vassalboro, Me., then Hallowell, Me. Elected 1880, 1881, 1882 as officer of NEFLL. Wrote supportive letters, but declined to contribute articles due to poor health.

Mrs. Lucy A. Ramsden, Danville [Dansville?], N.Y. Admirer of *CY*. Supportive letters to editor.

Georgia Replogle, Poughkeepsie, N.Y. Letter in support of the arrested Elmina Slenker (November 1887, p. 3).

Mrs. Sadie Rice, Northfield, Minn. Admirer of *CY*. Supportive letters to editor, including a poem.

Olive N. Robinson, Reed's Ferry, N.H. Spoke 1873 at NELRL.

Grace Royal. Spoke at a 1876 Sexual Science Association Meeting. Addressed 1881 NEFLL meeting. Addressed 1881, 1883, 1884, 1886 ADL Conventions. Attended 1884, 1885, 1888 Annual NEFLL Conventions. Addressed 1886 ATL Convention.

Mrs. M. A. Russell. Elected 1881 as officer of NEFLL. Elected 1883 as officer of NELRL.

Mrs. J. T. Sargent. Brief review of her "Sketches and Reminiscences of the Radical Club" (February 1881, p. 3).

Mrs. M. Saunders, Worcester, Mass. Addressed 1879 NEFLL Convention. Advertised as a clairvoyant.

Mattie E. B. Sawyer [Hull]. Associate editor of *Hull's Crucible*. Spiritualist. Free-love advocate. Attended 1876 NELRL Convention. Wrote to *TW*, "We lament that we could not have attended every session of the Labor Reform Convention; our sympathies are with the movement, and we are sure, the earnest active minds employed in this direction are destined to bring about a general revolution" (July 1874, p. 3). Spoke at 1876 Sexual Science Association and URL meetings. Attended 1876 NEFLL Convention where the honorary degree of "Her Royal Highness" was conferred upon her. Elected 1879 as officer of NEFLL. Elected 1877 as officer of ATL. Elected 1878 officer of new NDA.

TW followed her free-love advocacy: "Moses Hull and Mattie Sawyer propose to live together as they please without asking leave of a minister, or of that intrusive stupidity known as statute law...." (August 1874, p. 3).

Also announced "A Collection of *Original Songs* as Sung by Mattie Sawyer. Whether the product of spirits or not this charming little book shows genius and inspiration of remarkable delicacy and power. There is any amount of spiritual bosh called 'poetry' but this book will stand the test of criticism. Some of these songs, given off hand on Subjects selected by the audience, (both words and music being produced at the moment), are tests of ability which we would like to see Horace Seaver or any other materialistic speaker attempt to compete against.... If people know what's good, and how much the brave author needs money, they will see that the book has a large sale. Address Mattie Sawyer, 24 Newcomb St., Boston" (February 1875, p. 3). Brief review of her "Wayside Jottings," "... a collection of her Sketches, Poems, and Songs...." (December 1887, p. 3).

TW reported on a Social Freedom Convention, saying, "The Convention ... was a success, the prime movers therein, Hull, Sawyer & Co., having good cause to congratulate themselves on the result.... While we applaud Hull, Sawyer & Co. for bringing a great and grave question to the front, we dissent utterly from their tendency to force this grand reform into despotic grooves. They advocate 'true marriage' and a 'state nursery'; as well talk of true bondage and state-breeding!" (April 1875, p. 2).

When the couple incurred debts, *TW* declared "Moses Hull and Mattie Sawyer will start out on their missionary enterprise with their Large Tent about the 15th of May" (May 1876, p. 2). This was followed by the announcement, "Enraged by incisive criticisms of his revival-machine religion, the Rev. Ranter Hammond incited the arrest of Moses Hull and Mattie Sawyer for 'adultery' in Vineland, N.J.; Mrs. Sawyer was released but Mr. Hull was bound over for trial" (July 1876, p. 3).

The June 1880 issue took note of Sawyer referring to herself as "Mattie Hull." By 1887, the couple was living peacefully together; "Hull & Sawyer were unmolested in Massachusetts...." (May 1887, p. 2).

Olive Schreiner. Brief review of her book, *The Story of an African Farm*: "[It] shows the pious idiocy of much called 'religion,' satirizes marriage, personates Free Love in a physical sense...." (January 1889, p. 3).

Georgia Schumm [misspelled Shumm]. Copublisher of the *Chicago Radical Review* and coeditor of *Libertas*. Brief review of her translation of *The Rights of Women and the Sexual Relations* by Karl Heinzen, pub. by B. Tucker (September 1892, p. 2).

Dr. Juliet H. Severance [alt. spelling Severence], Milwaukee, Wisc., then Chicago, Ill. Her work *Financial Problems* briefly reviewed. (April 1884, p. 3) Among those announced as organizing an American Woman's Emancipation Society on December 7, 1873. Elected 1880 as V.P. of NLL. In 1887 assumed head of the NLL when Ingersoll walked out of conv. Elected 1881 as officer of URL.

Supported free love, with letters expressing such sentiments as, "... Our present marriage system is a slave institution and I abhor and detest it. It causes sickness, misery and death as I, who am constantly treating the sick, can testify. I could give cases of extreme cruelty and barbarity perpetrated under its 'sacred sanction,' that would surpass those of the master exercised over the slaves at the South...." (December 1880, p. 3).

"... Shall we speak tenderly of a system [marriage] that takes from woman the control of her person in the most important and sacred of all relations, forces upon her undesired maternity, gives man authority to perpetrate upon her the most revolting of crimes, which without its sanction would consign him to a prison cell, denies the mother the ownership of her own offspring, peoples the world with children begotten in disgust...." (August 1881, p. 3).

Supported EHH in imprisonments. Quoted her from *The Truth Seeker*, where she decried the NLL's backing away from former denunciations of Comstock. Also vigorously defended Lillian Harman and E. C. Walker in their imprisonment.

Olivia F. Shepard, Foxboro, Mass. Spiritualist. Active in 1874 formation of American Free Dress League, along with Benj. Tucker. Elected 1874 as officer of ALRL. Supportive letters to editor, often discussing dress reform. Also articles pleading that cause of dress reform.

TW quoted her from *W&CW*: "I must for the present devote myself to Dress Reform as a special branch of the central work of woman's emancipation.... Suggestions as to the best methods of procedure, how to raise money to be used in publishing and distributing tracts, or help to obtain a public hearing in any other way will be gratefully received and duly acknowledged" (October 1873, p. 3).

Brief review of her magazine, *The World's Friend, a Monthly Record of Light from Spirit Life, of fearless Thought & frank Criticism*: "... the welcome voice of Sheism in newspaperdom now excessively heistic" (May 1885, p. 3).

Belle C. Shull, Findlay, Ohio. Met EHH at the door of the State Prison upon his last release on May 13, 1892.

Elmina Drake Slenker, Snowville, Pulaski Co. Va. Editor of *The Little Freethinker*, "... a lively child, interesting age & youth...." (November 1892, p. 2). Advertised in *TW*.

Referred to as Aunt Elmina, because of such gestures as frequently sending gifts of yarn and knit goods to the impoverished Heywoods. Supportive letters to editor. For example, "I wish to tell thee that I am in deep sympathy with thee and thy work.... I have sold and given away many copies of 'Cupid's Yokes'..." signed herself "an Alphian Free Lover" (September 1880, p. 3).

When H. L. Barter was imprisoned for publishing *Libra Dawn*, she appealed to readers of *TW* to send money to his family who were in need.

Defended Chase's "Physiologist" against suppression under the Comstock laws. Wrote supportively about EHH's arrest for advertising the Comstock syringe. Appealed in *The Truth Seeker* for people to send financial support to the Heywoods.

TW briefly reviewed her book, *Little Lessons for Little Folks*, and her story, "Mary Jones."

Unfortunately, a letter to *TW* meant to be private was mistakenly printed. It discussed bestiality: "I'm getting a host of stories (truths) about women so starved sexually as to use their dogs for relief, and finally I have come to the belief that a clean dog is better than a drinking, tobacco-smelling, venereally diseased man is...." (September 1886, p. 3). In the next issue, Slenker clarified her position at length, "... I hold Diana Continence as the highest life under civilized conditions; that is, that there should be no coition save for parentage, but love should be trained into other lines..." (October 1886, p. 4). She explained that the letter had been private, but she had neglected to write the word "private" across it.

The censors noted Slenker's views. *TW* quoted the *New York Times* as saying, "Lynchburg, Va., April 28.—The arrest of Mrs. Elmina D. Slenker in the pretty little village of Snowville, Pulaski County, by United States Marshal J. R. Jordan created quite a sensation in that peaceful community.... He brought Mrs. Slenker here yesterday afternoon & lodged her in jail where she will remain, unless bail is furnished, until the United States District Court convenes at Abingdon. Mrs. Slenker has been suspected for several years of violating the postal laws by sending obscene matter through the mails...." (May 1887, p. 2). The obscene material was her book *Diana*, advertised in many issues of *TW*.

TW quoted *Winsted (Conn.) Press:* "Mrs. Slenker is no shrinking, obscure person on whom wrongs can be heaped without the world's being the wiser for it. Comstock could not have selected a woman better calculated to bring his infamous law into reproach; but to enable her to do her best her friends everywhere must show prompt sympathy & give her abundant financial support...." (May 1887, p. 1).

Elmina wrote, "I am *trapped by decoy letters*. Was taken to Lynchburg yesterday, with 15 minutes warning. Had a hearing today—documents pronounced *obscene* & am to be tried in June or July. It will be conviction, without doubt, as they have a mass of matter, from several sources. Let friends know of it" (May 1887, p. 2).

The May 1887 issue said she was out on bail and at home with a trial date of July 12. In the same issue, ATH had a defense entitled "Seductive Assault—Mrs. Slenker" in which she revealed that Slenker's mail had been "tapped" for three years. The September 1887 issue contained an article by EHH supporting Slenker "pure."

TW continued to quote her from *The Truth Seeker* and the *Winsted Press* where she explained her entrapment. It congratulated her on victory in the trial and recounted the dismissal of Slenker's case on the grounds that "the indictment does not set forth the offense with clearness and all necessary certainty so as to apprise the accused of the crime with which she stands charged...." (December 1887, p. 2).

In 1888 Slenker had three articles, all entitled "Motherhood," supporting *TW*'s plain-speech policy (July, August, September). She also wrote an article entitled "How to Love Wisely." "Woman's association with (but) one man produces a magnetic equilibrium that renders sexual contact (in any form) insipid, if not loathsome. The question naturally arises, why?..." In conclusion, she stated, "... it seems plain to me that Diana abstinence must be the highest realization of sexual love" (June 1889 p. 3).

Other brief articles included: "Modesty and Sex" (July 1889, p. 3); "Alphaism" (August 1889, p. 3); "Superiority of the Female" (September 1889, p. 3).

In an article on "Dianaism," she explained her sexual views: "Many think Dianaism is a cold, apathetic, distant, unnatural Love, one that is designed to crush all sex-feeling & reduce the race to Neuters. There is no reform less understood by the average reader than this phase of sex reform. We do not aim to eliminate Sex Love, or to suppress its manifestations; but we wish to foster & encourage it; we wish to make real love & true affection take the place of so much depletive, demoralizing, coitive love. We want the sexes to love more than they do; we want them to love openly, frankly, earnestly; to enjoy the caress, the embrace, the glance, the voice, the presence, & the very step of the beloved. We oppose no form or act of love between any man & woman, save the one creative act, which we declare sacred to procreation alone" (December 1889, p. 3).

Elected 1889 as president of the Fucking Trust of the URL.

Charlotte Smith. Editor of *The Working Woman*.

Mrs. E. D. Smith, Conn. Elected 1877, 1878, 1880, 1882 as officer of NEFLL. Attended 1879 URL.

Miss Isabella Smith. Elected 1876, 1880, 1881 as officer NELRL. Elected 1877 as officer of ATL.

Mrs. K. R. Smith. Elected 1880 as officer of ADL.

Miss L. E. Smith. Attended 1888 Annual ADL Convention.

Laura Cuppy Smith, McLean, N.Y. Supportive letters to editor. "I cannot do without your spicy little sheet...." (August 1873, p. 3). Quoted on free love.

Eliza F. Spencer. Elected 1880 as officer of URL.

Mrs. E. C. Stanton. Elected 1878 as officer of ALRL. Reprinted her from other periodicals.

Kate Stanton, Providence, R.I. Wrote, "I like your little paper exceedingly. Am talking Labor and suffrage on the 'Stump' and feel that I shall do much good" (October 1872, p. 3).

Mrs. L. G. Steinmetz. Attended trial of Bennett for selling *CY*.

Mary B. Steward. *TW* announced her death, "[She] ... was one of the most intelligent, devoted and tireless workers in the Eight-Hour movement" (April 1878, p. 2).

Dr. Emma R. Still. *TW* said, "[She] ... does efficient Greenback work in Maine" (September 1879, p. 3).

Josephine R. Stone. Mother of Geo. C. Van Benthuysen. Elected 1879, 1880, 1881 as officer of URL. Addressed 1880, 1881, and 1886 NELRL Convention.; elected 1883 as officer of NELRL. Represented the 4th Mass. Congressional District in the 1880 Chicago Greenback Convention. Elected 1880, 1881 as officer of ADL. Addressed 1881 ATL Convention. A Boston delegate to the 1880 Chicago Land Rally.

TW commented favorably upon her lecturing, especially on Labor. In a letter, she wrote, "I went to three land league meetings yesterday— spoke in one. Your prophecies about my work with the Irish women are all coming true" (June 1881, p. 3).

At first she supported the plain speech policy: "I think you [sic] paper is getting more and more interesting; am glad you are giving Mrs. Heywood's thought a substantial clothing of 'Printers Ink.' They are too near the centers of Persons and Things to be accorded any less honor. Her utterances are in a line new to me, and the style of expression is of a new type. She evidently stands in the vestibule of a temple of the universe whose portals are and have been closed to the most of us" (February 1880, p. 3).

Later, Stone became frustrated with EHH's frequent arrests. She wrote ATH regarding the 1883 arrest, "... why can't you learn a little worldly wisdom, say what you think privately, but don't try to instruct ignoramuses through the press ... I suppose ... you will keep right on trying to enlighten the ignorant, trying to free slaves who, hugging their chains, will only kick at and spit on you. I am sorry, but I can't say or do anything to help you" (October 1883, p. 3).

Mattie Strickland, St. Johns, Michigan. Attended 1877 NELRL meeting. Addressed 1878 URL meeting. Addressed 1878 NEFLL. "Mattie Strickland's first appearance on the League's platform is notable for

her spirited and telling addresses" (April 1878, p. 3). Secretary of the
NDA.

Arrested with Leo Miller on June 24, 1876 for living in sin. The
September 1876 issue featured an article by her entitled "Marriage Slaver":

> However devotedly I might love, I could not take upon myself the legal
> bonds of marriage, for I believe them to be founded on the principle of mas-
> ter and slave.... Living only a few years, and those in our quiet village, I
> have yet seen around me such ghastly spectres of buried hopes and lost
> ambitions as to make me shudder whenever the marriage bell pealed forth
> its hollow sounds. Bright girl-friends, who a few years ago laughed and
> danced in joyousness, now drag their weary bodies just this side of the grave,
> daily praying to die. Deny this not: *I know it,* and so do you all. The exces-
> sive demands of husbands, to whom they are not adapted; the constant
> blighting *fear* of maternity, which should be the golden hope of woman-
> hood; the soul-destroying subjection of one individual to another; the
> indifference and disgust that spring from enforced familiarity, are sapping
> the strength of body, mind, and soul of the women of our little town [p. 1].

Glowingly reviewed the pamphlet "Miller-Strickland Defense," and
reprinted Miller's appeal to radicals for help. Reported on the birth of her
son, Edwin Miller-Strickland, mentioning with approval the use of the
mother's last name as the child's primary one. She defended his "illegitimacy." "As the proud and happy mother of an illegitimate baby boy of
nearly two years, I must dissent from that opinion [that illegitimacy is
irresponsible.] While to be 'legitimate' is to be the offspring of parent who
have alienated ... the control of their own persons, it must be an equivocal honor to a freedom-loving soul...." (July 1878, p. 3).

TW announced her lectures and her enrollment at the State University, Ann Arbor, Mich. to study law. Then, "Mrs. Martha Strickland,
Atty. at Law, St. Johns, Mich. is prepared to speak on Reform subjects;
a woman of natural grace and power, she has well-informed & trained
ability to entertain & instruct audience, & deserves to have many paying
calls to Lyceum lecture platforms...." (December 1883, p. 2).

Mrs. Frances A. Stuart. Elected 1882 as officer of URL.

Mrs. M. Templeton, Vt. Elected 1880 as officer of ATL. Elected
1881, 1882 as officer of NEFLL.

Sarah L. Tibbals. Among those announced as organizing an American Woman's Emancipation Society on December 7, 1873.

Mrs. Mary E. Tillotson. Dress Reformer. Attended 1875 Dress
Reform Convention held in Worcester. 1876 became Corresponding Secretary of the American Free Dress League. Elected 1880, 1886 as officer
of URL. Addressed 1881 NEFLL.

Supportive letters to editor, often about dress reform. For example, "Permit a plea for the *bodily freedom* of the *enslaved half* of the world's laborers.... When to this is added bodily shackles that clog every exerted force, an impediment to every motion, a tax on every breath, philanthropists should help liberate them" (February 1876, p. 3).

Or, "In your kind notice of my book, *Love and Transition*, the mention of my leading speciality, suggests remarks of a much needed and important nature. True, dress reform has been my specialty, but not to the exclusion of other reforms, which I am glad you perceive...." (November 1879, p. 4). *TW* also favorably reviewed her book, *History of the Woman's Costume Reform*, and her *Poems*.

She was arrested for her wearing a "reform dress," although it fully covered her body. "Mrs. Tillotson, recently arrested and imprisoned in Jersey City, for wearing a reform dress, was liberated by the not quite idiotic judge who 'tried' her" (November 1881, p. 2).

She reported on her arrest:

> Ordering reformers to march off to stations is illegal, & should not be obeyed.... I knew the farce begun upon me meant that women's rebellion to present customs should not be advocated & resolved to test & stop it; hence I declined to obey.... While being carried I assured the trembling man of his legal liability, & he fled soon as he turned the key on me. By facts, reasoning to the sergeant through the grated window, I prevailed on him to call the judge, knowing he could but release me. The sergeant was stupid enough to ask if I had friends to bail me. I replied, I was under no obligation to get bail & should not ask friends to play a part in a farce like that, it was their business to simply release me & redress the vicious infliction. The judge was soon there, & all the trial he held was to order my door opened, assure the officers there was no law to justify them in disturbing me, nor to prevent women from wearing what style of clothing they choose, & asked the marshal to show me the way to my hotel. I was in the cell about an hour—long enough to contemplate the comforts innocence [sic] had been robbed of there [January 1882, p. 3].

She objected to the plain-speech policy: "In trying to popularize those three nerve-rasping ever-to-be deemed vulgar words [printed in *The Word* as c—-, c—-, and f—-], you not only smite the dear cause of social freedom, but your own respect & that of your paper; it puts a disgusting aspect on the whole movement.... The most charitable construction to be put on the offensive blanks in *The Word* is that it is a waggish retaliation for persecutions based on *proper* words; but the joke rebounds, & the fatal blunder will fall on the wag's head" (March 1887, p. 3).

ATH responded, "Mrs. Tillotson still talks *vs* the 'three words.' ... Mrs. Tillotson has done so much in Dress Reform for Free Legs as Jennie Doane phrases it, that I was surprised to find her bound in error...." (October 1887, p. 2).

J. Flora Tilton, Buffalo, N.Y. Sister of ATH. Elected 1877, 1882 as an officer of ATL. Elected 1878, 1879, 1880, 1882 as officer of NELRL. Elected 1878, 1879, 1880, 1882 as officer of NEFLL. Elected 1878, 1879, 1880, 1881, 1888 as officer of ALRL. Elected 1878 as officer of NDA. Elected 1879, 1880, 1881 as officer of URL. Attended EHH's hearing and 1883 trial. Attended trial of D. M. Bennett for selling *CY*.

One of the Lady Agents for Co-operative Publ., who traveled through the United States and Canada selling publications. She wrote letter from the road, including: "Not long since I was talking with a physician (old school) upon the social question. He bought three essays, and then, stepping forward, said, 'Just give me one *little kiss*.' As he was not an 'affinity' the 'little kiss' he did not get" (June 1875, p. 3).

Regarding a trip through Ohio, she wrote of a man on the train asking to see the books she was selling. He replied "Why don't you get married?" and offered himself as a prospect, citing his advanced years and large real estate holdings as incentives. She continued, "I blush with indignation when a man will say to me, as one did the other day, '... I *own my wife*, and she has the privilege of being 'ruled.''" She went on to say, "In all my travels I never met with men that seemed so low and ignorant in regard to women and their relations to society as I did in Ohio" (October 1875, p. 4).

She also reported on entering a large factory and asking to sell books to men there. She was told that the men did not have enough brains to read such material. "Yet these same men, without *brains*, are considered by their employers enlightened enough to vote for themselves and women also." She criticized capitalistic men who paid more to men for the same labor (November 1875, p. 3).

From Quebec City, she wrote of "an oppressor" who told her, "'*I* will not buy or meddle with such incendiary document. You aught to be arrested for selling such essays, sowing discord among the working men. *I* believe in a *hell* and those strikers and rioters will go there; destroying millions of property and putting the public peace in jeopardy.' I tried to convince him that such as he would ... be annihilated for not being on the side of truth and justice" (October 1877, p. 3).

Unsuccessful attempts were made to arrest her. "Comstock's stool-pidgion [sic], Britton set a trap to catch J. Flora Tilton in the N.Y. Labor Convention, assuming to be 'Mr. Young from the Sun Newspaper' wanting to buy *Fruits of Philosophy*. He did not succeed!" (June 1878, p. 2).

Josie (Josephine) S. Tilton, Bangor, Me. Sister of ATH. Among those announced as organizing an American Woman's Emancipation Society on December 7, 1873. Elected 1874, 1877, 1878, 1879, 1883 as officer of NELRL, attended 1876, 1892 Conventions. Elected 1874, 1888 as officer of ALRL. Elected 1877, 1878, 1879 as officer of NEFLL. Elected 1880 as officer of URL. Attended Heywood's 1883 hearing and trial.

She was a long-time radical, active during abolitionist period. On the occasion of Wendell Phillips's funeral, she reminisced about him: "The secured me a situation at the *Liberator* to learn the art of compositor; I was the last apprentice on that paper & the last person Mr. Yerrinton taught...." (March 1884, p. 3).

She and her sister J. Flora became traveling agents for The Co-Operative Publishing Co. "For nine years The Word has gone forth and from the same source hundreds of thousands of short essays have been distributed, mainly by the Tilton sisters...." (October 1881, p. 3). Frequent letters to editor, letters from the road, and detailed reports on her arrest for selling *CY*.

"Josephine S. Tilton, recently arrested in Newburyport, Mass., for selling *Cupid's Yokes* but let off for lack of a 'case' against her, goes East to Nova Scotia" (July 1877, p. 3).

"In the Newburyport *Herald* of June 8th, was the following: 'A rather interesting young lady, imbued with free love doctrines, was yesterday selling upon the street a pamphlet entitled *Cupid's Yokes....* The City Marshall, thinking the work had a corrupting tendency to the young, confiscated her stock in trade.... Miss Tilton is but the forerunner of the coming army of "young ladies" whose minds men must respect, and whose persons or business they cannot invade with impunity....'" (September 1877, p. 3).

"The 'Authorities' in Halifax, New Brunswick [sic] and Prince Edward island [sic], have been paying especial attention to Josephine S. Tilton, though they seemed hardly to know what to do with her. In Charlottetown, P.E., the City Marshal took from her, *Yours or Mine, Uncivil Liberty, Cupid's Yokes,* Mr. Tucker's *Radical Review, Hull's Crucible, The Word,* &c., &c., and burned them in the public square!... The object of these various publications is to abolish poverty and prostitution by *repealing certain laws.* Will some 'down East' lawyer show us wherein it is not as lawful to ask for the repeal as it is to ask for the passage of a law?" (October 1877, p. 2).

TW quoted *The Mayflower,* Halifax, N.S., as saying,

... We were honored with a call from the woman who sold *Cupid's Yokes.* A slight, active, comely, little brunette, apparently about thirty-five or forty years of age. [Editor's note: Mr. B. sets Miss Tilton's age rather high and probably his report is incorrect in several respects. We thank him, however, for his manly defense of the natural right of the people to acquire knowledge.] "Madam," said we, "do you really circulate these books to make a living, or to promulgate new doctrines? Are you a proselyte, or simply a book agent?" "No," she replied, "I am an educated woman, not dependent on the sale of these books. I believe implicitly the teachings founding *Cupid's Yokes*. I look upon marriage as a curse, a prostitution of our noblest passions. I believe in free love, Spiritualism, and affinity. My father and grandfather were atheists." "Have you ever been married?" we asked. "No, sir." "How many children have you?" "Sir," said she flushing-up. "With how many different men have you held the relations usually sanctified by marriage?" we continued. The woman's face was scarlet. "You are insulting me," she gasped. "Not at all madam," said we, blandly, "not at all; we are simply asking questions to see how far your practice and precepts join hands.... [November 1877, p. 3].

She was arrested, along with D. M. Bennett and W. S. Bell, for selling *CY*s. She pleaded "not guilty" and was held in the sum of one thousand dollars to appear before the grand jury. "Bennett and Bell are released on bail; but Miss Tilton, not caring to be put to the expense of paying her board while awaiting the tardy action of the Courts, has thrown herself upon the county for support, and is now confined in jail ... *Later.*—Some of Miss Tilton's friends insisting that she should accept bail, she has done so, and is now at liberty" (September 1878, p. 2). Trial deferred until February.

"Josephine S. Tilton, continues openly to sell *Cupid's Yokes* and other 'persecuted' books in New York City where irrespective of State and national 'law' she has many months vindicated Human Right to freedom of thought press and *the mails*. She, and her, our sister in Love and Labor, J. Flora Tilton, now canvassing in New England, 'sowing seed' as Parker Pillsbury says, in many States have quickened multitudes with new life...." (May 1880, p. 2).

Several exchanges with EHH were contentious, as when he used the male pronoun to refer to God. In another, the editor defended himself: "We 'rise to explain' to J. S. Tilton and others who arraign us for printing an advertisement of the Wyoming Lottery...." Apparently she believed such an advertisement backed "capital and interest." "Miss Tilton once burned some interest money rather than become a thief by using it; if she chooses to invest *her own* in a grab bag or lottery, it is her right; one may as innocently accept a prize or a blank as receive or bestow a gift" (February 1876, p. 2).

Indeed, for a brief period, she unsubscribed from *TW*. But she soon was writing detailed reports of conventions, which appeared in *TW*. For example,

Dear Angela:—I had thought I would not report my experiences at the Free Thinkers Convention at Hornellsville, as H. L. Green made an effort to apologize for his not only intolerant but unmanly behavior to me....

But to the Convention. I arrived there on Friday, Sept. 3rd. I went to the hall early in the afternoon. I had only reached the box office when I was met with: "Why have you not been here before? There are a great many inquiring for *Cupid's Yokes* and they want it. Nobody has it here, but I have said you were coming and most likely would have it." This was encouraging and I at once returned to my room and with several different pamphlets I supplied myself and retraced my steps to the hall. Sure enough I found a ready demand for it. Any why should it not be so?... [December 1880, p. 3].

One of the heads of the League, H. L. Green objected vigorously to the sale, and an altercation ensued. Tilton left, but a number of women assailed Green later that night, demanding a change in his policy.

TW reprinted Green's side from *The Liberal*: "With a little strong persuasive language, I prevailed upon the young lady to desist; but this was not the end of the trouble; about eleven o'clock at night I was called before a self organized tribunal to answer to the charge of the suppression of freethought; to save a volcano that was about to burst over my head and which I feared might destroy the convention, I made some concessions to the parties that had me in charge and that trouble was 'tided over' for that occasion." Then he encountered a "dress reformer," in a costume he considered scandalous, and in which he was embarrassed to have her speak in on the stage. He concluded, "The 'freelovers,' the 'communists,' the 'dress reformers,' and all other classes have their conventions, and no one should interfere or molest them, but our freethought associations are not strong enough to carry such loads even if they desired to, which I do not" (January 1881, p. 2).

She sent a telegraph of support to Parsons, imprisoned on Haymarket matter. One of several people who met EHH at the door of the State Prison upon his release on May 13, 1892.

Mrs. Lucy M. Tilton. Mother of Angela Heywood. Elected 1874, 1878 1880, 1881, 1882, 1884 as officer of American Labor Reform League. Elected 1880, 1881, 1882 as officer of the Anti-Tax League. Elected 1880, 1881, 1882 as officer of Union Reform League. Elected 1882, 1883, 1884 as officer of NELRL. She attended Heywood's hearing and his second trial under the Comstock laws. At the age of 83, she attended another hearing for Heywood on obscenity charges.

TW quoted Stephen Pearl Andrews from *The Truth Seeker* as saying

Mrs. Lucy M. Tilton, the mother, now more than seventy years of age, is a representative character of a peculiar kind, well worthy of notice; she is the only person I have ever met, except her daughter, Mrs. Heywood, distinctly and strongly imbued with the class of ideas I am about to mention which she holds in the deepest sincerity, and can state with a cogent conversational energy peculiarly her own. She is, in a word, what the world would call a fanatical opponent of books, literature, schools, intellectual culture, & what the world deems that higher enlightenment of education. She is the apostle, on the other hand, of persistent, useful, skilled labor, and a model teacher of every part and parcel of female industry in the family, which she has faithfully taught all her daughters. Born into the consciousness of being a person of more than ordinary native powers, and being deprived by conditions from acquiring book-learning in any large way, the supercilious assumption of superiority by the literary aristocracy burnt into her soul, until she came to hate the learned class as a set of snobs and tyrants to denounce & degrade whom, in comparison with the workers, is her special mission. She fairly hates the learned and their paraphernalia of books and bookishness while, with an admirable inconsistency, she reads everything and keeps up with the times.... [October 1883, p. 1].

She defended the plain-speech policy and openness in sex. *TW* explained, "One of the most serviceable lessons ever given children was when Lucy ... Mrs. H's mother, arranged chairs at a window, & called her little ones to see a stallion serve a mare...." (January 1890, p. 2).

Mrs. Francis W. Titus, Battle Creek, Mich. Attended trial of D. M. Bennett for selling *CY*. Edited and published a story of Sojourner Truth's life.

Mrs. M. S. Townsend [Wood], West Newton, Mass. Attended 1875 Social Freedom Convention. Attended 1876, 1877 NELRL Convention. Wrote poem celebrating EHH's release from prison (February 1880, p. 3).

Sara A. Underwood. Brief review of her *Heroines of Freethought* in February 1877 issue.

Virginia E. Vance, Concord, Ky. Supportive letters to editor. Admirer of *CY*.

Mrs. Dr. S. Alice Vibbert. Attended 1875 Dress Reform Convention in Worcester. Attended 1877, 1878 NEFLL Convention. Elected 1879 as officer of NEFLL. Addressed 1879 URL Convention. Elected 1880 as officer of URL. Addressed 1879 Temperance Convention in Princeton.

In a letter to editor from London, described it as "the richest and most cruel city of the world" (May 1889, p. 3).

Lois Waisbrooker, Columbus, Ohio, then Tama City, Iowa. Elected 1882, 1883 as officer of ALRL. Attended 1875 Social Freedom Convention.

She edited *The Foundation Principles*, "An Eight Page Monthly.... Advocates a Humanitarian Spiritualism, and holds it as a Foundation Principle that all gain coming from the use of natural wealth belongs to the party through whose labor it is secured, and not to some other claimant—that no man or set of men has the moral right to hold land not in actual use from those who need it, and that rent taken for the use of such land is robbery, and illegal when measured by the law of natural justice. Accepts no authority but that of Justice, and alive all through ... Clinton, Iowa" (April 17, p. 4).

Also editor of *Our Age*: "The paper I propose to establish is to be called 'Our Age' not the Present Age; and I believing that Spiritualism cannot move forward till the Red Sea of the social question is crossed, I shall make that a feature thereof. Yours for the New Heavens and the New Earth, where in dwelleth righteousness, or right conditions" (December 1872, p. 3).

Her work "From Generation to Regeneration: A Plain Guide to Naturalism" was advertised in *TW*.

Supportive letters to editor, but she did not support plain-speech policy. *TW* quoted *Foundation Principles* as saying, "A letter from Mrs. Heywood of Princeton, Mass., speaks of the organs of sex as 'Race Creating.' We like the term. It carries with it honor, dignity,—such as should ever be accorded to those life centers. 'Race Creating'; take in the full meaning of the term, and then think lightly—speak lightly— or act lightly in connection with those functions if you can. We believe in calling things by their legitimate names, when we speak of them; but we do *not* believe in (even privately) using the language of the street—of the rabble, simply because we can. Even allusions thereto hurt" (February 1885, p. 2). *TW* asked, "Will Mrs. W. please tell us what are 'legitimate,' proper names for the Sex Organs, & their associative use?"

When Moses Harman went to prison for the O'Neill letter (1892), she assumed editing duties of *Lucifer*.

Mrs. Cordelia Wales, Milford, Mass. Addressed 1876 Sexual Science Association Meeting. Addressed 1876 NELRL meeting. Spoke at 1876 and 1877 NEFLL Convention.

"Your new book, *Cupid's Yokes* was received to-night; Maria [Buxton] has read it through; we like it, and think it full of valuable information, and wish the world had known of its teachings years ago. How much agonizing misery it would have saved me and others" (March 1876, p. 3). She helped organize Love and Labor meetings addressed by the Heywoods in Marlboro and Milford.

Mrs. Dr. Walker. Announcement of her book *Charlotte Cushman, Reminiscences of her Earth Life with Some of her Spirit Experiences*, in March 1880 issue.

Helen M. Walton, New York City. Called a Woman's National Labor Convention to meet in Cooper institute of NYC in December.

Mrs. Humphrey Ward. Brief review of her book, *Robert Elsmere*, as a "religio-social novel which moves millions to no longer take mere belief as ultimate, but ask *what is true....*" (January 1889, p. 3).

Mrs. C. A. Warfield. Brief review of her "*A Double Wedding: or, How She Was Won*, which will be published by T. B. Peterson & Brothers, Philadelphia, on the 14th of July. She has also made an arrangement with this house, whereby they have become the future publishers of all her books...." (August 1875, p. 4).

Lydia M. Warner. Attended NELRL meetings. Attended Heywood's second trial.

Mrs. Hope Whipple. Attended NELRL meetings. Addressed 1876 NEFLL Convention. On January 30, 1882, she cabled the Irish working people, "The ten thousand workingmen gathered in Cooper Institute, representing American trade unions of all nationalities, ask Ireland to hold on with a deathgrip to the No-Rent Manifesto. The workingmen of America will stand by her. God save Ireland that Ireland may save humanity from Landlordism."

Lillie D. White. Helped to edit *Lucifer* during Harman's imprisonment over the O'Neill letter. *TW* announced, "Mrs. Waisbrooker has left *Lucifer*, & Mrs. L. D. White of Berlin Heights fame, succeeds her...." (November 1892, p. 2).

Mrs. Celia B. Whitehead. Dress Reformer. She criticized the plain speech policy. She wrote, "I fully recognize your *right* to publish all that you do publish, but to me it seems a grave and disgusting mistake to make footballs of the names of the reproductive organs & functions & kick them back and forth.... The greatest plainness of speech regarding sex matters does not offend me but a light & trifling tone regarding them is 'like smoke to the eyes or vinegar to the teeth'..." (October 1889, p. 3). *TW* deemed her criticism unbecoming to a woman of her "calibre."

Ironically, in one of Moses Harman's arrests for obscenity, a letter of hers was named in the indictment. *TW* described it as "a protest against the use of contraceptics & a plea for austerity of life; yet she is indirectly convicted of writing articles too obscene for public print" (May 1890, p. 3).

Mrs. M. J. Whitney, Salem, Mass., then Lynn, Mass. Addressed 1881 NEFLL Convention. Elected 1884 as officer of NELRL. Wrote supportive letters to Heywood on second and third trials.

Mrs. Dr. Martha Williams, Prospect, Conn. Aided in 1878 NEFLL Convention in Boston. Elected 1879, 1880, 1881 as officer of NEFLL. Elected 1879, 1880, 1881 as officer of URL. Elected 1882 as officer of ATL. Supported plain-speech policy. Letters to editor supporting EHH during his imprisonment.

Sarah R. L. Williams. Managing editor of the *Ballot Box*, which *TW* described as "a lively and convincing exponent of Stanton-Anthony Woman's Suffrage, issued monthly" (September 1877, p. 3).

Helen Wilmans, Chicago. Editor of *The Woman's World*. ATH wrote, "Breaking under heavy tasks Helen Wilmans is forced to suspend work and her paper, *The Woman's World*, three months; we deeply regret this, but hope that rest will return her with new vigor to editorial service.... I wrote Mrs. Wilmans a letter about the Penis & Womb which she did *not* quote from...." In the same issue, Wilman's letter appeared supporting ATH: "...You are the bravest woman living, I am a coward by the side of you.... Hammer daylight into the sleepy sculls [sic] of the nineteenth century idiots & poultroons...." (June 1883, p. 3).

Mary A. Winslow. A Signatory on the 1876 Call for a Woman's National Labor Convention.

Celia Parker Wolley. Brief review of her *Love and Theology* in November 1887 issue.

Victoria C. Woodhull. Coeditor of *W&CW* advertised in *TW*. She was often commented upon or reprinted in early issues. The August 1874 issue ran an article on the Woodhull and Beecher scandal.

The September 1874 issue criticized her as being hypocritical in denouncing promiscuity from the platform, yet living promiscuously in private. Nevertheless, *TW* later stated, "We attended Mrs. Woodhull's lecture on Social Freedom in Cooper Institute, N.Y. Friday evening, May 5th; the large audience was deeply interested in the speaker, and warmly applauded the many good points in her address" (June 1876, p. 2). And *TW* lamented the suspension of her periodical, "We regret that *Woodhull and Claflin's Weekly* is compelled again to suspend publication. It has done much to quicken thought on the social question, and its many friends will hail its reappearance with delight" (July 1876, p. 3).

TW reported that she had changed her name to Woodhall "and, over that name, writes in the London Court Journal that she has always entertained the profoundest abhorrence for the principles of the free love advocates." Elsewhere on the same page, announces that she is engaged to marry ... a London banker who "hesitates on account of reports that she once favored Free Love which she now denies!" (March 1881, p. 2). It added later, "Mrs. Woodhull issues *Woodhall & Claflin's Journal* from

12 York St., Covent Garden, London, England; this psychological marvel now says she never favored Free Love & curses Col. Blood for making her seem to...." (April 1881, p. 2). *TW* February 1882 announced that she was back in America, denying her freelove past.

TW quoted *Winsted Press* as saying, "Victory [sic] Woodhull puts up her hand as one who is willing to run the risk of being president of the United States during the next term; she proposes by circular to hold her convention in London, to pay the passage of delegates from this country one way and their expenses while there...." (September 1882, p. 3).

TW declared "Victoria C. Woodhull now fills a high place in English society. Her husband ... is the wealthy banker of 68 Lombard street" (August 1885, p. 2). She was quoted as saying "... I am fully persuaded, that the highest sexual unions are those that are monogamic, & that these are perfect in proportion as they are lasting" (*TW* November 1886, p. 2).

Nevertheless, *TW* gave her new periodical a positive review: "*The Humanitarian* by Victoria and Maud Woodhull, is an attractive exponent of Social Evolution, giving special attention to Stirpiculture and the endless themes Sex confronts us with. Monthly ... London" (January 1893, p. 3).

Mrs. Dr. S. E. Young. Attended Bennett's trial for obscenity (1879). Elected 1880 as officer of ATL.

Section II

Lucifer, the Light Bearer (1883–1907)

Editor: Moses Harman

"LUCIFER is a weekly Anarchistic Freethought Journal, deriving its name from LUX, *light* and FERRE, to *bear* or to *carry*; hence, LIGHT-BEARER.

"LUCIFER stands for Individualism, government from *within* as against Archonism or government from *without.*

"LUCIFER stands for *E*volution—for Peaceful Progressive Development, as against Despotic *Re*volution on the other.

"LUCIFER antagonizes ALL Paternalism—*all* authoritative government, and seeks by Educations Forces to Eliminate from out social system those Twin Representatives of Paternalism—Church and State" (April 3, 1885, p. 1).

As *Lucifer* became a target of the Comstock law, the periodical became more and more oriented toward a radical defense of women's rights through the advocacy of birth control and of marriage reform.

"Lucifer's specialty [sic] is freedom of women from sex slavery but under our present system how is a mother to support herself and the child when there are millions of able-bodied men who can't make a living for themselves? I'm ready to admit that, all things considered, marriage is no protection to a woman, but is often an extra burden. Both reforms must be brought about together. The laborers of the country should unite and contend for one *thing*, viz.: *The referendum.* When they get that, they can take the lines in their own hands and do the driving, but until they get it they may expect to be driven" (July 2, 1898).

3

Moses Harman: The Paradigm of a Male Feminist[1]

Moses Harman (1830–1910) is the sort of social visionary whom historians often overlook, even though his influence during his own lifetime was immense. (He also tends to be overlooked by feminist historians, perhaps because he is male.)

Neither a New England intellectual nor a West Coast radical, Harman lived most of his life in the Midwest, sharing many of the values that are associated with that region: He was a soft-spoken, hard-working, and devoted family man with an unswerving sense of right and wrong. He was also one of the most stubborn and persistent nineteenth-century Americans involved in the fight to advance the rights of women. Most of his writing remains buried in the pages of the now-obscure periodical he edited for twenty-four years: *Lucifer, the Light Bearer*. His main impact derives from his decades-long fight for freedom of speech, especially concerning birth control and the open discussion of other sexual issues. His persistence resulted in a series of imprisonments and culminated in his imprisonment in Joliet, Illinois, breaking rocks at hard labor, at the age of seventy-five.[2]

The British playwright George Bernard Shaw referred to Harman's last imprisonment in a letter to the *New York Times* of September 26, 1905, in which he explained why he would not be visiting the United States. Shaw declared, "The reason I do not go to America is that I am afraid of being … imprisoned like Mr. Moses Harman.… If the brigands can, without any remonstrance from public opinion, seize a man of Mr. Harman's advanced age, and imprison him for a year under conditions which amount to an indirect attempt to kill him, simply because he shares the opinion expressed in my *Man and Superman* that 'marriage is the most licentious of human institutions,' what chance should I have of escaping?"[3]

Harman and Shaw had an intellectual bond. They shared the same opinion of nineteenth-century traditional marriage: Namely, they believed such marriages were defined by laws and customs that enslaved women, who were stripped thereby of the right to their own wages, custody of their children, and the legal ability to defend themselves against sexual attack by their husbands. As an alternative, they favored "free love" unions in which there was no state interference into the voluntary sexual contracts of couples.

As a personal matter, Harman believed in monogamy. He conducted his life accordingly and without scandal. But as a point of social theory, he demanded that all voluntary sexual arrangements be legally tolerated and that women be treated as full equal partners. His insistence upon speaking out for "true" marriage and the rights of women led to his many years of legal persecution under the Comstock Act (1873), which forbade circulating obscene information—such as birth control advice—through the mails.

With the streak of hard stubbornness that often arises in the American personality, Harman simply would not be silenced. As he phrased it, "I believe in Freedom—equal freedom. I want no freedom for myself that all others may not equally enjoy ... The Spencerian formula: 'each has the right to do as he pleases, so long as he does not invade the equal right of others,' tells what freedom means. It is equivalent to saying that liberty, wedded to responsibility for one's acts, is the true and only basis of good character, or of morality."[4] This conviction lay at the heart of his lifelong battle to secure what he called the right of private judgment in moral matters.

Born in western Virginia to a poor family, Moses Harman grew up in Southern Missouri. Although he had only a few months of formal schooling, the young Moses became an avid reader, especially after an accident left him crippled with an enduring lameness. At sixteen he began teaching school and, then, went on to attend Arcadia College, Missouri. Harman soon became galvanized by the ideal of abolitionism—the pre-Civil War movement that demanded an immediate cessation to slavery on the grounds that every human being had a right to his (or her) own body. When the Civil War erupted, Harman was unable to enlist in the Union army due to his lameness. But he remained such an outspoken abolitionist that the proslavery county of Crawford, Missouri, held a vote and determined to "run him out" because of his unpopular sentiments.

When Harman married Susan Scheuck, the daughter of a Union sympathizer who had been executed by a roving band of Confederates, their marriage was a harbinger of his later commitments. Although the ceremony was conducted according to law, the young couple also entered into a personal contract that based their voluntary union on love, and not upon duty. Their two children, George and Lillian, were both born in Missouri. A third child died along with Susan during the birth process in 1877. One can only speculate on how deeply the death of his much-loved wife in childbirth influenced Harman's later insistence on the availability of birth control information to women.

In 1879 Harman took his young children to live in Valley Falls, Kansas, where his cousin Noah was a well-to-do farmer. Harman described his new home: "Valley Falls, a pretty little city, midway between Topeka and Atchison on the Santa Fe Railroad.

"It had then two weekly newspapers, five or six churches, several flourishing manufacturing establishments, good schools, as schools go, and was and is a very good sample of cities of second or third class in the young Commonwealth of Kansas, a name ever memorable for the bloody dramas enacted on its soil during the five or six years immediately preceding the great American Civil war of 1861."[5] Moses took a job teaching at the district school, and he soon became known for speaking his mind in a dignified but blunt manner. One exchange in particular would determine much of his future course.

Harman became involved in the Valley Falls Liberal League, a local branch of the National Liberal League, which sought to separate church and state, religion from politics.[6] This was an issue around which many figures in the American Individualist tradition gathered after the Civil War. In the words of Harman, the local "club was the successor of an older club ... which meetings were conducted on the plan of equal rights for all, regardless of race, color, party or creed." The League soon became involved in an exchange conducted with clergymen in the local Republican paper on "issues dividing the current and popular theologies from the deductions of modern science".[7] Although respectful of true (voluntary) Christianity—as he was respectful of true marriage—Harman argued the scientific point of view under the pseudonym "Rustic."

When the newspaper proved unwilling to continue the voluminous debate, the Liberal League issued its own periodical, the *Valley Falls Liberal*, in August 1880, with Harman serving as one of the unofficial editors. The new periodical became the foremost voice of liberalism in the 19th century sense within Kansas.[8] In 1881, it was rechristened the *Kansas Liberal*.

The *Kansas Liberal* eventually became the unfortunately named *Lucifer, the Light Bearer* (1883–1907), for which Harman would become notorious nationwide. The name was unfortunate because it raised suspicions within many religious-minded people. Indeed, since periodicals as controversial as *Lucifer* published without encountering the legal problems that plagued Harman, it is probable that some of his persecution was sparked by the provocative name. To voices of caution, Harman explained why he chose the title: "Lucifer, the ancient name of the Morning Star, now called Venus, seems to us unsurpassed as a cognomen for a journal whose mission is to bring light to the dwellers in darkness...."[9]

Perhaps his stubbornness came from receiving such as the following from a nurse who commented on his pamphlet "Motherhood in Freedom"[10]: "Most of my patients are women in confinement, and could I tell you all the pitiful stories I hear, of enforced motherhood, you would perhaps be startled more than you ever have been,—familiar as you are with the subject. My heart has ached for these helpless mothers and for the little unwelcome babes when I have taken them into my arms. So many of my patients have asked for knowledge in regard to prevention that I have decided, if I can obtain the desired information, that I will do what I can to prevent unwelcome babies and save worn-out women from this awful burden."[11]

If the gentle and cultured Harman had been the only one to choose the words printed in *Lucifer*, he might have escaped persecution for obscenity. For better or worse, however, Harman pursued a policy of not censoring the word choices of contributors. Harman believed that absolute freedom of speech cleansed society in a therapeutic manner: It allowed individuals to feel honestly drawn or repelled by certain ideas, and to understand their reactions rather than to suppress them.

In June 1886, *Lucifer* published "the Markland Letter," which described an especially brutal instance of forced sex within marriage and called it rape. Indeed, it may have been the first discussion of this subject in print on the American scene. The letter was graphic but used no words that were not to be found in a dictionary or a medical textbook. Markland asked rhetorically, "Can there be legal rape? Did this man rape his wife? Would it have been rape had he not been married to her?... If a man stabs his wife to death with a knife, does not the law hold him for murder?"[12]

In sending the issue of *Lucifer* containing the Markland letter through the mails, Harman ran afoul of the Comstock Act, which provided a penalty of up to ten years' imprisonment for anyone who intentionally mailed or received obscene material. Ominously, the word "obscene" had not been defined by the Act. But Anthony Comstock, the moving force behind censorship in late 19th-century America, defined obscenity in such a manner as to include the discussion of and protest against rape within marriage.

There is a sense in which *Lucifer* was an unlikely target for Comstock: It seemed to be an idyllic family business, a labor of love. Harman described the set-up: "I did the office work, assisted by my son George, aged fifteen, and daughter Lillian, aged thirteen, who had already learned to set type. We lived on a little fruit farm one mile from the printery at which the typesetting and press work were done. Editorial work was mainly done at home, in the early morning hours and late at night, while much of the day was spent by all three at work on the farm, raising fruits and vegetables, from the sale of which we supplied our own daily wants, besides helping to defray the expenses of publication; the folding and wrapping of the paper being done at night by the entire family, including wife Isabella, whom I had married since our removal to Kansas."

This contented picture was shattered on February 1887, when a warrant was served for the arrest of the editors and publishers of *Lucifer*: Moses Harman, Edwin C. Walker, and George Harman. Harman and his son were taken to Topeka where, upon executing bonds of $500 each to appear at the April term of court, they were allowed to go home. Ironically, E. C. Walker was already in jail when the warrant had been served. Both he and the sixteen-year-old Lillian Harman had been arrested and imprisoned for their non-State marriage, which Moses called an "autonomistic marriage." It consisted of an agreement, publicly declared in the presence of relatives and friends. Although there were no legal impediments to a traditional marriage, the couple preferred to enter into an entirely private and voluntary union. For their autonomistic marriage, Walker was sentenced to seventy-five days and Lillian to forty-five days in jail. Because they refused to allow court costs to be paid for them, the couple remained in jail for more than six months. Their imprisonment sparked widespread protest through radical communities, individualist or not.[13]

Moses and George Harman grappled with their own legal difficulties. After attending the April term court, they had been ordered to execute another bond and to reappear the following July. At the July term, they were told the weather was "too hot" to present the charges against them to the grand jury. They executed another bond to appear at the October term and went home. Over the next eight years, Harman was forced to waste a great deal of time traveling back and forth to Topeka at the legal whim of the court, and to spend scarce money in executing dozens of bonds, even though one bond alone would have answered the requirements of law.

Finally, in October 1887, the accused were allowed to know the specific charges brought against them—information that had been withheld. The grand jury indicted *Lucifer* on 270 counts of obscenity, which were eventually quashed because neither the judge nor the district attorney could discern a legally intelligible charge in any one of the counts. Not to be thwarted, the district attorney procured a new set of indictments, totaling 216 counts in all. The articles upon which the indictment was originally based were four in number: then the count was reduced to two: the Markland letter and a letter written by Mrs. Celia B. Whitehead, a well-respected mainstream reformer, which argued against the use of birth control devices.

Charges were dropped against George Harman and Edwin C. Walker in 1888. Moses Harman stood alone as the sole defendant, and a defiant one. In the June 22, 1888, issue of *Lucifer*, he reprinted the Markland letter: In columns running parallel to the letter, he also reprinted the thirty-eighth chapter of Genesis. His purpose was to demonstrate that the language of the Markland letter was no more offensive than that of the Bible. To declare the former obscene might lead to prohibiting the circulation of scripture through the mail.

Meanwhile, Harman's ongoing court process stirred up a storm of controversy. One of the protest letters written to presiding Judge Foster came from the indignant Celia Whitehead who demanded that the judge mark the parts of her letter he had declared as exciting "impure thoughts" in his mind. The district attorney was also deluged by protests from virtually every state in the nation. As a result, he continued the case over until 1890, at which point he was no longer in office.

In February 1890 Harman was arrested on fresh charges arising from "the O'Neill letter" written by a New York physician. Graphic in its language and speaking from nineteen years of medical experience, Dr. O'Neill spoke of witnessing many cases of the derangement or early death of women caused by "rape within marriage." Harman was escorted to Topeka once more and released on bail of $1,000 and a bond to appear.

Harman was finally sentenced to five years' imprisonment for mailing the Markland letter, but he was released due to a technical error in the proceedings. Then, in January 1891, Harman was sentenced to one year of imprisonment for the O'Neill letter. Another writ of error ensued in March. The legal harassment continued for years until, in June 1895, new sentencing placed Harman in the Kansas state prison at Lansing. Upon his release in 1896, the exhausted editor moved his family and *Lucifer* to Chicago.

Of this period, he later wrote, "… for more than nine years, I was never for one moment free from the 'shadow of the jail'—that is, I was either securely locked within prison walls or was under bonds outside of those walls, with the threat of imprisonment, like the sword of Damocles, constantly hanging over my head." He continued by proudly declaring,

"Meantime *Lucifer*, the real object of the prosecutors, did not die; *Lucifer* did not suspend; *Lucifer* did not retract; *Lucifer*, 'Son of the Morning,' did not cease to shine on friend and foe alike."

But some "friends" were becoming critical of Harman's insistence on discussing the sexual matters that impacted women. For example, George MacDonald, editor of *The Truth Seeker*, severely criticized *Lucifer*'s recklessness, but added, "Having thus expressed our opinion of Mr. Harman's offense, we are quite willing to go to his rescue. He is an earnest, honest, simple old gentleman with one idea, a little fanatical on that perhaps, but sincerely laboring for the good of the world, ever resolutely pursuing what he sees to be his work.... This is not a case for law; it is not a case for justice even, but for mercy. Every energy of Mr. Harman's friends should be bent to secure leniency for an aged & almost irresponsible gentleman, who has offended, not willfully but unwittingly, & through the best of motives."[14]

Benjamin Tucker, editor of *Liberty*, considered the "prosecution as [an] outrage," but warned, "Mr. Harman's act was a rash one, & he has no business to be disappointed if Liberals do not rally to his defense."[15]

Both defended and reviled, Moses Harman acquired the aura of a folk hero in which he began to appear in mainstream periodicals. Even the conservative *Woman's Journal*—the influential voice of the American Woman Suffrage Association—had some words of praise. "No one can have less sympathy than the editors ... with some of the views advocated in *Lucifer*; but on one point Mr. Harman's opinions are perfectly sound, and that is on the right of a wife to the control of her own person."[16]

The move to Chicago did not prevent the same sort of legal problems that had arisen in Topeka. Nor did Harman's dignified demeanor protect him. On writing of Harman's continuing harassment by the law, *Lucifer* contributor Jonathan Mayo Crane contended, "The writer of these lines has known Mr. Harman intimately for the last ten years and has talked with him on almost every conceivable subject of interest to humanity, including race culture and the relations of the sexes. In all that time never have I heard him tell a lewd story, or utter any word commonly regarded as vulgar or indecent."[17] Unfortunately, Harman had become almost a symbol to censors who did not feel able to ignore *Lucifer*.

Postal harassment preceded Harman's final arrest, with *Lucifer* being denied the use of second-class mail rates until the matter was appealed to Washington. Then, the Chicago post office began to confiscate and destroy issues it declared to be obscene. One issue was destroyed because it contained an article by the venerated feminist Alice Stone Blackwell—an article which had been reprinted from the well-respected and conservative

Woman's Journal. Another article declared obscene by the postal authorities was an excerpt from a United States Bureau of Animal Industry report, that had been issued by authority of Congress.

Finally, Harman was indicted and tried in May 1905 for mailing two articles: "The Fatherhood Question," which argued in an inoffensive manner that every prospective mother had the right to select the best possible conditions for procreation; and, "More Thoughts on Sexology" by the seventy-year-old Sara Crist Campbell, which argued that sexual ignorance inflicted needless pain upon women. The court refused to allow expert medical testimony on Harman's behalf, and the judge's instructions to the jury left little doubt as to his opinion that Harman was guilty. Thus, at the age of seventy-five, Moses Harman was sentenced to one year at hard labor.

From Cook County jail in Chicago, Harman wrote a "hail and farewell" letter to his friends, restating the object of *Lucifer's* publication, the object for which he was willing to endure yet another imprisonment: "… to help woman to break the chains that for ages have bound her to the rack of man-made law, spiritual, economic, industrial, social and especially sexual, believing that until woman is roused to a sense of her own responsibility on all lines of human endeavor, and especially on lines of her special field, that of reproduction of the race, there will be little if any real advancement toward a higher and truer civilization."

He requested friends *not* to "write in a vindictive or revengeful spirit" to those "who have been instrumental in putting me in prison." Quoting I Corinthians from memory, he reminded them, "Love suffereth long and is kind; love endureth all things, hopeth all things." He ended the letter, "I do not always agree with the Nazarene, but when he said, 'Father, forgive them; they know not what they do,' he showed a commendable spirit."[18]

Each issue of *Lucifer* after Harman's arrest carried a portrait of the imprisoned editor, with the heading "A Victim of Postal Inquisition." Under the portrait, his age and the length of his sentence served were listed like a clock going upward. For example, the June 7, 1906, issue declared, "Today Moses Harman is 75 years 7 months and 26 days old. He has served 101 days of his sentence to imprisonment for one year at hard labor. His task at present is breaking stone."[19]

Transferred to Joliet, where he broke rocks during the bitter winter months, Harman's health deteriorated disastrously. A transfer to Leavenworth—secured by the determined intervention of family and friends—probably saved his life. There, he spent a large portion of his remaining sentence in the hospital. Those expressing admiration for Harman and dismay at his continuing persecution ranged from the respected Clarence Darrow to the notorious Emma Goldman and Eugene Debs.[20] Journalists such as Louis F. Post in the *Public* and James H. Barry of the *San Francisco Star* wrote articles of staunch support. His case was discussed sympathetically in British, French, Dutch, and Japanese periodicals. Indeed, it was in discussing Harman's imprisonment that Shaw coined the term "Comstockery."

Upon his release from prison in 1907, the seventy-six-year-old Harman changed *Lucifer*'s name to the *American Journal of Eugenics*. The format became more scholarly, and the focus shifted more firmly onto eugenics—the study of how to improve reproduction and the human race—a subject that captured the imagination of many early-twentieth-century reformers.

On January 30, 1910, Moses Harman died in Los Angeles, where he had moved in 1908. The *American Journal of Eugenics* died with him. Although two memorial services were held for the venerated editor—one in Los Angeles, the other in New York City—the most fitting memorial may well be a letter published in *Lucifer*, August 1891, by Lizzie Holmes. Of *Lucifer*, she commented, "It is the mouthpiece, almost the only mouthpiece in the world, of every poor, suffering, defrauded, subjugated woman. Many know they suffer, and cry out in their misery...." Moses Harman and the circle surrounding *Lucifer, the Light Bearer* were among the brave social pioneers who fully acknowledged the suffering cries of women and attempted to heal their pain.

✳ ✳ ✳ ✳

The following reprints of articles by and about Moses Harman from *Lucifer* provide insight into Harman's philosophy and the extent of his activism on behalf of woman.

"A Free Man's Creed"

April 7, 1897, pp. 106–07, 109
by Moses Harman
My creed is short. Instead of "Thirty-Nine" articles, it has but three:
I believe in Freedom—the negation of all slaveries.
I believe in Love—the negation of all hate.
I believe in Wisdom, Knowledge utilized—the negation of all ignorance.

I put Freedom first, because, until freedom prepares the way, neither Love nor Wisdom can have room to live and grow.

If belief in this trinity, and if life regulated in accord therewith, constitute one a "Free Lover," then I do not object to that cognomen. Whether Free Lover is a title of honor or dishonor will depend upon what is in the mind of the speaker. "As a man thinketh in his heart, so is he." Names count for but little, and are apt to be misleading. For this reason I do not label or tag myself, and I object to being tagged by others. Freethinker, Rationalist, Libertarian, are good and expressive, but each has its limitations in the minds of most people. Free thought, to my mind includes and necessitates free action—free, non-invasive action. The thought that has not the courage of its convictions—that fears to practicalize and live what it believes to be right—is not Free Thought. It is thought under bondage to fear.

✷ ✷ ✷ ✷

Yes, I believe in Freedom—equal freedom. I want no freedom for myself that all others may not equally enjoy. It is, or may easily become, invasion, and invasion is the denial or the death of freedom. The Spencerian formula: "each has the right to do as he pleases, so long as he does not invade the equal right of others," tells what freedom means. It is equivalent to saying that liberty, wedded to responsibility for one's acts, is the true and only basis of good character, or of morality.

But to particularize:

I believe in Freedom to choose and to refuse in matters of food, of drink, of clothing, of books, of paintings, of amusements, of recreations, and—most important of all—I believe in freedom to choose and refuse in matters pertaining to companionships with the other sex. Freedom to choose our food and drink relates mainly to the life of the individual, but the choice of sex-companionship relates mainly to the life of the race, and is therefore incomparably the more important, inasmuch as the whole includes all the component units. Hence amative desire, or sex-love, is more imperious—less under control of calculating prudence, than is any other inherited desire or passion—and rightly so.

Freedom of choice—to be freedom—must be unlimited as to time. To be able to choose the kind or quality of one's food or drink but once in a lifetime would not be freedom. It would be the negation, the suicide of freedom. And so also is sex-companionships.

The right to make mistakes and to profit by them is vitally necessary to human happiness and progress, and pre-eminently is this true in the most important of all human relationships—that which grows out of the differentiation called sex, since this relationship concerns not only the happiness, the unfoldment, of each individual, but—for weal or woe, for success or failure, for uplifting or degeneracy, it is this relationship that reproduces the race—the larger selfhood.

I believe in Love; because love is the uniting, the combining, the organizing, the creative force of the universe. It is also the refining, the purifying, the uplifting, the glorifying, the happifying, force of the universe. Whoever or whatever debases or kills love, debases or kills life; for life is evolved and preserved through love. Without love life is a desert—not worth having.

I believe in Wisdom—knowledge utilized—because without wisdom to guide, both freedom and love may fail to bring happiness. I believe in wisdom; it is result of the exercise of love in freedom—love profiting by its mistakes; hence wisdom is the child of love in freedom.

It is because I believe in this trinity that I do not believe in marriage. These three are humanity's saviors and marriage crucifies them all. Marriage destroys freedom and compels slavery. Marriage kills love and incarnates hate. Marriage is the inveterate foe of wisdom and incarnates ignorance.

"Free Love" is tautological, since there can be no love where freedom is not. If love survives marriage it is not because of, but in spite of, marriage.

Bond love is a misnomer, an impossibility. The attempt to bind love kills it, or changes it to jealousy and hate.

Love, freedom, wisdom, constitute life's zenith, its sunshine; marriage, jealousy, hate, mean life's nadir, its darkness.

"Ignorance is the only darkness," says Shakespeare, and marriage promotes and compels ignorance, lest its victims learn how to gain their freedom.

I accept and heartily indorse [sic] Mr. Green's motto for the proposed new Free Thought organization, "Truth, Justice and Purity," and because I indorse that noble trinity I am an opponent of marriage and an advocate of love in freedom.

I oppose marriage because marriage opposes truth. Marriage is the hot-bed, the prolific breeding ground of deception, hypocrisy, falsehood. By its anti-natural requirements it compels men, and especially women, to dissemble and hide their real thoughts, their real characters, and after the fateful knot is tied the necessity for living a lie is often augmented manyfold. Whether they love or not, the married pair must still profess that they are true to each other and to their marriage vows; and this perpetual profession helps, of itself, to bring the disillusioning. But the disillusioning does not release from the necessity of deception, but rather increases it. The retroactive effect of this habitual deception is fatal to health and to noble development of the wedded pair themselves, and by inexorable causation the children born of such unions are hereditary liars and hypocrites. What wonder that there is so little of candor, of truth and of honesty in business, in politics, in religion, in love, and in all the relations in life?

I oppose marriage because it opposes justice. Marriage is unjust to women depriving her of her right of ownership and control of her person, of her children, her name, her time and her labor. Marriage is unjust to children—depriving them of their right to be born well through natural selection; depriving them of the right to be born of love—of love on all three planes, the physical, the intellectual and the psychic; and compelling them to be born of indifference or of disgust, on one or more of these planes; depriving them of their right to be reared in an atmosphere of concord and love, instead of an atmosphere of inharmony and hate. Unjust to woman and man alike, in that it deprives both of their natural right to correct their mistakes whenever they recognize them to be such; condemning them to a hell on earth until one or the other, in sheer desperation, shall commit what the marriage law calls a crime sufficiently heinous to release them—after passing through the added hell of the divorce court.

What wonder that the world is filled with hate, with greed, with strife, with wars—of households and of nations—when we remember how and where human beings are made and reared?

I oppose marriage because it opposes Purity. Purity in sexual-companionship is inseparable from love. Marriage does not recognize love as essential to purity, else it would demand that annulment of the marriage bond whenever there is a failure of love. Marriage unites "for better or worse," and marriage secures the worse by killing love. Marriage is ownership, especially the ownership of woman by man; marriage is force, authority, law, and love instinctively rebels against all force, all law, except its own.

Hence marriage fosters and compels impurity, prostitution, within its own pale—the worst of all prostitutions, since it is in marriage, mainly, that children are born. Marriage promotes impurity—prostitution—outside its own pale. Marriage is the prolific source of unmarried prostitution. The brothel is the legitimate outgrowth and complement of modern marriage.

I oppose marriage for much the same reason that I opposed its twin relic of barbarism, African slavery—because I believe it to be the "sum of all villainies," and I say of the laws made to enforce it, as Garrison said of the Constitution of the United States—they are a "covenant with death, an agreement with hell," figuratively speaking.

Many other indictments, equally damning might be made against this time-dishonored institution, but I have room only to say that I oppose marriage because I regard it the heaviest load that humanity has now to carry in its toilsome march from the lowlands of barbarism to the highlands of civilization.

It will doubtless be objected that evolution has been at work, and marriage is now only a "contract," to those who wish to make it such. Never was a greater mistake. The law dictionaries and the encyclopedias tell quite a different story. They tell us that "its complete isolation from all other contracts is constantly recognized by the courts." "In marriage every right and duty is fixed by law." And the law of marriage is based on the old Roman and the Canon law, both of which put the wife in the power of the husband—sink her individuality in that of the husband.

That marriage is less brutal than it once was is because man has risen faster than his institutions, and in spite of his institutions. Hence most husbands are better than the marriage laws authorize or allow them to be. But the same may be said of the old slave owners.

As Burke said of government, so we may say of marriage: "Talk not of its abuse; the thing, the thing itself, is the abuse." To abolish the abuses of marriage, then, is to abolish marriage.

"But what will you give us instead of marriage?" It will doubtless be asked. This is like asking what will you give us when you take away disease or superstition. The answer is, when disease is gone, health will remain; when superstition is gone, nature and reason will remain; when marriage is gone, Truth Justice and Purity will remain. Honor, candor, honesty, fidelity will remain. Fewer children will be born, because none will be born except such as are wanted, and they will be welcomed and cared for by mutual affection. The true, rational family will take the place of the narrowly selfish despotism now called by that name. Each member of the voluntary groups will drop to his place like stones in an arch when artificial props are removed. Government by authority will cease, because no longer needed.

Love, friendship, liberty, equality, fraternity, peace and happiness will take the place of hate, despotism, war and misery.

As to monogamy—a very different thing from marriage—under the reign of love, freedom and wisdom, there will be an opportunity for intelligent comparison, and if monogamy proves itself the fittest it will survive; otherwise it will give way to something better. What that something would or could be cannot be told until a fair comparison is possible.

Supplementary:

The foregoing article on what Editor Green calls a "Free Lover's Creed," though somewhat long, is really a condensation, a boiling down of a much longer and more elaborate statement. Many points were materially weakened, and some left out entirely, to fit the space allowed in the *Freethought Magazine*, and now that the fight is forced upon us,—not only by conservative Freethinkers, such as those who indorse [sic] the *Freethought Magazine*, but also by some of the radical reformers in the social realm who have been saying that Lucifer's attitude on this pivotal question is non-committal or "neutral," because of all these I think it best to insert here the substance of what was originally written for the *Freethought Magazine* and not published.

But before doing this I wish once more to remind all readers that I represent no one but myself, and that I represent myself for this day and hour only. *Tomorrow* my selfhood will probably be not the identical selfhood it is today. Or, perhaps more correctly, I can not honestly promise that the views I hold today will be held by me tomorrow. Like a planet or a sun, in its course through the skies, I expect to take a new departure every day, and perhaps every waking hour, of my life. With every new experience, and with every increase of light the sum total of my knowledge, of my thought, the sum total of all that makes up the ego—the me— is changed, and he who refuses to acknowledge the change, and who tries to hold himself to a creed or "confession of faith," stultifies his own reason, bars his future growth, denies and dishonors manhood, if he does not commit intellectual or moral suicide.

Elaborating some of my indictments against marriage, as it is defined in the Common Law, the Canon Law and the statutes of most of the states in this country, and perhaps adding a few new indictments, I would say:

I oppose marriage because marriage legalizes rape. The law does not recognize marital rape. "Once consent always consent," say the law and the gospel of marriage. If Webster is correct when he says rape is "sexual intercourse with a woman against her will," then "rape in wedlock" is almost universal at some time during married life, as nearly every wife could testify—if she dared. If the wife submits—surrenders her person— through fear, or because of a sense of duty, or for any reason except love, such surrender may be more properly called "prostitution" on her part, but on the part of the husband it is rape, pure and simple; and because I oppose both rape and prostitution I oppose marriage.

I oppose marriage because marriage is love's greatest enemy. "Marriage is love's miscarriage." The marriage bond is essentially *bondage*, and love will endure no bondage—except as itself imposes.

> Love's wing moults when caged or captured—
> Only free it soars enraptured.
> Can you keep the bee from ranging;
> Or the ring-dove's neck from changing?
> No, nor fettered love from dying
> In the knot there's no untying.

These lines do not voice simply the experience of the rover, the sensualist—him who knows nothing of love except in its physical manifestations, but they voice the honest verdict of all the ages and of all, or nearly all, who have surrendered freedom and self-ownership for married bondage; and the few exceptions which seem to disprove the rule can be shown to be not exceptions at all. When closely examined it will be found that the few married lovers live above marriage—that the ethics of their lives are the ethics of courtship rather than of marriage.

I oppose marriage because marriage is a yoke, and because the yoke is unequal, putting the heavier end upon the neck of the weaker yoke-fellow. Marriage is *conjugality*, and conjugality means being yoked together. *Juga* means a "yoke," and whenever the ancient Romans subdued an enemy they made the conquered to literally and really "pass under the yoke," to show to them that henceforth they were not free, but the slaves of the Roman people. When a woman marries she passes under the yoke, the yoke of marital bondage. The word "marital" comes from *mari*, the "husband," to indicate that marriage is *man's* institution—made for man's convenience and benefit, not for woman's.

The history of marriage shows this. The Jewish Decalogue extolled even by many Freethinkers, puts the wife among her husband's chattels. The Christian canon law, founded on the sayings of Jesus and of Paul does not put woman and man equally under the yoke. Shakespeare is noted for the fidelity with which he paints man and his institutions, and in the *Taming of the Shrew* he gives correctly the status of woman in his time, under Christian marriage, when he makes Petruchio to say,

> I will be master of what is my own:
> She is my goods, my chattels; she is my house,
> My household stuff, my field, my barn,
> My horse, my ox, my ass, my anything;
> And here she stands, touch her who ever dare.

And Katharina endorses what her husband says when she thus lectures rebellious wives:

Thy husband is thy lord, thy life, thy keeper,
Thy head, thy sovereign; one that cares for thee.
And for thy maintenance: commits his body
To painful labor, both by sea and land;
To watch the night in storms, the day in cold,
While thou liest warm at home, secure and safe;
And craves no other tribute at thy hands,
But love, fair looks, and true obedience;—
Too little payment for so great a debt,
Such duty as a subject owes a prince,
Even such a woman oweth to her husband;
...When they are bound to serve, love and obey.

And much more of the same tenor. All this is in full accord with canon law, as we have it today, built upon the sayings of Paul and of Jesus, who never put woman on equality with man; and therefore I oppose marriage because—admitting bondage to be necessary it is not right that bondage should be unequal. It is not right that the individuality of woman should be merged in that of man. Admitting that husband and wife should be one it is not right that the husband alone should be that one.

Those who may wish to know what marriage has done, and is now doing, for woman and her children, should read *Woman, Church and State*, by Matilda Joslyn Gage.

I oppose marriage because I believe, with Col. Ingersoll,—see his lecture, "Liberty for Man, Woman and Child," that the "unit of good government is the family," or that the family is the type and basis of government, of the "community," the state, or the nation. I recognize that the government of the United States is exclusive, jealous, partialistic, narrowly selfish, despotic, invasive, paternalistic, monopolistic, and cruel—logically and legitimately so because the unit and basis of that government is the family whose chief corner stone is institutional marriage.

I oppose marriage because I believe it to be the "Bastille," the last refuge and fortress, or stronghold, in, by and through which Ecclesiasticism hopes to perpetuate its power over mankind. All ecclesiastic organizations or nearly all, are now clamoring for more laws limiting divorce, thereby holding the oppressed and abused wives to their "duty" as breeders of the "unfit," breeders of the poorly endowed,—those who, like their mothers, will not have spirit enough to rebel against tyranny, and will be content with the lot in life "to which it has pleased God to call them."

I oppose marriage because the despotic and invasive "state" joins hands with the church to uphold and perpetuate its "peculiar institution," canon law marriage. Hence the statutes against the dissemination of knowledge in regard to sex, and in regard to "prevention of conception," which would lead to limitation of families, thereby depriving both state and church of their needful supply of submissive slaves. Church and state are Siamese twins, so inseparably connected that whatever threatens the life of one threatens the life of the other, and they both recognize that free motherhood—the abolition of marriage—would mean, in time, the abolition of both church and state.

✳ ✳ ✳ ✳

"Free Unions and Parental Responsibility"

October 16, 1901, pp. 324–26
by Moses Harman

A correspondent writes us in regard to social ethics in the far West, in part as follows:

"Editor Lucifer:—I was once an extreme monogamist and anti-divorce man, but experience compelled me to change my views. Custom is a great thing. In California the law does not interfere with men and women living together. Yet the opportunity is not embraced very often. I have known such couples, and women preferred it to marriage, and they lived together till death parted them. Still I believe there is less pain to marry than to have your children pointed to as bastards when at school and elsewhere. I say this in the face of the fact that I was compelled to leave ten children simply to get a little peace, and have been a hermit ever since. One child was only two months old—maybe three. Two days before I left I heard my wife say: 'you needn't fret, he'll not leave his babies'—this to a daughter who had remonstrated with her about some matter in controversy, when I had threatened to leave. I gave her and children all the property I had, and yet have the name of me a brute for abandoning my family."

The points most worthy of notice in this extract are these:

First. Comparison between legalized monogamy and "free unions."

Second. "Bastardy" as an objection to freedom in love.

Third. Responsibility for large families.

Fourth. Responsibility for care of children.

Our correspondent says the opportunity of living together without legal bonds is "not embraced very often" and yet the "women preferred it to marriage" in the few cases known by him.

Why did the women prefer illegal marriage to the legal sort?

Was it not because the masculine partner was put on his good behavior, and knew he must continue the ethics of courtship after he began living with his lover, and does not this tell us also why "they lived together till death parted them," as so many legally married couples do?

A little story just here is in point. It was told me by a lady lawyer in good standing, in the capital of Kansas. She knew the parties the question and said, "you can make what use you choose the facts."

In a western town, where people did pretty much as they pleased, a man named Jones led a reckless and "dissipated" life, until he fell under the influence of a woman of the "demimonde," called Madame Smith. They began living together and the daily lives of both became much improved. Jones was no longer the terror of the town but a quiet and useful citizen, and his partner a well-behaved and reputable home-keeper. Thus they lived and prospered for several years till in one of the periodic "devastations," or psychic epidemics known as a "religious revivals," they both "got religion and joined the church." Being now church members they must marry—of course; and marry they did, with the result that inside of six months they were separated, having quarreled, fought and returned each to the reckless and worse than useless life they had lived before they met.

My lady informant said for herself she preferred legal marriage. Why, she did not say, but looking for causes the reason is obvious enough. As a lawyer it was to her advantage to have many laws on the statute book, and the more irrational and invasive the law the better for the lawyer, because without a lawyer the unlearned and unsophisticated citizen cannot know how to defend himself.

But a more important reason is this: the ruling classes, that is the officials of church and state, will allow no man, and especially no woman to openly and avowedly antagonize the marriage institution. To be a heretic in regard to marriage is incomparably more dangerous to political, social and financial success than it is to be a heretic in religion, in politics, in finance or economics.

And why so very dangerous to oppose Institutional Marriage?

Again the answer is plain to be seen. In order that the ruling classes may have a sure hold on their positions and an easy time generally, they must be able to show that the masses of people are not able to rule themselves.

This means that the masses must be—as compared to themselves— weak, imbecile, intellectually and morally. The priest, the judge and the legislator must be able to point to the depravity, the sinfulness, the viciousness and the criminality of the average man and woman, the "natural" man and woman, and these ruling powers are shrewd enough to see that it is MARRIAGE—Institutional Marriage, canon law marriage, indissoluble marriage, that furnishes a perennial supply of material to prove

their claim that the masses of people are not able to govern themselves.
But more on this under another head.

"POINTED TO AS BASTARDS"

From time immemorial the terms "bastard" and "bastardy" have been used as whips by church state rulers, the archists, to hold woman in subjection and to drive the masses of people into the fold of matrimony, just as the words, "infidel," "atheist," "skeptic," "miscreant" (misbeliever) etc., have been the whips to drive people into the church. But from Shakespeare's time to the present—and doubtless long before the time of Shakespeare—it has been known that as a rule, "bastards" are brighter in mind and superior every way to the "legitimates," so much so that when a genius of any sort appears in a family of mediocre children the neighbors wonder who can be the father thereof.

But, as time wears on, the old whips, bogies and scarecrows of Archists in church and state, are gradually losing their terrors. The laity, the common people, the unprivileged masses, are slowly finding out that the words infidel, atheist, anarchist, bastard, etc., etc., have no such meanings as our power-loving, our cunning and unscrupulous rulers and their pliant tools, the publishers of daily papers, would have us believe, and hence we may reasonably expect that the time is not far distant when children at school will no longer point the finger of scorn at the free-born child, just as they now no longer voice that hatred of their parents toward their non-church-going neighbors by calling the children of these by such epithets as "little infidels," "young atheists," etc.

It should not be forgotten, however, that the fact alone that the mother is unmarried does not mean that her child is or will be born well, nor that it is a test case of free motherhood. Often it means the very opposite. So limited is the right of choice on the part of the prospective free mother, so easily victimized is she by the hypnotic power of sensuous men, and so sensitive to the scorn of "respectable" women, not to speak of financial dependence, that the wonder is that the child of the unmarried mother is not generally, if not always, inferior to children born in wedlock.

To make a fair comparison between free motherhood on the one hand, and married or enslaved motherhood on the other, social conditions—laws, customs and prejudices, must be wholly changed from what they are now.

RESPONSIBILITY FOR LARGE FAMILIES.

The "ten children" to one mother is significant, terribly significant of the married mother's enslavement, and at the same time her importance in the social, religious, political and economic systems that require the many to serve as hewers of wood, drawers of water, and also as lunatics, imbeciles to fill asylums, and as morally and intellectually inferior and weak, so that there shall never be lacking a good supply of candidates for penitentiary and houses of correction.

Without such supply it would be impossible for the archistic leaders of human society to point to such specimens as Czolgosz, Guiteau, Prendergast and the thousands and millions of petty thieves, burglars, tramps and "ne'er-do-wells," as proof that government of man by man is necessary, is indispensable, and that therefore the Anarchistic theory at its best, is wholly impractical, and would result in social chaos and ruin.

"Free Unions" do not produce a swarm of children, such as the husband and father, in the above instance, was compelled to abandon "in order to get a little peace." The free mother owns her body, her bed and the room occupied by her bed, and she admits no one to her room and bed as in matter of right, or of ownership.

This factor alone accounts for much of the disparity in the size of families of married and unmarried couples. I once asked the overseer of the poor, in Topeka, Kansas, why it is that the poor have large families while the rich have few children. His reply, in substance, was this:

"The poor have few sources of pleasure, of recreation or gratification, and hence they very naturally indulge to excess in the gratification of the reproductive appetite or instinct, and the temptation is always present. The rich can afford the entertainment of clubs, the Opera, summer vacations etc., and when at home, husband and wife usually sleep in separate rooms and beds, whereas the poor man and wife have one sleeping room and bed."

A Chicago lawyer speaking of his efforts to help the poor gave this as a typical case: "I told the father of many children that on one condition I would interest myself in his and their behalf, namely, that there shall be no more additions to the family. The promise was readily given, and with my help and the work I procured for him the prospects of the prolific couple were soon much improved; but before the first year was gone a new arrival claimed a share of the husband and father's earnings.

"'How is this,' said I. 'Did you promise there should be no more mouths to feed?'

"'Yes,' said he, 'but the fact is, the cold weather compelled us to sleep together to keep warm.'"

* * * *

While as a man and philanthropist this lawyer discouraged over production of children, as a member of the governing class his interests lay in the opposite direction. Hence early marriages and large families are constantly encouraged by both church and state authorities. Hence the pensioning of parents of exceptionally large families, as in some countries; also the custom of sending royal presents to the mothers of triplets or quadruplets, as reward for diligence in adding to the census rolls. Only a few weeks ago the mother of quadruplets here in Chicago, was made the recipient of many hundreds of dollars, and of much sympathetic, eulogistic notoriety, from rich and poor alike.

Numbers, numbers!—quantity, quantity, not superior quality, of population, is the goal sought for, the necessary condition and foundation upon which our archistic and capitalistic human society is based, and this fact, more than anything else, explains the unanimity with which the archistic religious and political organs oppose the freedom of woman, the self-ownership of woman, and clamor for more stringent divorce laws. Freedom in love—"the social side of anarchism," means an end to the archistic privileges of the present leaders, the drones and parasites of the great human hive.

As I see it, and, the cure for the evil of large families must come through freedom of motherhood, and with freedom motherhood must come RESPONSIBILITY of motherhood for the SIZE of the family. Robert G. Ingersoll was right when, in the last and greatest speech of his life, he said:

"There is but one hope. Science, the only savior of mankind, must make woman the mistress of herself; must put it into the power of woman to say whether she shall become a mother or not"—and having the power and the right to choose or to refuse, woman must be held RESPONSI-BLE—by an enlightened public conscience, NOT by laws, written or unwritten, for the manner in which she exercises that right and power, the most tremendously important of all human rights, powers, duties, functions, involving responsibilities.

RESPONSIBILITY FOR CARE OF CHILDREN.

Law and custom make man the head of the family, ruler of and provider for both woman and child, or children. Hence to desert wife and children is reckoned more than a misdemeanor; it is held to be a crime, than which few offenses are more heinous. Hence also to defend or excuse the deserter of wife and children is to invite the condemnation, the enmity and hate of all who up-hold our present political and societary institutions, based as they all are upon Institutional Marriage. But let us see:

If the husband and father is the head of the house, the ruler of the house and of these inmates, and if upon his shoulders rests the responsibility for support of the children and of their mother—especially during the child-bearing and child-rearing years of her life, is it not clear that just here is the logical reason for the subordination of woman to man in the realm of reproduction? That is, in the sex-life, the sex-power and functions of woman?

If then, woman is ever to be freed from sex-slavery, is not the first step, the first logical step, in her emancipation the removal of man's plea or claim that upon him rests the responsibility for her support? Including the support of her children during gestation and early infancy?

Consider carefully please, kind reader, before condemning. As I have often heard R. G. Ingersoll iterate and reiterate, "Let us be honest, let us be just"—and I ventured to add, LET US BE LOGICAL—RATIONAL.

When nature permits masculine man to gestate and give birth to a child, then he can logically claim the right of ownership and control of that child, and also the right to care for it until it can care for itself—all for the same reason that he claims the right to own, control and care for his own personal organism. Rights and duties are commensurable; they run parallel, or should so run, and therefore when man shall have acquired the right to own and control a child in nature's way, then and not until will the duty of caring for that child devolve upon him.

That this reasoning and its conclusion will seem cold, hard and cruel to many readers I have not the slightest doubt, but we all remember, doubtless, how cold and hard and cruel it seemed to part with many of the superstitions and illogical notions of our early childhood. For one I am not least afraid to trust to

LOVE IN FREEDOM.

For the care and maintenance of children. Masculine man can be trusted to do his part, as well as woman hers. When womanhood awakes in the "Land of Freedom," manhood will awaken, also, and the new man, the really free and manly man, will find his highest pleasure, his deepest and truest satisfaction in helping the woman he loves—the WOMEN he loves, if perchance he be a "pluralist" in love—to care for Her child or children, without the slightest idea that such help gives him a claim upon the person or service of the woman, or women—without expectation of REWARD of any kind except that which comes with the labor of love it self. He will feel and know that

"Love is life's end, an end yet never-ending—
Love's life's reward, rewarded in rewarding."

Herein, as elsewhere, "the letter (of the law) killeth; it is the spirit (of love) that maketh alive," paraphrasing the words of Paul.

By man's law the care of children has been made man's duty, man's responsibility. In all the past this law has been more or less a dead letter; nay, worse—it has been a fetter, a handicap, instead of a help to human progress. Remove the fetter, take off the handicap. No law but that of love is needed between woman and man, between child and man.

In the family, as in all other departments of associative life it holds good that

"If men relied on love to guide
    the world would be the better for it."

"But where is this Land of Freedom, and how do we get there?" It will doubtless be asked.

As yet the Land of Freedom exists only as a prophecy, a mental concept, in the minds of the few. But this is nature's way. First the ideal then the actual, the visible, the practical. As aids or pointers for those of our readers who are discontented with the present regime, and would be glad to help to inaugurate the reign of freedom and Justice, I will venture to name the writings of Leo Tolstoi, the grand old Russian thinker and iconoclast whose revolutionary ideas, and work among the poor peasants of his own country have caused his ex-communication by the national church, and the threat of banishment by order of the Czar.

Also I would recommend a little paper published at Home, Washington, called *Discontent*, which paper is the organ of a band of workers for freedom and justice on all lines, and who are trying to open the way for their practicalization on the Pacific Coast of the United States. The publishers of this paper are now under arrest for their radical utterances, as told elsewhere in this issue.

Now is a good time for the friends of progress everywhere to show their colors by sending for the paper *Discontent*—only 50 cents per year,— and also for some of the radical pamphlets and books sold by the same publishers, showing the road to the land freedom.

"To *Lucifer*'s Friends: Greeting and Farewell"

Cook County jail, Chicago, Tuesday morning, February 27, 1906.
Letter from Moses Harman
Dear friends all:

Again the expected has happened, and again I find myself behind prison walls.

Yesterday afternoon, about 5 o'clock, Deputy Marshall Wainwright called at 500 Fulton Street and very civilly and gently informed me that his orders were to conduct me at once to the Cook County jail and thence at 10 o'clock (next day) to the state penitentiary at Joliet. After a hurried consultation with Daughter Lillian and other inmates of *Lucifer*'s home the Marshall and I boarded the Lake Street elevated train and in less than one hour I saw and heard the heavy iron door close behind me, shutting me away from friends and the sweet light of Liberty.

Cook County jail, presided over by Warden John L. Whitman, has the reputation of being the best conducted and best managed jail in the United States. How true this may be I am not prepared to say, but from my short experience within its walls I am inclined to credit the claim.

Spent the evening writing letters to friends at a distance and in jotting down memoranda touching the business of *Lucifer*'s office, for though it is now nearly two months since all hope of the favorable verdict from the Court of Appeals has managed, I was not yet ready to turn over the publication business to other hands.

For more than a week I had spent most of the time sending out copies of the "Administrative Process of the Postal Department" and writing letters to editors and publishers in regard to this leaflet, so that the work of getting *Lucifer* No. 1060 to press was only fairly begun when I was told to stop work and go with the United States marshal. Several editorials were begun, but none finished; among these the one entitled "Ernest Howard Crosby in Chicago" was the longest and perhaps most important.

The chief aim of that article was to show that, great as was the work of William Lloyd Garrison as a reformer, as a destroyer of crystallized wrong, there still remains work to be done in the line of radical reforms—the line of destruction of crystallized wrongs—more difficult and requiring even more courage than was ever required to fight to the ages-old institution known as Chattel Slavery.

I had intended to trace some of the lines of resemblance between the enslavement of the African to the white man, and the enslavement of women in so-called Christian lands to her sexual master, masculine man, such as:

(1) The black man born of a slave mother was never supposed to reach an age at which he could be self-owning—the owner of his body and time. He took the name of his master, changing names every time he changed owners. So of woman. Until married her body is not her own to do as she pleases with. It belongs to her father, whose name she takes, or to society—that is, to the priest and Judge, who will not allow her to be self-owning. When she marries, the most orthodox of the Christian churches

require that someone must "give the bride away." "Who giveth this woman in marriage?" asks the priest—as when Alice Roosevelt, 22 years old, was married a few weeks ago. No matter how old, she has not reached her majority, as man reaches his majority at 21. Then, as in the case of the slave changing masters, she takes the name of the man to whom she is given, and every time she changes masters she takes the name of the new master. If she becomes a mother her children take the master's name.

(2) The crystals that hardened and solidified chattel slavery were partly theologic—that is, partly religious; partly economic or industrial, and partly "societary" or bon ton. The clergy quoted "Scripture" in support of chattel slavery; the man who wished to live without work supported the institution that compelled involuntary labor, and the man or woman who wanted entrance into the charmed circle of the best society knew that the "Open Sesame" to that exclusive circle was the ownership of slaves or the ability to use the slaves of others, coupled with undoubted allegiance to the slave holders' code.

And so likewise it is with the enslavement of woman. Marriage—legal marriage, Canon law marriage—is partly theologic (religious), partly economic (industrial) and partly bon ton ("societary").

The control of sex, of reproduction, is claimed by the priest and clergy man as pre-eminently their own province. They can show texts without number to prove that God ordained woman's subjection to man, from the time of man's entrance upon the earth, and since the clergy are the ministers of God, the ambassadors of God to man, of course, to know the will of God as to marriage the priest or clergy man must be consulted. He it is who must tie the hymeneal knot, and in order that his work be duly honored and respected there must be no untying of the hymeneal knot. "Marriages are made in heaven"; "whom God hath joined let not man put asunder."

Marriage is also an economic institution. Women have an industrial value, a financial value. Orthodox marriage makes man "the head of the house," "house bond" (husband), ruler of the house, while the wife is a "weaver," a producing servant, an "upper servant without wages." The husband holds the common purse and spends the common earnings, as he sees fit.

Marriage is a societary institution—pre-eminently so. He or she who would have entrance into "good society," to say nothing of the best, must be Orthodox in belief as to the sacredness of the monogamic marriage institution, however little his own conduct may agree with that belief. As in the case of belief and practice of religious creeds, while sins of conduct are easily forgiven, sins of belief are rarely or never forgiven. That is to say, man, the Lord and master, is not held to strict accountability for sins of conduct touching marriage; but not so with woman, the servant, the slave. Orthodox belief as to the marriage code will not save a woman from social ostracism, from a social hell, if her conduct is not in line with the code. Yea, more. Not only must her conduct be in strict accord with the code, but there must be no taint of calumny, no suspicion that her conduct is not strictly regular. Innocence is not enough. She must not only be "strictly virtuous, but clearly above suspicion," else social damnation is her life sentence.

I have written much more than I intended when this article was begun. Expecting soon-to-be called by Marshall Wainwright to go with him to Joliet, and expecting a friend to carry these lines to *Lucifer's* office, I close this "Hail and Farewell Greeting" by repeating what need not be repeated to those who have been constant readers of *Lucifer*, namely, that, next to the breaking of the chains that now prevent freedom of speech and of press, the object of *Lucifer's* publication is to help woman to break the chains that for ages have bound her to the rack of man-made law, spiritual, economic, industrial, social and especially sexual, believing that until woman is roused to a sense of her own responsibility on all lines of human endeavor, and especially on lines of her special field, that of reproduction of the race, there will be little if any real advancement toward a higher and truer civilization.

Thus far I wrote before leaving Cook County prison. I now add a line on train. My 17 hours' stay at the jail were not unpleasant hours. I slept but little, but it was not because of discomfort but because I wanted to write as many letters to friends and as much copy for *Lucifer* as possible.

Once more, as during my incarcerations in Kansas, I want to ask, as a special favor, that all my friends, far and near, will do me the kindness to write me words of cheer and hope—not so much that I expect to be despondent if I do not get the words of cheer but because I want to keep in close touch, close fraternal touch with all who labor and wait for the coming of the reign of truth, of honesty and justice. You need not write long letters, and especially I prefer that you do not write in a vindictive or revengeful spirit in regard to my imprisonment or the men who have been instrumental in putting me in prison. I do not always agree with Paul the Apostle to the Gentiles, but I do enjoy reading the thirteenth chapter of First Corinthians—I think it is—where he glorifies the spirit of love and forgiveness of injustice. "Love suffereth long and is kind; love endureth all things, hopeth all things," etc. Also when he says, "Count it all joy and gladness when men persecute you," etc.

Also I do not always agree with the Nazarene, but when he said, "Father, forgive them; they know not what they do," he showed a commendable spirit.

And now goodbye, goodbye dear friends all. I leave the work of *Lucifer* in your hands, confidently believing you will not let the work lapse for want of energetic effort. I am not a William Tell, nor Garrison, and yet I feel much as I think Tell felt—if the story be a true one—when he urged his friend not to let the common cause languish, whatever the result of that memorable day when he shot the apple from the head of his son; and I feel as I suppose Garrison did when he said:

"I am in earnest; I will not equivocate; I will not excuse; I will not retract a single inch, and I will be heard."

Again goodbye; the train whistles down brakes; the Joliet station is here. All good things to yours now and ever more.

* * * *

"Review of Prosecution in Kansas" [republished in *Lucifer* from *Advertisers' Guide* (Stanley Day, editor) of July, 1895]

The Persecution of Moses Harman

"When the innocent is convicted the court is condemned."

The purpose of this writing is to show by a simple statement of facts some of the grotesque inconsistencies of an attempt to enforce in this country the suppressive methods of an inquisitorial censorship.

In 1881 the publication of a radical newspaper, *Lucifer*, was commenced at Valley Falls, Kansas, the purpose being to provide a medium for the exchange and dissemination of radical thought and to stimulate progressive ideas in the social, economic, theological and philosophical fields of investigation. The merit of this unpretentious little paper lay in its fidelity to truth, and in extending hospitality to new ideas, and in candidly examining the value of their claims. No editors were ever more hearty, free or sincere than Moses Harman and his son George, and Edwin C. Walker.

While these men were quietly minding their own business and issuing *Lucifer* weekly they were arrested February 23, 1887, on a charge of violating the Comstock postal law, and taken before the United States Commissioner Wilson at Topeka, who held them to await the action of the grand jury, and upon executing bonds of $500 each to appear at the April term of court, they were allowed to go home.

Attending at the April term, they were told that nothing could be done with their care "on account of lack of appropriations," and again executing bonds to appear the following July, they went home.

At the July term they were told that the district attorney had decided not to present the charges to the grand jury "on account of the extreme heat," and for other frivolous reasons. Giving bonds to appear at the October term, they again went home.

This being forced to travel long distances fruitlessly, and to attend many terms of court accompanied by attorneys and bondsmen at considerable expense, was not the least oppressive of the many devices by which the prosecution exhibited its disposition to pester and annoy the defendants. Throughout the whole eight years of the outrageous persecution Mr. Harman has been compelled to give bonds a dozen or more times, a requirement as brutal as it was malicious, for one bond would have answered all reasonable requirement of the law. As the length of this narrative compels us to economize space, we cannot again refer in detail to each case in which a bond was required.

In October they again took the journey to court and were informed that they might return home and that they would be sent for if wanted.

A week after this adjournment it was discovered that they were wanted and they were accordingly sent for to come again to Topeka, where they were confronted with the most marvelous indictments ever incubated by a grand jury. These indictments, joint and several, charged the defendants with mailing a copy of each of five issues of their paper, to each of nine individuals, contrary to the statute. Ringing the changes and variations upon this theme amplified the indictments until they swelled up to 270 counts. The district attorney, like the drowning sailors, believing that some sort of ceremonial function was imperative at this juncture, required the defendants to execute another bond, which they did, and went home to unravel the intricacies of these complicated indictments.

Now, the purpose of an indictment is to inform the defendant what the charge against him is, but those indictments were drawn with the intention of concealing that information, and so effectual was the concealment that, neither the defendants, their attorneys, the judge, nor even the district attorney himself could point in any one of the 270 counts which contained any intelligible accusation against the defendants. So these indictments were quashed.

This would have been a good place for the prosecution to have stopped, but notwithstanding a remonstrance against the continuation of this farce, signed by one hundred of the best citizens of Valley Falls, the district attorney procured new indictments from a subservient grand jury.

By these new indictments, in 216 counts, the defendants were informed, for the first time, what articles they had published in *Lucifer* that had set the indictment mill agoing and produced such a plethoric grist of counts, 486 in all, whereby so much filing of bail bonds was exacted. The articles which it was now pretended were so shocking as to require the persecution of the publishers were only four in number. As, subsequently, upon the trial, the district attorney admitted that he and the grand jury were mistaken as to two of these articles, and withdrew the charges relating to them, it will only be necessary for us to concern ourselves with the remaining two as to which the charge was pressed. These were (1) The now celebrated "Markland letter." (2) A letter written by Mrs. Celia B. Whitehead.

These letters are too lengthy to be reproduced in our present limited space. Readers who are unfamiliar with them will find fair counterparts of the Markland letter in a "Special Report on Diseases of the Horse," published and gratuitously circulated by the United States department of agriculture, and in a little pamphlet entitled "Our Suffering Sisters," issued by the International Medical Missionary Society. The Whitehead letter is an argument rather in favor of the law prohibiting contraceptics than otherwise.

The usual annoyance of arrest and bond filing followed.

Thus it will be seen that although charged with an indictable offense, it was two years after the pretended committing of the offense, and over a year after their first arrest, and then only by fighting for it, that the defendants could find out from the prosecution what the charge against them really was, and when they did find out they learned that the original indictments embraced some pretended offense....

In May 1888, the defendants George Harman and Edwin C. Walker withdrew from the management of *Lucifer*, and Moses Harman continued as sole editor. By reason of this withdrawal proceedings against the junior editors were *nolle prossed* on the trial. From this point, therefore, our narrative will concern itself with the conduct and fate of Moses Harman.

As soon as the charges took definite shape, *Lucifer*'s friends clamored to know what it was all about, and on June 22 Mr. Harman reprinted the Markland letter in parallel columns with the 38th chapter of Genesis. This was done so that no one should be ignorant of the charge itself, nor of its frivolousness, that secrecy should not be added to the other disadvantages he would have to contend with, that it might be shown logically that, judged by the same tests which condemned the Markland letter, the Bible must necessarily be considered obscene, and furthermore, that something practical might be done to abolish such conditions as made possible the facts told in the Markland letter concerning the violation of a wife by a fiendish husband before her recovery from childbirth.

The other three indicted articles were republished July 20, August 3 and September 14, 1888, respectively, in especially large editions, thus demonstrating how difficult it is in this country to suppress thought, even though unprincipled men may be temporarily invested with power to hamper the press.

At the autumn term, 1888, the trial was put off until spring because everybody was so interested in politics that the administration of justice in court was set aside as a matter of secondary importance.

Meanwhile discussion of the indicted articles had been growing very active, whereby the frivolities of the charges became more and more palpable, and sympathy with the persecuted editor more and more earnest and general, and moral and financial support was advanced for his relief.

At the spring term, 1889, defendant demurred to the indictment and while this demurrer was pending Mr. Harman boldly advertised to send Lucifer for one year with "Irene" for $1.75. The point of this lies in the fact that the author of "Irene," Mrs. Fowler, had just been indicted under the flimsy pretense that her book was obscene. The indictment against Mrs. Fowler was never brought to trial.

On May 24, 1889, Judge Foster rendered an opinion overruling the demurrer, in which he criticized the prosecution with merited severity, saying, "I have but little patience with those self-constituted guardians and censors of public morals who are always on the alert to find something to be shocked at, who explore the wide domain of art, science and literature to find something immodest and who attribute impurity where none is intended." On the other hand, he went so far aside from the real issues, and so far violated judicial impartiality, as to make a gratuitous and premature statement, implying that the Markland letter and the Whitehead letter excited impure thoughts in *his* mind, and so were really "obscene."

Mrs. Whitehead, long, well and widely known among progressive people as a woman of sterling character, was naturally indignant at the judge's imputation that she had written an obscene letter, and clipping her own and the Markland letter from *Lucifer*, she mailed them to the judge with the request that he mark the parts in them which seemed to him indecent and return them to her. It might appear that, as the gravamen of the offense Mr. Harman was charged with was mailing these very articles, Mrs. Whitehead acted rashly in exposing herself to prosecution and inviting the judge to do likewise, but when we consider that all the obscenity there really was in the case lay in the prurient fancy of the judge and the prosecution, her act assumes a dignity far beyond any mere act of defiance.

Then followed a flood of criticism, and *Lucifer* and other radical papers were filled with opinions from many as competent to write opinions as Judge Foster himself, even though not clothed with authority, and the judge and district attorney were overwhelmed with letters from all parts of the country. There was no doubt a strong sentiment throughout the country that Mr. Harman would not be honestly dealt with. This sentiment came from observation of inconsistencies of the prosecution, as well as from a recollection of the outrage upon good old D. M. Bennett in a similar case. Under these criticisms the moral attitude of the prosecution became so contemptible that in autumn the district attorney washed his hands of the business by continuing the case to April, 1890, before which time his term of office would expire.

The attempt at suppression had resulted in widespread notoriety for the indicted articles. They had been distributed by Mr. Harman and his friends until they were well known and thoroughly discussed by all the well-informed radicals in the country. Some thought that not merely were the articles not detrimental to public morals, but that to amend public morals their publication was an eminently meritorious act. Some maintained that while the constitution guaranteed freedom of speech, and liberty of sentiment, with no restraint as to form of expression, it was still injudicious to print articles which might be objectionable to good taste. But while all censured officials so false to their obligations as to persecute Mr. Harman for printing matter of his own selection in his own paper for those who wanted to read it, there were some who considered such a publication unnecessary, on the ground that inhumanities like that described in the Markland letter were so rare that it was not worth while to combat them as it might be if they were more frequent. For the enlightenment of this latter class, and to meet their objection, many instances like that narrated in the Markland letter were detailed by *Lucifer*'s contributors, and among such contributions was a letter from Dr. O'Neill, describing a number of similar perversions.

Another arrest followed, February 18, 1890, on the O'Neill letter. Marshal Dillard, who had the warrant, was ordered to put Mr. Harman in jail in Valley Falls, and again in Topeka, but having no malice towards him, and full of confidence in him, he allowed him to go, unattended, on his promise to accompany him to Topeka next morning, but on arriving in Topeka the commissioner, to prevent his absconding, fixed bail at $1,000, and another bond was given.

On March 11, *Lucifer* contained a letter from Mrs. Waisbrooker quite similar to the O'Neill letter. Of this the prosecution, with its usual consistency, took no notice.

On April 17 a pretended trial took place, of a character grossly discreditable even to the system of jurisprudence under which such an outrage is possible. Of this farce the following are some of the main features: The new district attorney, Mr. Ady, had assured Mr. Harman that he should have sufficient notice of trial to enable him to prepare properly. This assurance he dishonorably violated, hustling on the trial at a time when Mr. Harman was unprepared, and showing thereby an entire lack of any honest intention to try the issues in the case with fairness. On the day in question Mr. Harman's counsel, Mr. Overmyer [sic], was in the deepest family affliction. His wife was not expected to live throughout the day and his child was dangerously ill. He was in no condition to try such a case. Other counsel was on the way from New York, intending in good faith to try the case upon its merits. These facts were fully detailed in affidavits on a motion to adjourn the case for one day, but while the prosecution had loitered along for four years, it now insisted that one day was too long a time for such an aggravated case of "obscenity" to go unattended to. No fair judge would have denied such an application for an adjournment. The application was, however, sneeringly denied by Judge Foster, who said to Mr. Harman: "if you have been as diligent in looking up counsel as you have been in instructing me in my duties you would not now be unprepared." Thus Judge Foster got square for some fancied slight to his ineffable dignity. No one has ever been able to tell with certainty what it was that piqued the judge and led him to take this mean revenge. Possibly something may have been written to him by some of Mr. Harman's friends which excited his spleen. Possibly it was the fact that just before the trial Mr. Harman had printed in *Lucifer* the oath of office taken by the judge. If it was this latter act that the judge resented he would better have deliberated long enough to realize that from the mere printing of the oath there was no implication that the oath was likely to be violated, but on the contrary, all the presumptions were that the judge would live up to his oath. The judge directed the trial to proceed at once, and assigned as counsel a lawyer entirely unfamiliar with the numerous details of the case, who, instead of setting up a proper defense and arguing on the law and the substantial merits, interposed the preposterous plea of insanity. Against this course Mr. Harman protested with earnest vigor, but his protest was treated as if it were mere contumacious disorder, and the judge presided over this hideous, wicked farce with as much gravity as if he were honestly trying the case.

It must have been gratifying to the judge that the conviction which ensued was upon just those articles which he had gratuitously characterized as obscene in his opinion a year before, but the obscenity of which he had omitted to explain to Mrs. Whitehead. As it was, the verdict was a compromise, three of the jurors being disposed to acquit.

Judge Foster imposed the most brutal sentence ever known in a case of this kind, five years' imprisonment and a fine of $300, and in doing so again manifested a pique and malignity which showed him entirely unfit to fulfill judicial functions. This manifestation of pique was accentuated by the fact that at the same term of court another defendant confessedly guilty of an offense of the same nature was allowed to go on payment of the minimum fact.

No stay was allowed, and Mr. Harman was at once committed to prison. His letters at this time are models of dignified protest against wrong. He remained in prison until August 30, when by virtue of a writ of error he was released, after seventeen weeks' imprisonment. A new bond was required.

On October 16, 1890, a curious proceeding was had before Judge Phillips, somewhat in the nature of a trial, on the O'Neill letter, yet without a jury. The defendant was examined before the judge for about an hour and adjournments were then had to December 29, when the law of the case was argued by counsel and submitted.

The appeal in the Markland letter case was adjourned at this time to the spring term of 1891.

January 15, 1891, Judge Phillips brought in a verdict of guilty against Mr. Harman, and without his being present in court sentenced him to one year's imprisonment. Comparing the Markland and the Whitehead letters on one hand with the O'Neill letter on the other hand it will be seen that the present case showed an improvement in judicial moderation. Another improvement was manifested, for, an appeal being taken, the monotonous formality of giving bonds was omitted, the marshal saying: "Go about your business as usual—when I want you I know where to find you."

In March, 1891, a writ of error as to the O'Neill letter case was allowed by Judge Caldwell, and another bond was required.

On June 1, Mr. Harman attended in court with counsel to argue the appeals, but adjournment was had to the latter part of November, when both cases were submitted to Judge Caldwell.

On April 15, 1892, while these appeals were yet undecided, a high-handed trick was played upon Mr. Harman. A whole edition of his paper was stopped in the post office at Topeka. This was the second time Mr.

Harman's enemies had recourse to this rascally trick, the first time being in October, 1890.

Early in June, 1892, Judge Caldwell filed his decision, setting aside Judge Foster's sentence in the Markland letter case. Thus it appears, while Judge Foster was so eager for conviction that he could not wait one day for the purpose of having a fair trial, that after six years of atrocious outrage, fiendish persecution, hideous perversion of justice, and contemptible trickery, the case stood just where it did in the outset, in June, 1886, when the Markland letter was first published.

June 13 Judge Caldwell filed a decision sustaining the conviction by Judge Phillips on the O'Neill letter and confirming the sentence, and a few days thereafter, to the eternal disgrace of our American judiciary, Moses Harman began a term of a year's imprisonment for exercising the American birthright of free speech.

On February, 16, 1893, on a petition for habeas corpus, Mr. Harman was discharged from imprisonment in the O'Neill letter case, upon the ground that the sentence of four months on each of three counts must either be held void for uncertainty, or else it must be held to mean that the sentences on all these three counts run concurrently, in which latter case the prisoner had more than served his term.

This left Mr. Harman with the old Markland letter case hanging over him—the case that was reversed and remanded "to be dealt with according to law."

After three years of inactivity and when everybody was in hopes this preposterous nonsense was so dead as to be incapable of resurrection, District Attorney Perry, who, with the change of administration, had been reappointed to succeed Mr. Ady, moved before Judge Phillips to correct the sentence and that an amended sentence be passed. This was very clearly inflicting two punishments for the same offense, but the district attorney seems to have had no shame and no moral sense to restrain him from making the contention that the previous proceedings were unlawful. The very proceeding that he instituted so dishonorably had not turned out as he expected, and so he declared it unlawful. The unlawfulness of the whole business was just what Mr. Harman and his friends had insisted upon from the outset. Had the case been "dealt with according to law" Mr. Harman would have been free from annoyance six years ago.

On June 1, 1895, Judge Phillips, the same judge who showed his incapacity for dealing with such cases "according to law" by his misfit sentence in the O'Neill letter case, undertook to correct the sentence inflicted by Judge Foster in the Markland letter case by the infliction of a new sentence, under which Mr. Harman was again arrested and at the present writing is lodged in the Kansas state prison at Lansing.

This is the history to date of one of the most flagrant violations of citizen rights ever perpetrated in this country. On a prosecution entirely groundless and unjustifiable an estimable old man, after being harassed unmercifully for eight years, has been swindled out of his liberty by a series of alleged trials which are a disgrace to our jurisprudence, and at last is in prison for having done an act for which humanity will long revere his memory.

That the publication of the Markland letter has resulted in great good no one who knows the facts can deny. But it ought not to be necessary in our civilization to make a martyr in order to take an advance step in the world's progress.

Mr. Harman in his persecution has the sympathy of all good men, and all to whom these presents may come are urged to respond in some form, spreading the light he has kindled, strengthening his hands for further conflict and helping to uplift humanity as he has done.

✳ ✳ ✳ ✳

"A Visit to the Prisoner"

March 29, 1906, pp. 489–90

by Lillian Harman

On Monday, March 26, I had a short interview with my father. His health has suffered from the confinement and prison diet, but in spirit is cheerful and hopeful. He feels, however, that if present conditions continue he will probably not outlive his term of imprisonment. There is a great deal of consumption in the Joliet penitentiary. He is confined in his cell nearly all the time, and his cell-mate, sleeps in the lower bunk with his head about three feet below father's, coughs a great deal of the time. I didn't understand whether he is a consumptive or not.

Father was compelled to submit to vaccination—the first time in his life in which he has undergone that operation. Because of trouble resulting from the vaccination, and the coughing of his cell-mate, he has not yet been able to obtain proper sleep. The general prison diet is better than in some other prisons, but is not suited to him, and he cannot have the food to which he is accustomed and which consists principally of fruit. The prisoners are permitted to eatenen while they are talking to their visitors, but can carry nothing to their cells. He had eaten nothing that day, hoping we would come. We took in some of the finest apples (his favorite fruit) that we could find. It was hard to be obliged to bring away all he could not eat while talking, when we knew he needed them.

He wrote a letter, about two weeks ago, but it was not permitted to be mailed, owing, I understand, to the fact that those through whose hands it passed considered that it contained criticisms of the management of the prison. Unless he obtains a special permit from the deputy warden he cannot write another letter until five weeks from the date of that letter.

He is allowed to receive magazines and books that are not considered improper by the officials through whose hands they pass. He has received the *Public, Tomorrow Magazine, Everybody's,* Shaw's *Plays Pleasant and Unpleasant,* the Chicago *Daily Tribune* and the *Record-Herald,* and other publications. He cannot receive *Lucifer,* the Chicago *Daily Journal* is barred, and understand the *American* and *Examiner* are classed with the *Journal. Lucifer* is barred because of his criticism of acts of governmental officials.

He has no employment, and is not allowed to have paper or pencil in his possession.

Some of the letters ... to him have not been delivered, owing to the fact that the writers have criticized the acts of officials or have attempted to "make a hero" of the prisoner. The prison officials feel that they have had nothing to do with sending prisoners there, but that, once there, all are to be considered equally guilty. The letters which are not delivered to him now will be retained and given to him on his release.

I've received a considerable number of letters that I have not forwarded. Some I wanted to copy before sending, and will send later. Others I did not forward because I felt sure they would not be given to him.

He is very glad to receive letters. In writing please let the penmanship be as clear and distinct as possible. Do not ask questions which require reply, as he cannot answer. Such questions should be sent to this office. All letters received will be acknowledged from time to time in this way. I hope no one will be deterred from writing by the limitations to expression which it is necessary to observe. Now that reading is practically his only occupation letters will probably be more welcome than any other time in his life.

I believe that this statement of facts is sufficient, and that comment is unnecessary. I have no desire to make an appeal for sympathy. Understanding as I do the feeling of love and admiration for him which so many of the readers of these lines share with me, I'll only express the hope that those feelings will be embodied, not in a "suffering sympathy," but in a "working sympathy." Life is sweet to Moses Harman. Liberty of body is dear to him. But the work to which his life is devoted is more to him than life itself.

4

Edwin Cox Walker
and Lillian Harman:
A Feminist Couple[1]

On September 19, 1886, Edwin Cox Walker and Lillian Harman, the daughter of Moses Harman, entered into an "autonomistic" marriage. That is, through a secular and non-State ceremony, Edwin and Lillian openly declared themselves to be husband and wife. This act violated the Kansas Marriage Act of 1867 and resulted in their being taken into custody by a constable on the charge of feloniously presenting themselves as man and wife without having been married as demanded by statutory requirements.

The couple was jailed on September 21, 1886, in the Oskaloosa county jail, though Lillian was released to await trial in her family home. On October 6 she was imprisoned once more, then taken to Topeka for a trial that began eight days later. On October 19 the court rendered a verdict of guilty. Edwin was sentenced to seventy-five days in county jail, Lillian to forty-five. Part of the sentence, however, included a demand that they pay court costs before obtaining their release. The couple refused.

In January 1887 the Kansas Supreme Court considered an appeal of the case known as "State v. Walker and another." On March 4, the appeal was denied. The couple remained in jail, unwilling to pay court costs, until April, when the arrest of Moses and George Harman left no one at the helm of *Lucifer, the Light Bearer*.

The following self-explanatory legal document is a record of the couple's appeal to the Kansas Supreme Court.

State v. Walker and another [Lillian Harman]

(Supreme Court of Kansas, March 4, 1887)
13 *Pacific Reporter* [Kan.] 279 (1887) pp. 280–89

Appeal from Jefferson county.

E. C. Walker and Lillian Harman were prosecuted in the district court of Jefferson county for a violation of section 12 of the marriage act, which reads as follows: "That any persons, living together as man and wife, within this state, without being married, shall be deemed guilty of a misdemeanor, and, on conviction thereof, shall be fined in a sum of not less than five hundred dollars, nor more than one thousand dollars, or be imprisoned in the country jail not less than thirty days, nor more than three months." Com. Laws 1879, p. 539. At the trial, which was had with a jury, Moses Harman, the father of Lillian Harman, testified that on September 19, 1886, his daughter, Lillian, and E. C. Walker entered into what he called an "autonomistic marriage," at his home, in the presence of himself and two other persons. On that occasion, a statement concerning the compact or union about to be entered into was read by the witness, then followed a statement made by E. C. Walker, which was responded to by Lillian Harman, and the ceremony was terminated by another short statement from the witness. These statements were published in the *Lucifer*, a newspaper edited by the witness, and the account there given was read in evidence, and is as follows:

"AUTONOMISTIC MARRIAGE PRACTICALIZED"

"While distinctly denying the right of any citizen or citizens, whether minority or majority, to inquire into our private affairs, or to dictate to us as to the manner in which we shall discharge our private duties and obligations to each other, we wish it understood that we are not afraid nor ashamed to let the world know the nature of the civil compact entered into between Lillian Harman and Edwin C. Walker, at the home of the senior editor of *Lucifer*, on Sunday, the nineteenth of September, 1886, of the common calendar. As our answer, then, to the many questions in regard thereto, we have reproduced as near as possible the aforesaid proceedings.

"(1) M. Harman, father of Lillian Harman, one of the parties to this agreement or compact, read the following, as a general statement of principles in regard to marriage: 'Marriage, by which term we mean the various attractions, sentiments, arrangement, and interests, psychical, social, material, involved in the sex-relations of men and women, is, or should be, distinctively a personal matter, a strictly private affair. There are, or should be, but two parties to this arrangement or compact—a man and a woman; or perhaps we should say, a woman and a man, since the interests, the fate of women is involved for weal or woe in marriage, to a far greater extent than is the fate or interests of man. Some one has said, "Marriage is for man only an episode, while for woman it is the epic of her life." Hence it would seem right and proper that, in all arrangement pertaining to marriage, woman should have the first voice or control. Marriage looks to maternity, motherhood, as its most important result or outcome, and, as dame nature has placed the burden of maternity upon woman, it would seem that marriage should be emphatically and distinctively woman's work, woman's institution. It need not be said that this is not the common, the popular, and especially, the legal, view of marriage. The very etymology itself of the word tells a very different story. Marriage is derived from the French word "*mari*," meaning the "husband." And never did the etymology of a word more truly indicate its popular and legal meaning than does the etymology of this one. Marriage, as enforced in so-called christian lands, as well as in most heathen countries, is pre-eminently man's affair, man's institution. Its origin—mythologic origin—declares that woman was made for man, not man for woman, not each for the other. History shows that man has ruled over woman as mythology declares he should do; and the marriage laws themselves show that they were made by man for man's benefit, not for woman's. Marriage means, or results in, the family as an institution, and the laws and customs pertaining thereto make man the head and autocrat of the family. When a woman marries, she merges her individuality as a legal person into that of her husband, even to the surrender of her name, just as chattel slaves were required to take the name of their master. Against all such invasive laws and unjust discriminations, we, as autonomists, hereby most solemnly protest. We most distinctly and positively reject, repudiate, and abjure all such laws and regulations; and, if we ever have acknowledged allegiance to these statute laws regulating marriage, we hereby renounce and disclaim all such allegiance. To particularize and recapitulate: Marriage being a strictly personal matter, we deny the right of society, in the form of church and state, to regulate it or interfere with the individual man and woman in this relation. All such interference from our standpoint, disregarded as an impertinence, and worse than an impertinence. To acknowledge the right of the state to dictate to us in these matters is to acknowledge ourselves the children or minor wards of the state, not capable of transacting our own business. We therefore most solemnly and earnestly repudiate, abjure, and reject the authority, the rites, the ceremonies of church and state in marriage, as we reject the mummeries of the church in the ceremony called baptism, and at the bed-side of the dying. The priest, or other state official, can no more prepare the contracting parties for the duties of marriage than he can prepare the dying for life in another world. In either case, the preparation must be the work of the parties immediately concerned. We regard all such attempts at regulation of the part of the church and state as not only an impertinence, not only wrong in principles, but disastrous to the last degree in practice. Here, as everywhere else in the realm of personal rights and reciprocal duties, we regard intelligent choice,—untrampled voluntaryism,—coupled with responsibility to natural law for our acts, as the true and only basis of morality. As a matter of principle we are opposed to the making of promises on occasions like this. The promise to "love and honor" may become quite impossible of fulfillment, and that from no fault of the party making such promise. The promise to "love, honor, and obey, so long as both shall live," commonly exacted of woman, we regard as a highly immoral promise. It makes woman the inferior—the vassal—of her husband, and when, from any cause, love ceases to exist between the parties, this promise binds her to do an immoral act. viz: It binds her to prostitute her sex-hood at the command of an unloving and unlovable husband. For these and other reasons that will readily suggest themselves, we, as autonomists, prefer not to make any promises of the kind usually made as part of marriage ceremonies.'

"(2) E. C. Walker, as one of the contracting parties, made the following statement: 'This is a time for clear, frank statement. While regarding all public marital ceremonies as essentially and ineradicably indelicate,—a pandering to the morbid, vicious, and meddlesome element in human nature,—I consider this form the least objectionable. I abdicate in advance all the so-called "marital rights" with which this public acknowledgment of our relationship may invest me. Lillian is and will continue to be as free to repulse any and all advances of mine as she has been heretofore. In joining with me in this love and labor union, she has not alienated a single natural right. She remains sovereign of herself, as I of myself, and we severally and together repudiate all powers legally conferred upon husbands and wives. In legal marriage, woman surrenders herself to the law and to her husband, and becomes a vassal. Here it is different; Lillian is now made free. In brief, and in addition, I cheerfully and distinctly recognize this woman's right to the control of her own person; her right and duty to retain her own name; her right to the possession of all property inherited, earned, or otherwise justly gained by her; her equality with me in this copartnership; my responsibility to her as regards the care of offspring, if any, and her paramount right to the custody thereof, should any unfortunate fate dissolve this union. And now, friends, a few words especially to you. This wholly private compact is here announced, not because I recognize that you, or society at large, or the state, have any right to inquire into or determine our relations to each other, but simply as a guarantee to Lillian of my good faith towards her. And to this I pledge my honor.'

"(3) Lillian Harman then responded as follows: 'I do not care to say much; actions speak more clearly than words, often. I enter into this union with Mr. Walker of my own free will and choice, and I agree with the views of my father and of Mr. Walker as just expressed. I make no promises that it may become impossible or immoral for me to fulfill; but retain the right to act, always, as my conscience, and best judgment shall dictate. I retain, also, my full maiden name, as I am sure it is my duty to do. With this understanding, I give to him my hand in token of my trust in him, and of the fidelity to truth and honor of my intentions towards him.'

"Then M. Harman said: 'As the father and natural guardian of Lillian Harman, I hereby give my consent to this union. I do not "give away the bride," as I wish her to be always the owner of her person, and to be free always to act according to her truest and purest impulses, and as her highest judgment may dictate.'"

It was expressly admitted that no license for the marriage of the defendants had been obtained, and that no marriage ceremony was performed by any judge, justice of the peace, or licensed preacher of the gospel, and that neither of the defendants belonged to the society of Friends or Quakers. The proceedings mentioned were followed by the matrimonial cohabitation of the defendants. Upon this testimony, the jury returned a verdict of guilty. Motions in arrest of judgment, and for a new trial, were filed and overruled, and judgment of the court was that the defendant E. C. Walker be confined in the country jail for a period of 75 days, and the defendant Lillian Harman for a period of 45 days, and that the defendants pay the costs of the action, and stand committed to the jail of the county until payment is made. The defendants appealed.

Overmeyer & Safford and *G. C. Clemens*, for the appellants. *S. B. Bradford*, Atty. Gen., and *W. F. Gilluly*, for the State.

J. JOHNSON rendered the first opinion which concluded as follows:

"… Gen. St. *c.*31, art. 7. Under that act severe punishment is measured out to those who marry or live together as man and wife where there is a legal impediment to their marriage. For these offenses there is a maximum punishment prescribed of from five to seven years imprisonment, while a conviction under the provision of the marriage act which we are considering, subjects the parties to a mere fine, or to imprisonment in the county jail not more than three months.

"The exception made by the statute in regard to marriages solemnized among the society of Friends or Quakers, lends support to the view which we have taken. Marriage with them is based on consent, publicly declared in one of their meetings, and has all the elements necessary to make it good at common law. According to the defendants' theory, they would not be liable to the penalty written in section 12, because marriage celebrated in accordance with their usage is valid at common law. But to relieve them from complying with the formalities of the statute, and to exempt them from the penalty provided, the legislature deemed it necessary to except their informal marriages from the operation of the act. The argument made that, to require an observance of the statutory regulations, trenches upon the liberty of conscience guaranteed the constitution, is not sound. Although marriage is generally solemnized with some religious ceremony, it is not under the control of ecclesiastical or religious authority. No religious rite or ceremony is prescribed. The intervention of a preacher or priest is not essential, and no religious qualification is required. So careful was the legislature to guard against any such invasion, that no particular form of ceremony is prescribed; and in the first section of the act it is declared that the ceremony may be regarded either as a civil ceremony or as a religious sacrament. The regulations prescribed are neither burdensome nor unreasonable. These parties may go before a probate judge, and obtain a license for a nominal fee, and there, in his presence, and without further rite or ceremony, perfect the marriage by declaring that they take each other for man and wife. The so-called 'mummeries of the church' against which the defendants so strenuously object and protest may be wholly omitted, and they may be married in as plain, and with as short and simple a ceremony, as can be desired, by a justice of the peace or other magistrate. It cannot be doubted that the purpose of the statutory regulations is wise and salutary. They give publicity to a contract which is of deep concern to the public, discourage deception and seduction, prevent illicit intercourse under the guise of matrimony, relieve from doubt the *status* of parties who live together as man and wife, and the record required to be made furnishes evidence of *status* and legitimacy of their offspring. In the accomplishment of this purpose it was just as necessary to provide a penalty against parties who contract marriage in disregard of the rules prescribed, as against officers and ministers who only perform a minor part in the proceedings; and we have no doubt that this was the legislative intention in the enactment of section 12 of the marriage act. We see no reason to declare the act invalid, and finding no error in the record, we must affirm the judgment of the district court."

"HORTON, C. J. *(concurring.)* Upon the record, as presented to us, the question, in my opinion, for consideration is, not whether Edwin Walker and Lillian Harman are married, but whether, in marrying, or rather in living together as man and wife, they have observed the statutory requirements. The language of the statute is: 'The marriage relation shall only be entered into, maintained, or abrogated as provided by law,' and 'any persons living together as man and wife, within this state, without being married, shall be deemed guilty of a misdemeanor.' Section 12, *c.* 61, Comp. Laws 1879. My construction of these provisions is that a ceremonial marriage must be celebrated in conformity therewith; and that any persons living together as man and wife, without being married according to these directions, are liable to the penalty thereof. I do not say, nor do I intend to intimate, that a 'consensual marriage' is not valid; but the legislature has the right to require parties assuming the marriage relation to have the marriage entered into publicly, and a record made of the same. This I think the purpose of the statutory regulations [sic]. Whatever command the state may give respecting a formal marriage, the courts usually hold a marriage at common law to be good, notwithstanding the statute, unless it contains express words of nullity; yet persons who marry without conforming to the statutory regulations, may be punished, although the marriage itself be valid.

"The consequences of marriage, as to conjugal rights and the rights of heirs, are so momentous that the interests of society may properly require a witness to the marriage, and a record of its acknowledgment. This much is required in the acknowledgment and registration of an ordinary conveyance of real estate. If there be no registration, no officiatory, and no eye-witness of the marriage, the woman is placed at the mercy of the man, who may deny the 'consensual relation,' and repudiate her; and, on the other hand, a man may be blackmailed by an adventuress, who may declare there was a 'consensual marriage' when there was none; therefore, the statute requiring the registration and acknowledgment of marriage is for the benefit of the parties, as well as their heirs. No man, who desires in good faith to make a woman his wife, will object to obtaining a marriage license, and going before some person authorized to perform the marriage ceremony, and acknowledge the marriage. The fees for a marriage license, and its return, are only two dollars. The acknowledgment of the marriage relation may be made for a trifling sum, unless the parties voluntarily donate a liberal fee.

"As a rule, I do not think that any woman who has reached the years of discretion, and has a full appreciation of the marriage relations, will demur, when it is proposed to clothe her matrimonial association with the forms of law. If the man objects to having his marriage public, he tacitly admits that he intends to cheat her whom he has privately promised to make his wife. It is only just that the acknowledgment and registration of the marriage relations should not be left to the whim and caprice of the parties, because no transaction in the life of a man or woman is more important, or fraught with more significant consequences; and society is supremely interested in having a marriage entered into publicly and to have a record thereof.

"But counsel claim Edwin Walker and Lillian Harman should not be imprisoned on account of their non-observance of the statutory provisions regarding marriage, upon the ground that the statute 'is an interference with their conscience,' and therefore unconstitutional. Section 7, Bill of Rights. The assertion that the acknowledgment and registration of a marriage conflicts with any right of conscience, is wholly without foundation....

"If Edwin Walker and Lillian Harman are suffering imprisonment, it is because they have willfully and obstinately refused to conform to the simple and inexpensive regulations of the statute directing marriage. In the non-observance of these regulations, they have exhibited neither good sense nor sound reason. For purposely and publicly defying the law, enacted for their benefit, and the benefit of their offspring, if they shall have any, they are not punished; and if they persist in the future in living together as man and wife, without complying with the statute, they deserve, and undoubtedly will receive, further punishment, if criminal proceedings be instituted against them. They can at any time easily procure a license to marry, go before an officer, and acknowledge their marriage; and then they will become, within all of the terms of the statute, husband and wife. Then over their union there can be no contention; then the wife may be to the husband, in law and indeed,—

"A guardian angel o'er his life presiding,
Doubling his pleasures, and his cares dividing."

VALENTINE, J. CONCURRED.

Section III

Liberty: Not the Daughter But the Mother of Order (1881–1908)

Editor: Benjamin R. Tucker

"Our Purpose:

"LIBERTY enters the field of journalism to speak for herself because she finds no one willing to speak for her. She hears no voice that always champions her; she knows no pen that always writes in her defence; she sees no hand that is always lifted to avenge her wrongs or vindicate her rights. Still fewer have the courage and the opportunity to consistently fight for her. Her battle, then, is her own to wage and win. She accepts it fearlessly, and with a determined spirit.

"Her foe, Authority, takes many shapes, but, broadly speaking, her enemies divide themselves into three classes: first, those who abhor her both as a means and as an end of progress, opposing her openly, avowedly, sincerely, consistently, universally; second, those who profess to believe in her as a means of progress, but who accept her only as far as they think she will subserve their own selfish interests, denying her and her blessings to the rest of the world; third, those who distrust her as a means of progress, believing in her only as an end to be obtained by first trampling upon, violating, and outraging her. These three phases of opposition to Liberty are met in almost every sphere of thought and human activity. Good representatives of the first are seen in the Catholic Church and the Russian autocracy; of the second, in the Protestant Church and the Manchester school of politics and political economy; of the third, in the atheism of Gambetta and the socialism of Karl Marx.

"Through these forms of authority another line of demarcation runs transversely, separating the divine from the human; or, better still, the religious from the secular. Liberty's victory over the former is well-nigh achieved. Last century, Voltaire brought the authority of the supernatural into disrepute. The Church has been declining ever since. Her teeth are drawn, and though she seems still to show here and there vigorous signs of life, she does so in the violence of the death-agony upon her, and soon her power will be felt no more. It is human authority that hereafter is to be dreaded, and the State, its organ, that in the future is to be feared. Those who have lost their faith in gods only to put it in government; those who have ceased to be Church-worshipers only to become State-worshipers; those who have abandoned pope for king or czar, and priest for president or parliament,—have indeed changed their battle-ground, but none the less are foes of Liberty still. The Church has become an object of derision; the State must be made equally so. The State is said by some to be a 'necessary evil'; it must be made unnecessary. This century's battle, then, is with the State; the State, that debases man; the State, that prostitutes woman; the State, that corrupts children; the State, that trammels love; the State, that stifles thought; the State, that monopolizes land; the State, that limits credit; the State, that restricts exchange; the State, that gives idle capital the power of increase, and, through interest, rent, profit, and taxes, robs industrious labor of its products.

"How the State does these things, and how it can be prevented from doing them, Liberty proposes to show in more detail hereafter in the prosecution of her purpose. Enough to say now that monopoly and privilege must be destroyed, opportunity afforded, and competition encouraged. This is Liberty's work, and 'Down with Authority' her war-cry" (August 6, 1881, p. 2).

5

Sarah Elizabeth Holmes: The Study of a Silenced Woman

Traditionally, American feminism has been a by-product of broader social movements in which women have played supportive but background roles. The activities and attitudes of these women generally became feminist in reaction to the slights they received from male counterparts. That is, the women tended to split away in disillusionment and organized among themselves. For example, the pivotal Seneca Falls Conference (1848) directly resulted from the public shunning that female abolitionists had received from male counterparts at the 1840 World Anti-Slavery Conference in London. Equally, Second Wave feminism—the feminism that erupted in the '60s—was fueled by the resentment women activists felt toward their antiwar antiestablishment male counterparts who viewed them as typists and bed warmers, not as equals.

After achieving a platform of their own, the voices of these emerging feminists often resounded with pent-up talent, passion, and idealism. Until then, however, many of the best minds in radicalism—that is, the women—labored in the background, never receiving the acknowledgment they deserved. Those women brave enough to stand up and voice their opinions were often ridiculed or ignored by those who should have encouraged them: namely, the men beside whom they labored.

Sarah Elizabeth Holmes,[1] a contributor to *Liberty*, is an example of one woman who was silenced by her male counterparts—that is, by the group of radical individualist men who gathered around Benjamin Tucker's periodical. Her dismissal is all the more egregious because Holmes was one of the few activists whose contributions—whether prominently or behind the scenes—almost spanned the twenty-seven years of *Liberty*'s publication. Perhaps her brief role as Tucker's "intimate" prevented others from taking her seriously—a fate that has befallen the partners of many men.

Before appearing within *Liberty* in her own voice, Holmes made significant contributions to the literature of liberty through her translations and her publication of the works of others. In 1887, for example, Holmes published Olive Schreiner's feminist prose-poem "Three Dreams in a Desert" in pamphlet form,[2] and a four-page tract, "The Socialistic Letter" by Ernest Lesigne under the title "The Two Socialisms: Governmental and Anarchistic." Two years earlier, Holmes had translated from the French a work by George Sauton entitled *Ireland*, which had run serially in *Liberty* in 1885. This was followed by her translation, *The Wife of Number 4,237* by Sophie Kropotkin—wife of the famed French anarchist—serialized in 1886, then "The Political Theory of Mazzini and the International" by Michael Bakounine, serialized in 1886 and 1887. These publications often constituted the first appearance of key political tracts in America.

In terms of original material, Holmes's first contribution to *Liberty* was an article entitled "Shall Woman Beg for Liberty?" (February 25, 1888). Holmes took another woman contributor, "Henrietta," to task for admitting that she desired the "social support of respectable society." Holmes's article ended with a ringing cry for the "plumb-line" approach so favored by Tucker who was renowned for demanding absolute adherence to principle. Refusing to credit the opinions of society, Holmes wrote, "Either our ideas are better or worse than those of society. If worse, let us submit without complaint to our deserved doom. If better, let us not apologize for them, or beg society to excuse and tolerate us in spite of our living on a higher plane than the rest of the world."[3] Even Gertrude B. Kelly—known for taking the hardest of hard lines on theory—had paid more homage to the psychological role that social ridicule played in intimidating women into silence.

Holmes's most important original contribution to the literature of individualism appeared on May 26, 1888, under the pseudonym "Zelm." Tucker enthusiastically endorsed the article: "For an article compact with original, suggestive, valuable, and lofty ideas on one of the most delicate of questions read Zelm's 'Reply to Victor'...."[4] The exchange between Holmes and Victor Yarros—a coeditor of *Liberty*—was widely read and became a "classic," assuming a life of its own beyond the pages of *Liberty*. For example, eleven years later, Tucker announced that a Berlin publisher had just issued a seventeen-page pamphlet in German entitled "Die Frauenfrage. Eine Discussion zwischen Victor Yarros and Sarah E. Holmes." It constituted a German translation and reprint of the exchange.[5]

The opening volley of the dialogue between Zelm and Victor had started on May 12, 1888, with Yarros's article entitled "The Woman Question." Yarros began by describing the condition of women as an "economic slavery" more acute than that experienced by men. Given the current political system, he posed the following dilemma: If "Women must enjoy equal rights and equal freedom, and must in all respects be the equal of man," then how can they "attain and presumably maintain this condition" if they could not sustain themselves? Without independence, he believed women would be "the property, tool, and plaything of man" without "power to protest against the use, nor remedies against the abuse, of their persons by their male masters."

Having posed a dilemma, Yarros answered it by returning to the opening assumption that men and women must be equals. He questioned whether this assumption was valid. Arguing from the ideology of Stirnerite egoism—from the principle that "might makes right"—Yarros concluded that by the standard of "might" women were severely disadvantaged. He was not merely pointing to the greater size and strength of men. Yarros claimed that woman's reproductive functions weaken her position in society. "In order to enter into one of her strongest natural desires [sex]," he explained, "she is compelled to enter into relations with man of which the burdensome and painful consequences she alone has to bear. While man's part in the relation is pleasurable throughout, woman purchases her enjoyment at an enormous price."

The price was children, and their existence placed the mother who was responsible for their care at a great economic disadvantage. At this point, Victor contended that the woman's "equality of powers for self-support" along with "all other equalities" disappeared.[6] A woman with children became inherently unequal to and weaker than man.

Yarros briefly considered that the inequality created by motherhood might be solved by "fewer children"—that is, by the woman using birth control. He quickly dismissed the solution as ineffective and, perhaps, undesirable.

Instead of pursuing a solution further, Yarros announced that he was leaving the question for others to resolve in the stated belief that many arrangements would spring up in a free society, each depending upon "the temperaments and tastes of the individual persons." Nevertheless, Yarros ended the article with a clear indication of his preference in arrangements: "[W]hy a man should not 'make a home' for the woman he loves, I am unable to see. While he is providing the means, she is educating the children and surrounding him with comfort. When they cease to be happy together, they separate."[7]

The subsequent issue of *Liberty* carried the lengthy response from Zelm (Holmes). Entitled "A Reply to Victor," it would become a classic within individualist feminist literature. Holmes immediately introduced a harsh note of practical reality into Yarros's vague musings on sexuality. She demanded that the discussion deal from the outset with "the number of children desirable in the future family" which was "so essential an item in the consideration of the social problem of the future."

Oddly, Holmes did not raise the question of contraception even though the repressive Comstock laws, which prohibited the spread of birth control information, had made it a prominent issue within radical circles for over a decade. Instead, Holmes chose to comment on Yarros's almost pastoral analysis of a brutal reality: Women were forced to bear children whom they could not support. With reference to Yarros's poetic waxing about Apollo and Venus, she observed, "On his [Yarros's] theory of life ... every Apollo will find his Venus before she is older than twenty-five." Holmes pointed out that this meant Venus would have twenty years more of fertility and would be likely to have as many as ten children. Nevertheless, Yarros still expected her to educate them and to surround him "her lover with comfort!" Holmes concluded wryly, "If I have not misunderstood him in this, he has been looking at the subject from a man's standpoint."

Most of Zelm's "Reply" focused on similar down-to-earth issues, such as the specific arrangement which provided the best education for children, and whether the right to control the children should rest with the mother or the father. Although her discussion often slipped into romanticized language as well, Holmes remained practical enough to offer an extremely early feminist defense of day-care centers for working mothers. Indeed, when Charlotte Perkins Gilman made much the same recommendation over a decade later, in her book *Women and Economics*, she created a sensation. Holmes anticipated this reaction as well. Regarding the suggestion that working mothers leave their children with trained strangers, she predicted she would "encounter on this point a remonstrance in the minds of many women" who believed a true mother would never leave her child, except with family. Nevertheless, Holmes insisted it might be best to look outside the family structure for "trustworthy people who would find in it [child care] ... attractive labor, for which they would receive due remuneration."[8]

Unfortunately, Holmes's budding argument for day-care centers was ignored in a reply entitled "The Rights of Babies," written by fellow *Liberty* contributor A. Warren. Warren picked up on a more fundamental question raised by Holmes, a question that haunts the issue of children's rights to this day. Warren addressed the issue of who should control the child. Clearly, an infant required someone to exercise protective control, even though control would clearly be a violation of right if applied to an adult.

Holmes had claimed that such control should be vested in the mother alone. Warren replied, "I do not deny the *right* of the mother to control her child...; but it is not *her exclusive right.*" Control of the child could not only be rightfully exercised by the father, but by third parties as well. He reasoned in the following manner: "If freedom is to be universal, children are sovereign from the moment of birth. If not, then who shall say when their freedom shall begin? But if the child is sovereign, the mother can have no authority to control it, any more than can any other person." If the child is not sovereign, then anyone could act to protect it.

In a patronizing tone that contained no sarcasm, Warren went on to compliment Holmes on the "sensitivity" that caused her to overlook the rights of children. "Her soul went out to the mother only," Warren explained Holmes's oversight. "I am sure that, when she comes to turn her attention to this branch of the subject, she will agree with me."[9]

Holmes's immediate reply was unresponsive to Warren's main argument, but a more thoughtful article by her appeared several issues later. By then, her "Reply to Victor" had been roundly criticized within *Liberty*, and Holmes seemed acutely sensitive to the backlash. With a diplomacy rare in anarchist circles, Holmes confessed, "My own words express my thoughts so clumsily, it may easily be that theirs [her critics] have at least in some degree failed also in revealing their own conceptions. That is, we may have mistaken each other." She graciously refused to consider an odd argument advanced by the veteran anarchist J. Wm. Lloyd in which he contended that a child be required "to pay for its life," preferring instead to believe that "Mr. Lloyd was dreaming of a glorious anarchical future...."[10]

On the heels of a public criticism that clearly embarrassed her, another distressing situation emerged. The event may well have convinced Holmes to contribute little else to a forum in which she was treated with disrespect. Tucker explained the offending situation: "It was agreed between Victor and Zelm ... that he should write a statement of his views on the subject in question, and submit it in manuscript to Zelm; that she should then write a statement of her views as a contrast to his, and in turn submit it to him; that he should then revise his manuscript in the light of hers ... that she then should have a similar privilege; and so on, until each should be content to let his or her statement finally stand for comparison with the other's.... [T]he original articles were to end the matter between Victor and Zelm."[11]

Nevertheless, and knowing that Holmes would not have "entered into the arrangement" had she known it would become an extended debate, Tucker published a follow-up piece by Yarros, in which he further critiqued Holmes's article. She declined to contribute a second piece, perhaps hoping to cut short an acrimonious dispute. Her strategy did not work. In the following issue, Yarros felt it necessary to provide yet another commentary entitled "A Word of Explanation," in which he defended himself against the comments Tucker had made about his last article. Yarros stated that the misunderstanding "was not my fault, sure, but her [Holmes's] own."[12]

With such bitterness following her major appearance in *Liberty*, Holmes published very little of her own work in the periodical thereafter. Instead, she contributed to *Liberty* through her translations and the publication of various pamphlets, most of which were advertised in the periodical. For example, she published a second edition of Stephen Pearl Andrews's libertarian classic, *The Science of Society*.

Sadly, Holmes's withdrawal from discussion about the control of children probably doomed the early seed of a debate on children's rights within *Liberty* to wither. Other women fared no better in their attempts to discuss children's rights within Tucker's periodical. Clara Dixon Davidson, editor of the short-lived periodical *L'Enfant Terrible*, broached the issue anew in a *Liberty* article entitled "Relations Between Parents and Children." Davidson returned to the key question: What of infants who are too young to care for themselves? "Who shall decide upon the permissible degree of freedom? Who shall adjust the child's freedom to its safety so that the two shall be delicately, flawlessly balanced?"[13] Davidson contended that parents had no inherent or legal duty to support their children. Their only duty was to not aggress against them.

Abiding strictly by the principle of equal liberty, she reasoned, "While a cursory glance at the subject may seem to show a denial of equal freedom in the refusal of a parent to support his child, a more careful study will reveal the truth that, so long as he does not hinder the activities of any one nor compel any other person or persons to undertake the task which he has relinquished, he cannot be said to violate the law of equal freedom. Therefore, his associates may not compel him to provide for his child, though they may forcibly prevent him from aggressing upon it."[14]

Tucker declared the issue in which Davidson's article appeared to be "devoted to" the question of the status of the child under anarchy. Yet Tucker's dismissive attitude toward women was evidenced even when he attempted to praise Davidson. Announcing that her article had laid unopened in an envelope "for several months," he patronizingly confessed to being "delighted to find that a woman had written such a bold, unprejudiced, unsentimental, and altogether rational essay on a subject which women are especially prone to treat emotionally."

After years of slighting "the woman question," *Liberty* seemed poised on the brink of exploring it. In the next breath, however, Tucker pushed the issue of children's rights into the background of anarchism by observing, "In one view the question of the status of the child under Anarchy is a trivial one" whose chief value lay "in the light which it throws on the matter of equal freedom."[15]

The issue "devoted to children" occasioned little comment. Another piece by free-love advocate Lillian Harman that questioned age-of-consent laws also sparked little controversy despite its provocative content.[16] Even the well-reasoned article by Mona Caird, entitled "Ideal Marriage," did not prompt debate. Caird argued that mothers had a superior "claim" over their offspring—that is, a claim superior to that of the father who, in turn, had a claim superior to that of a third party: "[O]ver and above … unpaid labor, the wife has borne and reared the children, and from the very nature of the case has therefore a superior claim. An uncle or a friend might work for the children far harder than the father ever works, but he could not by that means assume rightful authority to direct their career, although the parents would naturally take the benefactor into their counsels. The mother's right rests upon her unique relationship to the child…. The bread-winner, of course, has a strong claim to be consulted…."[17]

Again, Caird's article stirred little interest. In short, although it was the women of *Liberty* who broached subjects of vital interest to women, such as the status of children under anarchy, the real exchanges arose independent of and despite their efforts. The women were ignored or treated disrespectfully. When a full-blown debate over children's rights finally erupted within *Liberty*, it was conducted by—or, perhaps, more accurately abandoned to—the men. And so the discussion centered around the ideological points of concern to them: Stirnerite egoism versus natural rights. Holmes was still a presence at *Liberty*, but she did not join the debate. She did imbue it with the humanity and common sense which she had brought to the earlier discussion, which the later debate lacked.

* * * *

The following reprints of articles by Sarah E. Holmes (Zelm) from *Liberty* indicate the quality of the voice that was silenced.

"Shall Woman Beg For Liberty?"

February 25, 1888

I am surprised and puzzled at Henrietta's letter to Gramont in No. 117. Why in *Liberty*? I can find no liberty in it; only a pathetic appeal to be let alone if one should want a little. If "nothing can be better and more laudable" than for women to voluntarily submit to the bondage from which men have delivered them why is the letter written? Is this presumably emancipated woman making society not to censure conduct which she does not consider laudable? Somehow I am reminded, by all such entreaties to that world still in the bondage of old ideas, of the chorus in "Princess Ida." They are all lovely girls and they have put on shining armor and come out to fight. They are well drilled and delight the audience with their martial bearing and the beautiful precision of their military evolution. Then they make a curtsy and sing a little song:

> If you please, sir, do not hurt us,
>   Do not hurt us, if you please.

How can women who really believe free love better than slave love beg for the social support of respectable society? How can anyone, finding spontaneity in love better than the disposal of one's self for a consideration, mercenary or moral, desire this support? Can a woman with any real self-respect and dignity beg for the favor of those who are capable of thinking only lightly and scornfully of her highest thought?

I am thinking now only of social support, of which, as I understand it, Henrietta is speaking. If a woman finds herself boycotted in consequence of the expression, in language or life, of her ideas, or if she has reason to fear such boycotting, certainly that is a different matter, requiring deliberate consideration and choice. I might choose to forego the expression of my ideas rather than to starve; but, given food, can I not dispense with the rest? I will ask only for bread, not for smiles. A musician does not love discords. If because he is honest enough to say so, he loses a pupil and has no other means of earning a living, let him consider carefully before expressing himself. Better that one musician should live than that the world be given over to discord alone. But if he secures the pupil, let him not also beg for the social privilege of listening to his practising rather than going to the theatre.

Either our ideas are better or worse than those of society. If worse, let us submit without complaint to our deserved doom. If better, let us not apologize for them, or beg society to excuse and tolerate us in spite of our living on a higher plane than the rest of the world.

✱ ✱ ✱ ✱

The Exchange (Partial) Between Victor and Zelm "The Woman Question"

May 12, 1888
by Victor [Yarros]

Possibly at the expense of my reputation as a radical, but certainly to the entertainment and interest of *Liberty*'s readers, I intend to express in this article some conservative thoughts on the so-called Woman Question. This I will do, not so much because of my desire to present my own views, but because it appears to me a good way of eliciting elaborate statement and clear explanation from those with whom I shall take issue. The discussion (if such it may be called) of the Woman Question has so far been confined to platitudes and trivial points, while it has been deemed one of the absolute requisites of an advanced, Progressive, and liberal thinker to believe in equality of the sexes and to indulge in cheap talk about economic emancipation, equal rights, etc., of the "weaker sex." Declining to repeat this talk in a parrot like fashion, I asked to be offered some solid arguments in support of the position which I now, with all my willingness, cannot consider well grounded.

But let me state at the outset that I have not a word to say against the demand—which, alas! is not very loud and determined—on the part of women for a "free field and no favors." I fully believe in Liberty for man, woman, and child. So far as I know of Proudhon's views upon the function and sphere of woman I utterly oppose it, and his exclusion of the relations of the family institution from the application on his principle of free contract I regard as arbitrary, illogical, and contradictory of his whole philosophy. Nor, on the other hand, am I jealous of the privileges and special homage accorded by the bourgeois world to women, and do not in the least share the sentiments of E. Belford Bax, who declaims against an alleged tyranny exercised by women over men. Not denying that such "tyranny" exists, I assert that Mr. Bax entirely misunderstands its real nature. Man's condescension he mistakes for submission; marks of woman's degradation and slavery his obliquity of vision transforms into properties of sovereignty. Tchernychewsky takes the correct view upon this matter when he makes Vera Pavlovna say: "men should not kiss women's hands, since that ought to be offensive to women, for it means that men do not consider them as human beings like themselves, but believe that they can in no way lower their dignity before a woman, so inferior to them is she, and that no marks of affected respect for her can lessen their superiority." What to Mr. Bax appears as servility on the part of men is really but insult added to injury.

Recognizing, then, this fact of injury and insult which woman complains about, I sympathize with her in the aspiration for self control and in the demand to be allowed freedom and opportunities for development. And if this desire to work out her own salvation were the whole summit and substance of the "Woman Question" that would have been to me a question solved.

Women, in the first place, are the slaves of capital. In this their cause is man's cause, though the yoke of capitalism falls upon them with more crushing effect. This slavery would not outlive the State and legality for a single day, for it has no other root to depend on for continued existence.

In addition to this burden of economic servitude women are subjected to the misery of being the property, tool, and plaything of man, and have neither power to protest against the use, nor remedies against the abuse, of their persons by their male masters. This slavery is sanctioned by custom, prejudice, tradition, and prevailing notions of morality and purity. Intelligence is the cure for this. Man's brutality and cruelty will be buried in the same grave in which his own and woman's superstitions and fixed ideas will be forever laid away.

Normal economic conditions and increased opportunities for intellectual development are in this case, as in all others related to the social problems, the indispensable agents of improvement. It would be idle to discuss the possibility of any change under the present industrial and political arrangements. Woman must now content herself with indirectly furthering the cause nearest to her heart; she must simply join her strength to that of man—and even the most selfish of us will wish more power to her elbow—in his effort to establish proper relations between capital and labor. And only after the material foundations of the new social order have been successfully built, will the Woman Question proper loom up and claim attention.

Let us attempt here to briefly summarize the problem, the remedy, and the reasoning process by which the same are formulated, so far as we understand the position of the most extreme radicals in our ranks.

"Women must enjoy equal rights and equal freedom and must in all respects be the equal of man. They must contract on absolutely equal terms." How to attain and permanently maintain this condition?

"Economical independence is the first and most important thing to women who would be and remain free. When a woman ceases to be self supporting and begins to look to man for means of life, she deprives herself of independence, dignity, and power of commanding respect.

Complete control over her own person and offspring is the next essential thing. With this right of disposing of her own favors she must never part, and to no one must she delegate the privilege of determining the circumstances under which she shall assume the function of maternity. Eternal vigilance is the price of Liberty.

"Communism being the grave of individuality, woman must beware of ever abandoning her own private home, over which she exercises sovereign authority, to enter into man's dominion. Someone is bound to rule in the family, and chances are decidedly against her gaining the supremacy, even if this be considered a more desirable issue than the other alternative.

"The ideal, then, is: independent men and women, in independent homes, leading separate and independent lives, with full freedom to form and dissolve relations, and with perfectly equal opportunities and rights to happiness, development, and love."

Beautiful as this ideal may seem to some, I confess that it inspires me with no enthusiasm. On the contrary, it seems to be unnatural, impossible, and utterly utopian. While welcoming liberty, I do not anticipate such results.

Pray, let no reader hastily condemn my lack of sober judgment and pronounce me a sentimentalist and a dreamer. I am the most prosaic and unemotional of mortals. I utterly lack the "moral sense." Crime arouses no indignation in my breast, and vice fills me with no abhorrence. "Virtue" has a very half hearted champion in me. For instance, I am never moved to any outburst of intense feelings by the hue and cry against prostitution. I cannot help regarding it as entirely proper and natural for a woman to accept pecuniary remuneration for sexual intercourse with man, just as she accepts it for other services involving surrender of time or labor-power. The idea of sacredness of sex appears to me a survival and result of antique worship of the sexual organs, which Christian theology unconsciously assimilated and made part of its own mystical teachings. And, though the mysteries of love are as yet unexplained, nevertheless it is safe to say, *a priori*, that a large proportion of what has been written about it is nonsense and pure imagination. Thus it will be seen that what I have to say on this subject is born, not of sentiments, but of thought and dispassionate reflection.

"Right" is not a euphonious equivalent of "might"—a melodious and gentle term substituting the harsh "might" to the religious Bunthornes. A "right" to thing means the capacity to profitably secure it. The rights of an individual are fixed by his powers of body and mind. He has a right to appropriate and enjoy all that he can. If all men were intelligent and mentally free, no need of theoretical enlightenment and urging as to the principle of equal rights would exist. Each would naturally remain in full possession of his own. But in the absence of this intelligence, chaos is the rule. Some manage to obtain shares far beyond their individual capacity of procuring wealth, and many ignorantly and stupidly suffer themselves to be most unceremoniously used and abused by cunning people. Consequently it becomes necessary to open their eyes to this fact of their getting results utterly disproportionate to their expenditure of energy, and of their perfect ability to get and keep the entire amount without any external aid. Instead, however, of saying, "you can take it," we are obliged to speak of their "right" to take it,—so have the jugglers and tricksters confused their ideas of true and real titles to property. But it is evident that no one would stop to argue about the right to do a thing which cannot be done.

From this standpoint, what becomes of the demands of equal rights and opportunities in the relations of men and women? "Words, words, words," without meaning or significance. Nature having placed woman at such a decided disadvantage in the path of life, of what avail are her protestations and cries for equality with man? In order to gratify one of her strongest natural desires, she is compelled to enter into relations with man of which those burdensome and painful consequences she alone has to bear. While man's part in the relation is pleasurable throughout, woman purchases her enjoyment at an enormous price. A woman's loss here is man's clear gain. Up to the moment of her contracting to cooperate with men in the production of offspring woman may be considered as man's equal,—ignoring the question of physical vigor, weight and quality of the brain, etc., which cannot and need not be discussed here. A younger girl would, under proper and normal conditions, enjoy equal opportunities with the young man in the matter of providing for her material and intellectual wants. Economic independence, education, culture, and refinement,—all these would be fully within her individual reach. But let her enter into love relations with the young man and resolve upon all assuming parental obligations and responsibilities, and all is changed. She is no longer the equal of her male companion. For sometime before and longtime after giving birth to a child, she is incapable of holding her independent position and of supporting herself. She needs the care, support, and service of others. She has to depend upon the man whom she made the father of her child, and who suffered no inconvenience from the new relation. With the equality of powers for self-support vanish all other equalities,—a fact of which believers in the equality of the sexes are not only well aware, but one which they continually use as an excellent argument for economic independence of women. Surely, then, they ought not to overlook this cruel, illusion-breaking fact of natural equality of men and women resulting from the wide difference in the consequences which reproductive sexual association entails respectively upon the partners to the same. Women must either look to their male companions for making good the deficit thus occasioned in their accounts,—in which case the foundation is laid for despotism on the one side and subjection on the other,—or else find the means of support in excessive labor or in economy of consumption during the intervals of freedom from the restraints and burdens mentioned above,—which are what make the burden of life heavier to her and so reduce her opportunities for development and recreation. In both cases—inequality.

"Few children" will no doubt be suggested as the solution of this difficulty. But is this desirable and compatible with our conception of a future happy condition? Children all are a joy and a blessing to parents whom poverty, or the fear of poverty, does not transform into unnatural, suspicious, brutal, and eternally-discontented beings. I do not exactly entertain Mr. Lloyd's doubts as regards the superiority of the motto, "More and better children," over "Fewer and better children"; for, though not a Malthusian, I believe that some classes in society might well moderate their activity in the matter of reproduction. But I cannot think human happiness would be subserved by carrying the limitation to extreme. Moreover, this control over nature can only be successfully maintained by either the employment of artificial checks and preventives or by the practice of abstinence,—methods which nobody will recommend except as necessary evils, but which should never have been resorted to in the absence of serious reasons.

Of course, if—as seems fairly established—mental exertion, access to other pleasures, and comfortable surroundings generally are really important factors in checking fecundity and frequency in the matter of offspring, this last problem will of itself be most happily solved under the new conditions of life. But this prospect, while it may cheer the hearts of believers in small families, scarcely affords relief to those with whose position we are now mainly occupied.

Assuming sexual passion to be no stronger in women than in men (some are of the opinion that it is much stronger), there will always be a preponderance of forces and tendencies in favor of men in this natural antagonism. Man has no motive to deny himself gratification of his sexual desires except his dislike to be the cause or even the witness of the pain and suffering of those whom he loves, whereas woman, as we have seen, stakes her most vital interests when she follows her natural impulse.

Leaving it for advocates of independent homes to settle these difficulties for me, I may ask here, wherein would be the evil or danger of family life when, as the economic necessity for it having disappeared, so far as the woman is concerned, under a more rational industrial system, it should be maintained in the highest interests and free wishes of both parties to the contract? Why should not the love relations remain much as they are today? With the tyranny and impertinent meddling of Church and State abolished, would not the relation between "man" and "wife" always be the relation of lover and sweetheart? Between true lovers who are really devoted to each other relations are ideal. But legal marriage is the grave of love; material conditions and the current notions of virtue and morality destroy the individuality of the married woman, and she becomes the property of her husband. Remove these, and living together ceases to be evil. The family relation in that state will continue to be perfect as long as they will continue at all.

Readers of *What's To Be Done?* know how Tchernychewsky's heroes arranged their married life. To that and similar plans there can be no objection. It depends upon the temperaments and tastes of the individual persons. But why a man should not "make a home" for the woman he loves, I am unable to see. While he is providing means, she is educating the children and surrounding him with comfort. When they cease to be happy together, they separate. And, as in the commercial sphere, if the air of probable competition suffices to prevent monopolistic iniquity without necessarily calling forth actual competition, so in family life under freedom the probability or rather certainty of the woman's rebellion against the slightest manifestation of despotism will make the man very careful in his conduct and insure peace and respect between them.

I am not blind to the fact that my ideal contains the element of Communism, and also involves the concentration of love upon one person of the opposite sex at a time. But, as long as these are a spontaneous result of freedom, they are no more to be theoretically deplored than especially recommended. Personally I hold, however, that some sort of Communism is inevitable between lovers, and that "variety" in love is only a temporary demand of a certain period. A certain degree of experience is just as necessary in the matter of love as it is in any other branch of human affairs. Variety may be as truly the mother of unity for duality, rather as Liberty is the mother of order. The inconstancy of young people is proverbial. But when free to experiment and take lessons in a love, the outcome might be that finally each Apollo would find his Venus and retire with her to a harmonious and idyllic life.

Upon the last two phases of the question a great deal more might be said. I will return to them at some future time.

My remarks are far from being systematic or clear, but it is not my purpose to put forth anything positive and conclusive. I merely desire to provoke discussion and call out some explicit and elaborate statements from those of Liberty's readers who, unlike the writer, have in their minds a more or less complete solution of the "Woman Question."

"A Reply to Victor"

May 26, 1888
by Zelm [Sarah E. Holmes]

"Independent men and women, in independent homes, leading separate and independent lives, with full freedom to form and dissolve relations, and with perfectly equal opportunities to happiness, development, and love." I leave out the word "rights," doubtful I can use it without being misunderstood. Perhaps I can succeed in dispensing with its use altogether. This ideal, so stated, is attractive to me and completely in harmony with my idea of the course in life which will best further human happiness.

I am not sure I quite understand Victor's position in regard to the number of children desirable in the future family. Yet this seems to me so essential an item in the consideration of the social problem of the future that it must be dealt with at the outset. If the greatest amount of happiness can only be secured by obedience to the "natural" sexual instincts, unrestrained by consideration of any other pleasures which are renounced for their sake, then I can but admit that there seems no escape from the perpetual dependence of woman upon man. Of whatever form the new organization of society may be, it is not likely to be one in which one can "have his cake and eat it too." And, allowing considerable margin for the "certain period" at which, Victor claims, "variety is only a temporary demand," it is not too much to suppose, on his theory of life, that every Apollo will find his Venus before she is older than twenty-five. She has twenty years of child-bearing possibilities before her, and the simple gratification of by no means abnormal sexual impulses might result in her giving birth to ten children. During twenty years of her life she will have held, borne, and nursed these children. And yet his plan involves that, during this time, when, he asserts, she "needs the care, support and service of others and is therefore unable to support herself," she is nevertheless "educating the children and surrounding her lover with comfort," it seems to me that, if I have not misunderstood him in this, he has been looking at the subject from a man's standpoint.

But I do not see why we should let this sexual impulse lead us where it may. All our life is a foregoing what we are inclined to do for the sake of a future happiness we may thereby gain or a future pain we may thereby avoid. I do not always eat whenever I see appetizing food; I refrain from sitting in a draught and drinking ice-water when I am too much heated; I sometimes get up when I am still sleepy; and I do not stay in the ocean long enough to risk a chill. And I know the consequences of following the simple sexual impulses to be more serious than any other.

I may consider many of nature's methods exceedingly wasteful and clumsy, and I may believe that, if I had made the world, I would have made it otherwise, that I would have made our simple, spontaneous, first, and most keenly-felt desires those which, if blindly followed, would result in the greatest conceivable happiness. But nature and the laws of the universe and of our own selves are facts which we cannot alter and to which we can only study to adjust ourselves. "If God exists, he is man's enemy"; woman's even more. Finding no escape from this conclusion, I no longer treat nature as my friend when she betrays me. I do not even insist upon trying all experiments for myself. When they are too costly, I am sometimes content to learn from the experience of others. Nor, for the women, the consequences of simply obeying the sexual impulses are the bearing of children. That means risking her life. It also means the endurance of intense suffering, such suffering as she has never before been able to conceive. In the future social condition I believe every girl will be taught this. Nevertheless, I believe there will still be children in the world. I believe that, when a woman no longer looks upon bearing children as either a duty or a slave's necessity in the service of her master, it is not impossible that she will consider it the greatest privilege life may hold out to her. And with her claim to this child which has cost her so much once recognized by all men and women, why may it not be that she would choose this luxury rather than other "opportunities." A woman will no longer look upon it as a more or less unfortunate natural consequence of the satisfaction of a strong desire, but as a blessing—yes, the very greatest in life to any woman with the mother-instinct—to be secured with full purpose and careful choice, with a complete understanding of all else that must be given up for its sake. Victor has not made it clear to my mind that the woman is the loser who chooses this. It is hard to find the measure of other development or luxury that will be compensation for a woman's loss of this possibility.

But I do not admit that she must needs sacrifice her independence to secure this end. Under normal conditions a woman is by no means unfitted for any productive labor during pregnancy. It would be an exceptional case in which she would be unable to perform the three hours' daily work necessary for self support during the whole period. This is adding one hour to the limit set in the "Science of Society," in which Mr. Andrews claims that two hours' daily labor will be more than sufficient to support each individual in average comfort. I do not even admit that the woman "has to depend upon the man whom she made the father of her child for some time before and a long time after giving birth to a child." All that is needful is that she have the service and help of someone. It is even impossible that he can give her the real sympathy of one who can understand just this. I think it must have been the experience of every mother, however tenderly cared for by her husband, that, after all, only some other mother could or did understand, and that all his offered sympathy was really only pity.

After the birth of a child, a woman may be unfitted for any productive labor for two months. And we must add to the list of expenses the support of a nurse during this time and the physician's fee. During another seven months she will nurse her child and, perhaps, will do no other work except directly caring for him. But I am taking this for granted rather from a desire not to underestimate the needful expense of child-bearing than because it seems to me surely the better way. There is a strong feeling among advanced people that a women ought to do nothing whatever during pregnancy and child-nursing but fold her hands and look at beautiful pictures and listen to beautiful music. But I think this is largely reactionary. The pendulum has swung quite over. It is like saying: "Women have done too much; therefore they should do nothing."

It is a safe estimate, it seems to me, to say that it will cost not more than half as much to support a child for the first ten years of its life as to support an adult. That is, a woman will be obliged to work four hours and a half a day instead of three for ten years in order to support each child. And she must have previously saved money enough for the child-bearing expenses which I have just indicated. After ten years, in the new order of economic life, a child may be self-supporting.

I cannot see how all this can seem to anyone an impossibility or even an undesirability. When the nursing period is at an end, the mother engages in the four and a half hours' daily employment, leaving for this time her child in the care of others. These others may be friends who assume this care because it is to them a delight and a rest or, in the absence of such friends, it may be simply trustworthy people who would find in it, not rest, but attractive labor, for which they would receive due remuneration. I am almost certain of encountering on this point a remonstrance in the minds of many woman. A true mother will never leave a young child, they will say. But I am almost as certain that every mother who is thoroughly honest with herself will admit that it would have been better, both for herself and her child, if she could have left him in safe hands for a few hours each day.

Victor's plan involves the education of children by the mother, and I am quite sure that he is positive about every true mother desiring to educate her children herself, and that it will be her most ardent wish. I am less confident about that being the case. I can only admit that it may be her greatest desire that they be well educated. But the ideal mother, in my mind, is one whose most ardent desire is to be her children's closest, dearest, best friend; that, in all their life, in all trouble and sorrow, they will look first to her with that sweet serenity of confidence that can only come of having never looked in vain. And I hold it to be a simple utter impossibility for most women to stand in this closest and best relation in a child's after-life if, throughout its childhood, she has wasted herself in attempting to be its sole educator. If the mother's arms must ache for every hour of rest the child enjoys, if the tired, dull brain must be worried and strained to answer the many, many eager, carefree questions which are so easy to ask, so hard to answer,—there is nothing left for sympathy with the young, fresh, growing life. And the mother who, because of all the long, close first life with the baby heart [sic] and because of all which that little baby has inherited of her own nature, might stand in a special, peculiar relation to the little growing individual, is often farther off, actually, than any other friend. And I believe it to be a truth that many, perhaps most people, will silently verify that, when the stress, when the crises of life come, however much the mother may yearn to help, however sorry she may be for all the pain her child must bear, the sympathy she has to offer is not that which alone has worth,—the sympathy of an understanding heart.

Although, in a sense, education begins at birth, we may speak of it now beginning with a child's first questions, and, from this time, to secure its best possible development, it should have the help of real educators. Now, real educators are born, not made. And there are very few born. The ability to bear healthy, strong, beautiful children by no means argues any ability whatever to educate them. I do not say that any mother may not be able to answer a child's questions somehow, but to answer them truthfully and in a manner fitted to the child's just-dawning understanding is another matter. And that is education. It is a well established belief amongst the most advanced minds that the best teachers are needed most in Kindergarten. Older children are better able to dispense with the best of guidance. But this belief is a new, not an old idea; a product of evolution. A still later product, I believe, will be the discovery that the best of teachers are needed to answer a child's first questions, and that the mother of any special baby is as little likely to be possessed of the requisite qualifications for success in that direction as she is to be able to teach the higher mathematics.

The feeling is sometimes expressed that it is hard and unjust for a mother to pay all the cost of her children. That is, I think, because, in family life as it has always existed, except in those cases where the mother has been left a widow, she has never known what it was to have what she had purchased. Consequently, in the minds of most people, there is no conception of the reward that might be hers. All that a woman may hope for, under present conditions, is that the father will be so occupied with outside cares that he will be content to leave the control of the children in her hands. But the fact that he is their father and supports both herself and them leaves him in no doubt as to his right to interfere. The suffering she endured in bringing them into the world is a cost which he can never estimate. Even if he has once witnessed it, and if it has made such an impression on him that he would never risk another such possibility for her, he does not consider it as giving her a right to anything.

Now, I do not feel that it is a blessing to a woman to bear children whom she cannot control. I believe that their existence is a joy to her only just so far as their existence is a happy one. That to be forced to see them harshly or unjustly treated, or even treated in any way other than what she conceives the best, is to be forced to endure greater suffering than could come to her in any other way. "Mothers never do part bonds with babies they have borne. Until the day they die, every quiver of their life goes back straight to the heart beside which it began."

Suppose, some day, little Frank throws his ball through the window. It is papa's window, bought with the money earned by his own labor. Frank has been told not to throw his ball in that room. And papa thinks he will never remember not to do it again until he is whipped. So he whips him. Mamma does not agree with papa about this. Indeed, when they used to talk about how children should be treated, papa was always quite sure that a child should never be whipped. But in this emergency he has abandoned this theory of education and adopted a new one. It is not enough to put this illustration by with the reflection that a more careful investigation into the possibility and probabilities inherent in papa's nature would have avoided the difficulty. It is impossible that a woman can know what any man will do in any position until she has seen him just there. We all know that no theory of education exactly fits all children; that is, in actual life, circumstances are constantly arising where the long cherished theory must be set aside for this individual child in just this individual case. And I am not claiming that a mother can ever secure herself against witnessing some suffering on the part of her child. It is only that if, in all cases, the course followed is chosen by her, unconditionally, uninfluenced by consideration for any other opinion than her own, she may then feel confident that, whatever pain has been caused, a greater has been avoided; and in that reflection lies her comfort and compensation.

On any theory of mutual control and paternal support, or maternal control and paternal support, or mutual control and mutual support, how will these questions be answered? Is Frank to be put to bed in a room by himself and obliged to lie there until sleep comes, or is he to be rocked and sung to? When he is sick, are physicians and drugs to be summoned, or is heroic cold water and hygienic treatment to be solely relied upon? Shall he be vaccinated? Shall all attention be paid to his physical development for the first few years, or shall he be given early opportunities for mental discipline? Shall he be allowed without remonstrance to follow his own will, or is he to be resisted when he becomes an invader? Shall this resistance be offered when he makes his first attempt to possess himself of another's property, or must one wait until he threatens to throw the looking-glass out of the window? May he pick berries and chop wood for the neighbors if he prefers it to attending school? Must he learn to swim or go into the water first? Is he to have both a bicycle and a pony, or to go barefooted in summer? Is he to dress in crimson velvet or in dark-blue overalls? Is he to be fitted for a surgeon or a book-agent? Is he to have a private tutor and a hundred dollar microscope, or to go to the village-school?

Even apart from the consideration of definite questions, it seems to me impossible that any but the most self-controlled man who has any claim, even a fancied one, shall refrain from continually interposing more well-meant suggestions which must oftener bewilder and hopelessly entangle the originally clear plan of the mother than serve any useful purpose.

This theory of independent living does not seem to me to involve any loss of the "home" which the family relation has always, it is assumed, been alone able to secure. There would always be, for the little children, the safe, sure mother-home. And, besides this, there would be the father-home, somewhere else, and as many friend-homes as there were dear friends, to which the little children would lend their sunshine whenever their wish so to do met with the mother's consent.

I cannot readily understand anyone but a Communist being ready to favor "a sort of communism between lovers." In every other social relations an Individualist would have the strongest faith in every plan which conduced to the greatest development of individuality as most certain to bring happiness. But in this relation, in which, of all other in life, mistakes result in the sharpest suffering, this general principle is set aside, and the development of individuality, at least of womanly individuality, less carefully considered than the securing for her of certain luxuries and other material advantages. It is true that, when one is in love, it is impossible to conceive happiness in any other form than the constant presence of the loved one. Nevertheless, I believe that neither the finest nor the keenest happiness lovers are capable of yielding each other will result from following this wish blindly, without reason or thought. I am even disposed to find fault with Victor's saying that "between true lovers who are really devoted to each other the relations are ideal." I do not think that "devotion" is any element of an ideal relation between grown-up people. A mother or father or adult friend may be devoted to a helpless baby, to a child, or to a weak, sick, afflicted man or woman. But only weakness has need to devotion, or desires it. What strong men and women want, in either the relations of friendship of in that fervid, passion-full form of friendship known as love, is simply to feel the "home in another heart"; a home not made, but found. Apollo's Venus is doubtless altogether lovely in his eyes, but that fact is only tiresome or amusing to the rest of the world, and must inevitably tend to fill Venus with a narrow vanity which effectually checks all desire or capacity for growth. I no more admire a blind love than a blind hatred. Either is below the plane on which developed men and women will find themselves. That youth is inconstant is proverbial, but not all proverbs are quite true. Youth is the age of hero-worship, and the tendency of that period is to idealize the object of love. Today young people, experimenting in love, begin by finding an Apollo or Venus in every beautiful face, and end—in what? In finding the true one at last? Not at all. In finding that they were mistaken, but in concluding that this one will do. Having reached this conclusion, their inconstancy hides itself from public view under the veil of married life, and these young people become constant, but not always constant in their love. My prophecy of the future is that, after love has been left free long enough (I do not mean an individual man or woman, but all men and women), Apollo will find that he has no Venus. Because it seems to me that, as human life advances and human beings differentiate, there becomes less and less possibility of finding any one with whom one is completely in sympathy.

Nevertheless, I believe there will always be love. Indeed, I believe in love. I do not see why hating should be so free and so—it would seem—comparatively virtuous. If one hates, it is a matter of course. But if one loves, it is something to be looked into, and there is probably something wrong about it. Now, I am going to assume, in spite of all public sentiment to the contrary, that love is not a bad thing, but a good thing; that it is a normal, healthful, strength-giving, developing force among the condition of human existence; that it is called forth by the perception of lovable, admirable, fine qualities, wherever they exist; that in its intrinsic nature it is a blessing, and not a curse, wherever it exists; that it does not need to be sanctified by a marriage rite or even by the approval of friends; that if, in its results, it leads to suffering, it is because our own reason, not the authority of others, has not rescued us.

When a man "makes a home" for a woman in the way Victor proposes, he makes it impossible that either shall know any other love without calling upon the other to bear a certain amount of deprivation. For me, any arrangement which would involve the love of only one at a time would be sufficient to condemn it. Not to be free to love is the hardest of all slavery. But marriage is like taking a path in which there is only room for two. And a man and woman cannot take up a position before the world as dearest friends or lovers—call the relation by any name you choose—without by that action cutting themselves off from all fullness and spontaneity of other love and friendship. By the very announcement of their mutual feeling—in whatever form the announcement may be made—they have said: "Everything in my life is to be subordinated to this." To voluntarily and deliberately "make a home" is to say that nothing foreign to either can enter.

The result in life today is commonly this: Of the old friend of either only those enter the new home who have a sufficient number of qualities that are equally attractive to both to make them welcome and who can be content to continue friendship on the basis of those qualities. If John does not like music, Ellen gives up her musical friends. Why should he be asked to hear the piano, when it is only so much noise to him, or even hear music discussed, when it is a bore to him? Why should Ellen be called upon to breathe tobacco-perfumed air, because John and certain of John's friends feel restless and uncomfortable without their after-dinner cigar? Things are mainly either pleasurable or painful; not indifferent. If John and Ellen are honest with each other, they will discover that John dislikes music and Ellen dislikes tobacco, and that to lay aside their sensitivities on one occasion may be a slight matter, but that to be called upon to lay them aside at any time is a really serious mater. But Victor perhaps thinks the home need not be like that. John may have his smoking-room and Ellen her music-room. In that case the smoking room would be, after dinner, John's home, and the music-room Ellen's home. The place where we are free,—that is home. That is perhaps the secret of all home feeling. The presence of our dearest friends helps it only when their mood meets ours.

But this is not "making a home." To make a home, in the popular sense, is to buy land and build a home which is ours, buy dishes and furniture which are ours, agree to have children which are ours, and to make no change in our life arrangements except by mutual consent.

Victor puts the case simply, and it sounds easy: "When they cease to be happy together, they separate." Is it so simple? It is not enough to say: We are not bound together one hour longer than our mutual love lasts. Mutual love does not come and go, keeping step like well-trained soldiers.

As the first flush of love passes away, people begin to discover each other. After all, they were not one. In very many cases it was only the blinding force of the sex element which retarded this discovery. There was no conscious deceit. But the discovery is apt to be a painful one. And the old hunger for sympathy in all things returns. If we are still free to seek it, no harm comes. There may even be no pain in the slow discovery that in no one other soul can it be found. But if we are not free, and if, by some chance, one, not both, comes to believe that the love was founded on a mistake? Jealousy is only pain at a loss suffered or threatened. It need not be angry pain. We have come to apply the word only to angry pain, but the anger is in the individual and not an inevitable result of the condition. And people are not commended, do not receive the support of public sentiment, when they are angry at the loss of something to which they have never claimed a right,—or more, have never believed they possessed a right. We all understand that in *What's To Be Done?* the marriage of Vera Pavlovna and Loponkhoff was simply a form, demanded by conditions of their environment which they were helpless to resist. Law and custom necessitated her going through the form of making herself his slave. Being a slave in her own father-and-mother home, it was only on that condition that he could give her liberty. Later, when he discovered her feeling for Kirsanoff, his love for her liberty was greater than his desire to preserve an outward form of home from which the home has fled. Both he and Kirsanoff saw or dimly felt that she was not a woman who would love more than one at once. Their future showed that she could not even believe in a love she could not understand. In the fullness of her lighthearted content with Kirsanoff, she decides quite positively that

Loponkhoff really did not love her. We are all a little inclined to the view that real love is only that which we feel or have felt.

It is very true of love that we know not whence it comes or whither it goes. It is sometimes more sadly true, and makes one of life's problems far more intricate, that we know not when it comes or when it goes. Its death is as incomprehensible as its birth. Sometimes it is drained away, silently and unsuspectedly, by the thousand wearing trifles inevitably attendant upon the constant companion which the torrent of new-born love so imperiously demands. Sometimes it is swept away in one instant by the discovery of some quality of character of whose existence we have never dreamed. Sometimes, as in *What's To Be Done?* the constant need of one is identical only with the temporary need of the other, and the discovery can not possibly be made until the temporary need has passed. All life is either growth or decay,—that is, change. And with every change in the individual there is change in his love. In the happiest lives and the longest loves its proportion and depth and character are perpetually changing.

Victor says: Variety may be as truly the mother of duality as liberty is the mother of order. Has he forgotten that this mother does not die in giving birth to her daughter, and that this child does not thrive well without the mother?

"The Problem Which the Child Presents"

September 1, 1888, p. 7
Zelm [Abridged]

In attempting to give utterance to some of the many thoughts suggested to me by those who have found much to take exception in my ideas about love and the life in love and the life that comes from love, I would rather it were not looked upon as an *answer* to my critics. I have read no comments which have not seemed to me to hold some germ of truth. While I differ with them, I also feel that in many ways they have expressed phases of thought with which I can feel much sympathy. If we are not in the same truth, we have certainly touched truths here and there, and this touch has not been, with me, without its glad inner recognition of a common fellowship. Even if it were less so, my own words express my thoughts so clumsily, it may easily be that theirs have at least in some degree failed also in revealing their own conceptions. That is, we may have mistaken each other.

When anyone claims that men will have no motives to beget children whom they cannot control, does he not forget how many women, today, bear children gladly, even although they know that law and society may at anytime give the control of them into the father's hands? Loving him, they trust in him, and believe that he could never be cruel or hard to his children. The fathers of the future will have no less confidence in the mothers of the future.

I have heard it urged against the new plan of social life that the fathers will have an altogether too delightfully easy time of it to the world, with no care or responsibility. Well, I can't be very sorry about that. I have no great veneration for care or responsibility. I hate careless and irresponsible people only because they shirk what they have assumed, but I do not want more care and responsibility in the world, but less. My own life as a worker and one of the exploited class, having been not without its burdens which have seemed "too grievous to be borne," has brought me into great sympathy with others who are weighted down and into very little sympathy with careless, frivolous, or every light-hearted man and woman.... But it is not because I feel burdens and bowed forms the greatest and best and most to be desired things in life. It is only that, being ill myself, I am greatly in sympathy with others who are ill, and that I am very sorry for anybody who is in pain. I do not exactly understand how you, who are well, can be very jolly and hilarious while I am sick. Nevertheless, I believe in health, and, although I am a little cross with you now, in your insolent unconsciousness of the existence of pain or disease, I shall work, with whatever strength is in me, for the banishment of physical ills from the earth. I shall also work for the abolishing, as far as possible, of anxiety and painful care-taking; and this, I believe, is one of the results which will flow from the new order of things. There will be no further attempt to divide responsibility, because it will be perceived that the peculiar arithmetic of responsibility is that division is always multiplication. A kindergartner may keep six children busy, happy, and in the conditions most favorable for their education for three hours; but if six people have charge of one child, there will be six different opinions with regard to what shall be done with the child. If there are, five people will have to waive their responsibility before anything can be done with it. And all the six people will have to keep the child constantly in mind that it may not fall or hurt itself, I am afraid, if such division of labor were to be instituted in all departments of human activity, our future economic conditions would not be materially improved. We must come to learn, I think, that in this, as in all else, individual initiative, individual lead, individual responsibility, are the essential conditions to all progress.

And not only will responsibility be concentrated, and so lessened, but it will be placed just where it can never be felt as a burden. When a lover promises to spend the evening with the woman he loves, does he remember or think of it as a promise? *Could* he forget it? A mother is responsible, doubtless, for her child's nourishment; but only a wholly world-corrupted mother, an unnatural mother, ever can think of anything but the delight of feeling the clinging of the baby lips and the pressure of the little head against her heart. It is not nursing, but weaning, that calls for heroism, for thought of future good instead of present joy.

It seems to me that we desire and conceive children, firstly and mainly, for ourselves. We wish to live again in them, to live with them; to take up this old, tired world and look at it once more through their fresh, young eyes that have yet known few tears. The old dream of immortality comes again in the longing to feel that something of ourselves may still exist in the world after we are no longer here, that a life something like our own, with something of our real selves in it, will perhaps, love and take up our work where we are forced to leave it. We want the warm, soft, tender grace of their baby bodies and the truth of their fearless, uncorrupted minds. With it all and in it all we wish for them,—not alone for our selves in them, but for their *selves*,—the best that life can hold for anyone. Please fate, we will do our best to secure it for them. But I do not think we bring them into the world for the world's sake or even for their sakes, but simply for the joy of perpetuating ourselves.

There are two phases of feeling in regard to the question of ownership which I am not in the least inclined to set aside as unimportant or meaningless. The first is the revulsion which all tender natures instinctively feel at the suggestion that a child is in any sense property or is owned by any one. "A child is not a slave," Mr. Lloyd says. It is true; but a child is none the less a product for which a price has been paid. Suffering endured is *cost* in the same sense that repugnance overcome is *cost*. And this forever establishes the claim; this product is not *anyone's* or *everyone's*; only the mother's. A gypsy may steal my child on the day of its birth, may nourish it and support it until it becomes self-supporting. All her care and all its dependency do not make it belong to her, simply because it was originally stolen. And yet all our sentiment is opposed to its *belonging* to any one, except as Mr. Lloyd uses the word, as the fruit to the tree. We are shocked at the idea of a human being as property, and if it could be, as Mr. Warren would have it, that a baby could be born sovereign, it might and would belong to itself from the moment of its existence. But it is simply a fact that, if its life is to be preserved at all, if it is ever to be able to reach its power of sovereignty, it must be cared for and educated by some adult mind and to that end controlled by some adult will. Whose mind and whose will be this to be? This little life being here, is it to be destroyed or saved? Has any one a right to insist that it shall be preserved until it shall attain the power of self-preservation; and, since it must always be a matter of varying opinion as to what means must be employed to accomplish this and, has any one a right to insist upon his decision in the matter? Or would it be better, think you, that there should be a "consensus of the competent" to decide who shall have it in charge?

I admit that the possession of power over a becoming individual is a dangerous thing, a demoralizing thing, but the greatest possible safeguard against this is tenderness, and I most earnestly believe that all the pure, unadulterated tenderness which human beings are capable of feeling mothers must feel for their children.

The second phase of feeling is the sense of injustice to the father. His part in the production of the child being is as essential as the mother's, although destitute of the element of cost, and his desire for a child as great, perhaps, is it quite fair, it is asked, to deny him all right, and is it not a miserably inadequate social condition which leaves a man practically childless? To this it can only be said that the mother has the right to give her child to whom she will; nor do I know that she may not sometimes desire that it become the father's. Yet I do not feel that, whatever any "court of equity or arbitration might decide," there would be any justice in the child's transference to the father, on the mother's death, if this were against her wishes. Her choice of him as a father rested on her faith in his worth and her conception of the integrity of his character. If this faith is lost and this conception changes, she has the same right to appoint another guardian that would be hers in regard to any other possession. Suppose, for instance, that Romola had conceived a child before her discovery of Tito Melema's share in the betrayal of Savonarola; or that the wife of the governor who did not commute the sentence of the men at Chicago had conceived a child three months before the execution; those children should belong to their fathers, do you think?

It is feared that a father will be less with his children, and that fatherly love will die out. But all this fear rests upon the idea that love is a less powerful motive in the world than the sense of obligation or duty or responsibility. A mother will certainly not wish less than he be with them. Nor are his opportunities less than before, but, on the contrary, as much more as the leisure of a man who is supporting only one instead of two or three or four.

Tell me, you who are afraid, does a lover spend less time with the woman he loves than a husband? After the first joy of long-delayed possession is past, where, in the scale of pleasant things, does a husband place an evening with his wife? Ellen was always well cared for in her father's house. John never felt the slightest shade of responsibility for her support in those old lover days. Was she less to him, do you think? Did he care less for a look from her eyes? Did he wonder with a less eager wonder what she would think about the book they were reading together? Did a cloud of tiredness or despondency on her face pass unnoticed by him then? Did the least touch of her hand thrill him less? Did he care less for her confidence, her trust, her restful, unwavering faith in his manhood?

In regard to what a father may do for a child (supposing always that he has kept the mother's love and confidence), he would naturally be checked or limited in nothing which did not interfere with the mother's plan for the child's education. And here again, if you believe that the mother will refuse everything on this plea, you can only do so because you can believe that a woman will cease to love a man as soon as she feels herself under no obligation to love him; that she will be ready, on any pretense, to deny him the blessedness of giving; that she will love him less because he loves her child; and that she will hasten to think him unworthy as soon as she is no longer dependent upon him for her existence.

There is, and I suppose there always will be, a great margin in our book of wants after the text page of necessities is written out; a wide range of things we would like, although we can do without them. I think the father may find scope enough for his generosity. He need not quarrel with a system which lets all that he does take the form only of gifts. Gifts are the only precious things in the world. It is well when a man pays his debts; indeed, it is very bad when he does not; but it calls forth neither love, nor gratitude, nor, in fact, any pleasant emotion whatever. A lover's gifts, so long as they are gifts, are only treasures. But, in our present social system, they soon become no longer gifts, but only symbols of a claim. In the world's code of honor, they are to be returned as soon as the engagement is broken. That is, they were not gifts, but mortgages.

A married lady who had preserved something, at least in her longing, of the romance and poetry of her first love feeling, said reproachfully one day: "George brought Clara some violets last night; *you used to bring me violets.*" "I bring you beefsteak now," he said, smiling playfully, perhaps a little teasingly.

And no violets.

Now in the world's glorious future, in which I believe, the love of men and women will not take the form of violets first, and beefsteak, but no violets ever after. And for my little girl my most yearning wish, could be, not that she may never be really hungry before the dinner is quite ready; or that she may never work hard—scrub floors, if need be—to earn the money for beefsteak; but that she may never, in all her life, look into the eyes of an old-time lover and say: *You used to bring me violets.* I want men and women to keep their love as fresh as the baby-life to which such love gives birth; to be true, honest, strong, self-sustaining men and women first; and then to love; to love one or to love many—fate and the chances of life must settle that—but, one or many, I want each love to be as full of its own essential fragrant essence as a violet's breath.

From such love—of one or many, again—will come into the world glad little children, conceived with the sunshine of life's best gift. And they will come into a world of homes—true homes, violet homes. And there will be one guiding hand, holding in it the thread and purpose of their education, trusting them to others who are to be trusted, but always and only of its choosing; and as these young lives grow into conscious-ness of love, they will find themselves in a world full of lovers,—not hus-bands, wives, families, duties, claims, responsibilities,—but, only and always, love and lovers.

6

Gertrude B. Kelly:
A Disillusioned Woman

While some women seem to have been intimidated into silence, others walked away from *Liberty* in disillusionment. One such woman was Dr. Gertrude B. Kelly.

In the opinion of Benjamin Tucker, editor of the pivotal individualist periodical *Liberty*, "Gertrude B. Kelly, ... by her articles in Liberty, has placed herself at a single bound among the finest writers of this or any other country...."[1] From her first article in *Liberty* (September 1885) to her bitter split with that same periodical over its debate on egoism versus natural rights (August 1887), Gertrude Kelly (1862–1934) was one of Tucker's most dynamic writers and, certainly, its most frequent female contributor and a strong champion of Natural Law.

In particular, her articles brought a unique perspective on labor and women, for she was one of the few feminists of her time who believed "... there is, properly speaking, no *woman question*, as apart from the question of human right and human liberty."[2] She looked forward to a society comprised of individuals in which such secondary characteristics as sex or race had no impact upon the equal rights enjoyed by each person. As Kelly phrased it,

"The woman's cause is man's—they rise or sink
Together,—dwarfed or god-like—bond or free."[3]

The general cause shared by woman and man was the drive for "universal liberty, equality of rights, individual responsibility" as "the moving principles of societary progress."[4] The specific social injustice upon which Kelly focused her considerable energy and insight was what she called "the plight of the working-class."

As a medical doctor who worked in the tenements and as the Secretary of the Newark Liberal League, Kelly displayed a special concern for the debilitating effect of poverty upon the laboring woman. Indeed, her first article in *Liberty*, entitled "The Root of Prostitution," argued

164

that the inability of women to make an adequate living through respectable forms of labor was the cause of this profession. She wrote, "We find all sorts of schemes for making men moral and women religious, but no scheme which proposes to give woman the fruits of her labor."[5]

The condemnation aired in this article expressed two themes that were common to most of Kelly's analyses of poverty and of women:

First, women had been oppressed by cultural stereotypes created primarily by men. She declared, "Men ... have always denied to women the opportunity to think; and, if some women have had courage enough to dare public opinion, and insist upon thinking for themselves, they have been so beaten by that most powerful weapon in society's arsenal, ridicule, that it has effectively prevented the great majority from making any attempt to come out of slavery." She leveled this charge equally at the supposedly enlightened men in her own political circle, whom she claimed, would "immediately change not only the serious topics of conversation, but change the very tones of their voice" when wives or sisters entered the room.[6]

Second, charitable organizations created by the rich were hypocritical in their attitudes and behavior toward the poor, who needed to become self-sufficient and not to be further victimized by misguided benevolence. She particularly ridiculed the philanthropic groups so popular in her day in which working "girls are given lessons in embroidery, art, science, etc., and are incidentally told of the evils of trade-unions, the immorality of strikes, and of the necessity of being 'satisfied with the condition to which it has pleased God to call them.'"[7]

Like most radical individualists of nineteenth-century America, Kelly viewed capitalism as the major cause of poverty and social injustice. This conviction sprang from two other beliefs. First, she accepted a particular version of the labor theory of value that was espoused by the path-breaking individualist Josiah Warren: This version is commonly expressed in terms of "Cost Is the Limit of Price." Second, she shared the popular radical belief that capitalism was an alliance between business and government, in which the latter guaranteed legal privileges to the rich. In essence, Kelly considered all forms of capitalism to be what contemporary individualism calls "state capitalism."

Accordingly, she believed that interest, profit, and rent were usuries through which capitalists exploited laborers by usurping the product of their labor. Although it sounds ironic to modern ears, Kelly—along many other early individualist theorists—considered the free market to be a cure for capitalism. She considered voluntary cooperation, unregulated by anything but the laws of economics and the desires of individuals, to be the solution to this social injustice.

For example, in her article "The Unconscious Evolution of Mutual Banking," Kelly suggested a remedy for the state monopoly of money which caused the usury of "interest": her remedy was the establishment of privately controlled currency (or currencies). She exuded, "…The free monetary system with its destruction of interest and profit, looms up before us! The exchange of product against product is inaugurated! The social revolution accomplishes itself!"[8]

In other words, to sever the alliance between government and business that constituted capitalism, it was necessary to deny government any power over the economic arrangements of individuals, for "… all the laws have no other object than to perpetrate injustice, to support at any price the monopolists in their plunder."[9] In her opinion, a free market in which individual contracts—and not government—set prices would eliminate practices such as charging interest.

But what if she were proven wrong? What if interest and other forms of usury continued to exist within the framework of a free market? Contributors to *Liberty* were clear and consistent on at least one point. Individuals had the absolute right to enter into agreements which *Liberty* contributors considered to be foolish and self-destructive. Any interference into such voluntary contracts constituted the use of force which was the more primary evil. As Kelly commented, "…We realize the labor question can never be solved by force…. You cannot shoot down or blow up an economic system, but you can destroy it by ceasing to support it, as soon as you understand where its evils lie."[10] But if a free individual could not be persuaded away from paying interest, then that individual would have to live with the folly of his or her own actions.

It is important to understand Kelly's history in order to fully appreciate her opposition to usuries such as rent and interest. As an immigrant from Ireland, Gertrude Kelly's introduction to individualistic philosophy was probably through the columns of "Honorius" in *Irish World*—an organ of the Irish No Rent movement. Honorius was, in fact, a pseudonym for the American natural rights advocate Henry Appleton who contributed frequently to the early issues of *Liberty*, both under his own name and under the pen name of "X."

Kelly could not have been indifferent to the absentee British landlords whose claims to most of Ireland's fertile soil came from conquest and legal privilege. The exorbitant rent and interest they charged the Irish for use of land and money were a major cause of that country's poverty. On coming to America, Kelly did not seem to think that the differing histories of the two nations required differing economic and political analysis.[11] She applied the same general principles to both—principles she had derived partly from reading English classical liberals such as Herbert Spencer and John Stuart Mill, both of whom her articles often quoted.

In articles that displayed a deep breadth of reading that ranged from Proudhon and Godwin to Malthus, Kelly also displayed a level of common sense uncommon among political visionaries. She advised the fellow individualists who wanted to pursue dubious reforms to ease the immediate problems of female labor and to educate themselves, instead, by listening to the voices of working women. Reformers with grand schemes should take "lessons from Miss Corson on how to make a neck of beef last a family of six persons for three weeks."[12] Only by understanding the daily realities faced by working women with hungry children could radicals address the needs of this class of labor.

In short, Kelly infused the nineteenth-century individualist dialogue with a refreshing though harsh dose of women's reality, both in her discussion of issues and of events.

Kelly's insistence upon principle linked to common sense helped to anchor radical individualism to the goal of non-violence, especially when the movement was pressured to respond to violent events of its day. Her influence may be judged by her response to one particular event which history calls "the Haymarket Incident." In the wake of this event, most radicals—including other prominent feminists and some individualists—cried out for blind vengeance against the State. Kelly offered a voice of reason.

The Haymarket Incident: On May 4, 1886, a large crowd of laborers assembled in the Haymarket Square of Chicago to protest against recent police brutality. As the meeting began to break up peacefully due to rain, the police hurried the process along. From the sidelines, someone threw a bomb toward the police, who opened fire at the laborers. The shots were returned. In the final count, seven policemen and an unknown number of protesters died.

The police rounded up labor leaders, with no regard to whether they had been involved in the violence or not. Eventually, seven men were tried for murder in a court case that has been generally accepted as a wholesale travesty of justice. For example, the jury was not chosen in the normal manner: A bailiff was instructed to go out into the street and select whomever he wished from the passers-by.

Most feminists responded with shock, outrage, and bitter pain. For example, upon reading a newspaper headline stating that the Haymarket protesters (communist anarchists and labor radicals) had thrown a bomb into an assembled crowd, the teenaged individualist-feminist Voltairine de Cleyre had exclaimed aloud, "They ought to be hanged!" She keenly and instantly regretted the words, and assumed the opposite position with equal vehemence. Fourteen years later, de Cleyre remained sorely haunted by her words: "For that ignorant, outrageous, blood-thirsty sentence I shall never forgive myself...."[13] Much of de Cleyre's political activity in the ensuing years can be seen as an attempt to expiate her sin. Her most passionate addresses were delivered as lectures at the yearly memorials to the Haymarket martyrs that she attended.

In *Living My Life*, the socialist feminist Emma Goldman described her reaction to the judgment in the Haymarket trial: Five of the men were condemned to death. After becoming hysterical, Goldman was put to bed where she fell into a deep sleep. Upon awakening, she discovered something new and wonderful within her soul. It was "a great ideal, a burning faith, a determination to dedicate myself to the memory of my martyred comrades, to make their cause my own...."[14] She left her newly wed husband and proceeded to New York to prepare for the task that would consume the rest of her life.

Against this backdrop of passionate and profound reaction among feminists, Kelly called for a calm and measured response. She refused to consider retaliation in kind against the State because force could never be an appropriate means by which to achieve social ends. In an appeal for restraint, she wrote, "Oh my brothers! let no blind feelings of revenge against the state and its tools lead you to play into its hands by attempting to meet force with force.... Remember that the employment of force leads to the redevelopment of the military spirit, which is totally opposed to the spirit that must exist in the people before anything that we wish for can be brought about."[15]

Over and over again, Kelly stressed education. Enlightenment and persuasion had to be the paths employed by individualists because ignorance was their main opponent. Although the content of the education was an essential factor in the process of educating people, the method was equally important. It not only had to be nonviolent, but also privately funded, since taxation and the public funding that sprang from taxes were the sort of violence against property known as theft.

On June 1, 1887, Kelly delivered a remarkable speech entitled "State Aid to Science" before the Alumnae Association of the Women's Medical College of the New York Infirmary for Women and Children, at which she had studied. It was remarkable because—at a time when feminists called out for various forms of state assistance to educate women—Kelly addressed the destructive consequences of governmental attempts to promote knowledge. It was remarkable because Gertrude Kelly was a medical doctor and, as such, she was expected to tolerate, if not to revere outright, the institutions that conferred social status upon her profession.

Published as an article in *Liberty*, this speech presented two themes: "first, that progress in science is lessened, and ultimately destroyed, by state interference; and, secondly, that even if, through state aid, progress in science could be promoted, the promotion would be at too great an expense of the best interests of the race."[16]

Kelly argued for the impossibility of government promoting knowledge by pointing out, "It seems to be generally forgotten by those who favor state aid to science that aid so given is not and cannot be aid to Science, but to particular doctrines or dogmas, and that, where this aid is given, it requires almost a revolution to introduce a new idea."[17] Such an arrangement of government patronage creates "a great many big idle queens at the expense of the workers."

But, even granting for the sake of argument that state aid could promote knowledge, Kelly contended that the cost of this promotion would enormously outweigh any advantage. The cost would be the violation of property rights through the taxation that would be necessary to support the government's program. If ordinary people sufficiently valued the service being funded by the State, then public funding wouldn't be necessary. If they didn't value it, then the government had no right to take money from the worker to finance officially desirable knowledge. "I maintain," Kelly insisted, "that you have no right to decide what is happiness or knowledge for him, any more than you have to decide what religion he must give adherence to. You have no right to take away a single cent of his property without his consent. Woe to the nation that would strive to increase knowledge or happiness at the expense of justice. It will end by not having morality, or happiness, or knowledge."[18]

On the state funding of education, as in all issues, Gertrude B. Kelly demanded "no compromise" with the principles of individual autonomy and individual responsibility—in short, with the doctrine of individual rights. Indeed, it was her devotion to Natural Law that led her to depart from *Liberty* when it became a forum for Stirnerite egoism. Kelly contributed, instead, to the brief journal entitled *Nemesis*, then began to write for the periodical *Alarm* under the editorship of Dyer D. Lum. Her departure from *Liberty* robbed that periodical of an able defender of natural rights theory and robbed it of its most forceful voice for women. In a similar manner, Gertrude B. Kelly's absence from the pages of feminist history impoverishes that movement.

Disillusioned with the "philosophical individualism" of *Liberty*, Kelly went on to express her principles through action and became the director of a clinic for the poor in the Chelsea district of New York city. As an outlet for writing and theory, she turned to the cause of women's suffrage and of Irish independence, becoming a prominent member of the Irish Women's Council. Two years after her death in 1934, Mayor Fiorello La Guardia honored her work with poor children by dedicating the "Dr. Gertrude B. Kelly Playground" on 21st Street.

✳ ✳ ✳ ✳

The following articles by Gertrude B. Kelly from *Liberty* have been edited solely for the purpose of omitting confusing or obscure references. For example, references to articles or comments that appeared in earlier issues of the periodical have been removed.

"'Culture' and Thought"

December 12, 1885
"They are but giants while we kneel."
Having heard all my life from those who claimed to know that the difference between the rich and the poor was due to the superior thinking powers of the former, I went to a meeting of the Newark Bureau of Associated Charities, where it was advertised that the Rev. Edward Everett Hale would speak on the "Abolition of Poverty." The meeting, which was a very large one, was held in a church, and there were none of those poor coats and bonnets which we have been taught to associate with lack of brains, but a grand array of costly over-coats, and seal skin sacques, and Paris bonnets, which evidently denoted in their possessors an unusual amount of intelligence. Here, thought I, is a grand opportunity for hearing words of wisdom; now that the cultured classes are awakened to the fact that there is poverty, and that it is removable, the solution of the labor question will receive a wonderful impetus, and the only reason that this question has not received its solution before is that these powerful minds have been directing their attention elsewhere.

The meeting opened by the president stating that the object of the society was the Abolition of Poverty, surely a very large object, and one well worthy of our support, and that its methods of work consisted in Investigation, Cooperation, and Sympathy. The investigation was designed to discover the causes of poverty, but I noticed that the society, which has four paid superintendents who devote their whole time and energy to the work, and an executive committee of forty ladies who have nothing else to do, after four years' investigation, has not yet discovered that monopoly has any share in the production of poverty; strange, is it not, with such brains! The cooperation consisted in focusing the rays of the organization on any object considered "worthy of charity"; and the sympathy,—I have forgotten how the sympathy acted, probably a tear dropped now and then.

The annual report of the society was then read, showing that in this city of Newark 3,147 families, representing 13,798 persons, had applied for relief. It certainly is time that the question of the abolition of poverty were taken into earnest consideration, when one in every eleven of the population of a small city like this, is so reduced as to have to solicit relief from a charitable society.

The first speaker, a Rev. Dr. Wilson, told us that poverty and riches were increasing simultaneously; that every day the rich were growing richer and the poor poorer; that the gulf between them was widening, etc.; and that the most touching sight in the world was that of the laboring man up with the lark (Do larks inhabit the tenement-house region?) and away to work, but unable by the most unremitting toil to earn enough to keep body and soul together: it almost made him shed tears to witness it. But as it was a natural law that things tended to propagate themselves, he could see nothing through the ages but wealth multiplying on the one hand, and poverty and crime on the other, unless we took in the holy power of prayer. The reverent gentleman did not say to whom or how or how often the prayer should be administered, nor how its curative effects would manifest themselves.

Then appeared Monsignor Doane, a very much over-fed and sleek-looking man, with a very low brow, but who nevertheless represented abstinence and culture, who talked about the intemperance of the working-classes. One higher than us had said, "the poor ye shall have always with you," but he thought there was a necessary and an unnecessary poverty, the unnecessary poverty being caused by drinking; for instance, he knew a mechanic who was earning fifteen dollars a week, and who lost twenty-two and one-half dollars by being idle ten days after a spree. There was a great deal of talk about abolishing poverty, as there was about abolishing landlordism, but poverty and landlordism were both legitimate, and could never be abolished. Perhaps they can, some day, Monsignor, and you and *your* intemperance with them!

Next was Mr. Lyman Abbott of the "Christian Union," who was the only man that showed any comprehension that there was a labor question, and who consequently did not at all appeal to the sympathies of the audience. He called attention to the fact that crime and intemperance were almost entirely dependent on poverty; that poverty could not be

relieved by a soup-house here, or a dollar there, or a sewing-society somewhere else; that there was a broader, a deeper, and a greater question to
be solved than the relief of the mere temporary needs of the people, when
statistics showed that in Germany the wages of the skilled mechanics
were only $105 a year, that in Italy and France and Austria things were
very much the same, that in England many thousands were on the verge
of starvation, and that in this country, which claimed, and claimed truly,
twenty-five years ago, that no man able and willing to work, and no
woman capable, strong, and well, but could find bread and butter too,—
that this claim could no longer be made, for there were now at least five
hundred thousand people in this rich country of ours who could find neither bread nor work, who were in what Carlyle called the Englishman's
Hell, the hell of enforced idleness. This question of ill-paid, under-paid,
or no labor, which soup-houses or organized charity will not solve, Mr.
Abbott said, is making itself heard in St. Louis in dynamite under the
cars, in Cleveland, Cincinnati, and Chicago in armed men patrolling the
streets, and in New York in street processions advocating the hanging of
Jay Gould. Unless the Church can produce its Savonarola, who will have
purification at all hazards; unless the State can produce statesmen who
are pledged to lessen the burdens of the poor, and put down the gambling in Wall Street,—society is doomed…. Abbott drew a very vivid picture of what it is to be a man face to face with the terrible question of
finding bread for his wife and little ones, near and dear to him as the best
beloved darlings of the rich, and unable by the most strenuous exertion
to keep the wolf from their door. Is it any wonder that such a man walk-
ing along one of the well-lighted avenues of an evening, and looking into
the beautifully-curtained windows where everything seems to delightful,
should harbor dangerous thoughts against society, and should ask himself why they should have so much and he so little, who is every bit as
good as they are. Then he pictured the pure young girl with a mother and
little sister looking to her for support, who sees on one side of her the
false bad man with gold in his hand, and, on the other, a *respectable, virtuous* life for *sixty-five cents a day*. What wonder that she succumbs, and
that a pure woman, with noble instincts and generous heart as ever beat
in human bosom, is lost to herself and to society forever because she must
take to the only means which will support life in her and her loved ones!

Then came the climax, culture shone forth resplendent, and the great
question was illuminated in a manner truly wonderful. Mr. Hale proved
that five hundred thousand out of work was not very much in such a large
country as this (I hope the five hundred thousand will take this to heart;
it may help to allay the pangs of hunger); that organized charity was

capable of settling the whole question; that what was wanted was compulsory education in technical schools, ladies' societies in which working girls who earned only sixty-five cents a day should be taught to sew better so that *in time* they might earn seventy or *even* seventy-five cents; and that what paupers and criminals needed were personal friends,—gentlemen, and especially ladies, who need not give up their society connections to do it—to go down to them in a spirit of friendliness, and with the Holy Spirit! I wonder how much Holy Spirit it would take to prevent Mr. Hale's descent into vice if he were earning sixty-five cents a day. Mr. Hale spoke against the old system of charity, the system of out-door relief, etc. under which men went from one distributing place to another to draw wood, coal, provisions, etc. much, my dear friends, as you go from place to place to draw your dividends. I wonder if the reverend gentleman saw how very apt his illustration was, how the cases were, in fact, identical, both the drawing of dividends and the drawing of wood, coal, and provisions signifying the taking something and giving nothing in return.

The only gleam of comfort to be derived from such an affair as the above-described, to a hater of the existing social order, is in the recognition of the fact that we are not governed by an aristocracy of intelligence; that, if there is any difference in intelligence between the governing and the working classes, it is in favor of the latter, despite all their disadvantages; that the power of original, independent thought amongst the cultured classes is very rare; and that their morality is at as low an ebb as their intelligence. It is a significant fact that the word *justice* never once occurred in their immense avalanche of language; perhaps it is too hard a word; it certainly is not so soft and pretty as *charity*, to be touched by those with soft hands.

It is comforting, on the whole, to reflect that true culture, true intelligence, and true morality can never be gained at the expense of our fellow-creatures, and that, if the exploiters succeed in dwarfing our growth, they none the less surely dwarf themselves, and inevitably tend to their own destruction.

✳ ✳ ✳ ✳

"A Woman's Warning to Reformers"

January 23, 1886

> Can man be free if woman be a slave?
> Chain one who lives, and breathes this boundless air,
>   To the corruption of a closed grave!

Can they whose mates are beasts condemned to bear
Scorn heavier far than toil or anguish dare
To trample their oppressors? In their home,
Among their babes, thou know'st a curse would wear
The shape of woman—hoary Crime would come
Behind, and Fraud rebuild Religion's tottering dome.

Another instance that no wrong can be done to any class in society without part at least of the evil reverting to the wrong-doers is furnished in the fact that women always have been, and still are, one of the most important factors in the counter-revolution.

Men, for some purpose of their own, which they probably best understand, have always denied to women the opportunity to think; and, if some women have had courage enough to dare public opinion, and insist on thinking for themselves, they have been so beaten by that most powerful weapon in society's arsenal, ridicule, that it has effectually prevented the great majority from making any attempt to come out of slavery. Woman, entirely deprived of all intellectual enjoyment, and of all opportunities for mental growth, has been forced back upon her emotions for all the pleasure that there is in her life, and it is in this that the church always has had, and always will have, its strongest support. If you men are so constituted that you are satisfied to meet daily in the most intimate relationship persons who have no sympathy with any thought, hope, or aspiration of yours; if you are satisfied that your own homes are just the places where you are least understood; if you have no interest in the emancipation of woman for her own sake,—you ought to have some for the sake of your sons, for the sake of the cause to which you profess to be attached.

Look around you, and see how many of the children of reformers enter the reform movement. Scarcely one in a hundred; and why? Because the influence of the mother has been acting in a contrary direction. The church is wiser than you; it knows the influence of the mother on her children; it knows what a great force is needed to shatter the ideas formed in early life; it knows that its power can never be broken as long as the women are within its folds, and consequently exerts all its influence to have the future mothers entirely under its control. Do you know that there is a large society of working-girls, directed by philanthropic ladies in New York, Yonkers, and Hoboken, and probably in other cities, in which the girls are given lessons in embroidery, art, science, etc., and are incidentally told of the evils of trades-unions, the immorality of strikes, and of the necessity of being "satisfied with the condition to which it has pleased God to call them?" Do you know that it is the very best and brightest of the working-girls that are being entrapped into these organizations, the girls with a yearning for higher culture, greater growth, than the narrow conditions of their life afford them?

How long are you going to be blind to the fact, which the backward Russian long ago recognized, that, unless you convert the women, you are engaged in but a Sisyphus labor, that what you gain in one generation is lost in the next, and all because women are supposed to have no intelligence to which you can appeal. You do not know whether they have no intelligence to which you can appeal. You do not know whether they have intelligence or not, for you have never tried to find out. There are even Anarchists of my acquaintance who, when their wives or sisters enter the room, immediately change not only the serious topics of conversation, but change the very tones of their voices, in order to come down to the level of the supposed inferiority. Well, I give you warning of what persistence in this line of action will lead to; what you build up, the women will pull down. On your own heads be the penalty, if you fail to heed it.

"State Aid to Science"

[Speech to Alumnae Association of Women's Medical College of the New York Infirmary for Women and Children, June 1, 1887]

If what I say to you today should seem to you out of place, you must blame the chairman of your executive committee and not me; for, when she asked me to contribute something for this meeting, she assured me that anything which affected the relation of medical women to society, anything which related to the advancement of science, was a proper subject of discussion at the annual meeting of the Alumnae Association.

Herbert Spencer closes the second volume of his *Principles of Sociology* with these words:

"The acceptance which guides conduct will always be of such theories, no matter how logically indefensible, as are consistent with the average modes of action, public and private. All that can be done, by diffusing a doctrine much in advance of the time, is to facilitate the action of forces tending to cause advance. The forces themselves can be but in small degrees increased, but something may be done by preventing misdirection of them. Of the sentiment at any time enlisted on behalf of a higher social state there is always some (and at the present time a great deal) which, having the broad, vague form of sympathy with the masses, spends itself in efforts for their relief by multiplication of political agencies of one or other kind. Led by the hope of immediate beneficial results, those swayed by this sympathy are unconscious that they are helping further to elaborate a social organization at variance with that required for a higher form of social life, and are by so doing increasing the obstacles to attainment of that higher form. On a portion of such the foregoing chapters may have some effect by leading them to consider whether the arrangements they are advocating involve increase of that public regulation characterizing the militant type, or whether they tend to produce that greater individuality and more extended voluntary cooperation characterizing the industrial type. To deter here and there one from doing mischief by imprudent zeal is the chief proximate effect to be hoped for."

In these times of ours, when all classes in society, from the Bowery Socialists to the highest professors of science, seem to vie with one another in demanding State interference, State protection, and State regulation, when the ideal State to the workingman is that proposed by the authoritarian Marx, or the scarcely less authoritarian George, and the ideal State to the scientist is the Germany of today, where the scientists are under the government's special protection, it would seem idle to hope that the voices of those who prize liberty above all things, who would fain call attention to the false direction in which it is desired to make the world move, should be other than "voices crying in the wilderness." But, nevertheless, it is not by accident that we who hold the ideas that what is necessary to progress is not the increase, but the decrease, of governmental interference have come to be possessed of these ideas. We, too, are "heirs of all the ages," and it is our duty to that society of which we form a part to give our reasons for the "faith that is in us."

My endeavor today will be to prove to you two propositions: first, that progress in medical or any other science is lessened, and ultimately destroyed, by State interference; and, secondly, that even if, through State aid, progress in science could be promoted, the promotion would be at too great an expense, at the expense of the best interests of the race. That I shall succeed in convincing you of the truth of these propositions is too much to hope for, but at least I shall cause you to re-examine the grounds for the contrary opinions that you entertain, and for this you should thank me, as it is always important that the position of devil's advocate should be well filled.

It seems strange that it should become necessary to urge upon Americans, with their country's traditions, that the first condition necessary to mental and moral growth is freedom. It seems strange in these times,— when all the unconscious movements of society are towards the diminution of restraint, whether it be that of men over women, of parents and teachers over children, of keepers over criminals and the insane; when it is being unconsciously felt and acted upon, on all sides, that responsibility is the parent of morality,—that all the conscious efforts of individuals and groups should be towards the increase of restraint.

A knowledge of the fact that all the ideas prevalent at a given time in a given society must have a certain congruity should make us very careful in accepting ideas, especially as regards politics, from such a despotic country as Germany, instead of receiving them with open arms as containing all the wisdom in the world, which now seems to be the fashion. As Spencer pointed out some time since, the reformers of Germany, while seeking a destruction of the old order, are really but rebuilding the old machine under a new name. They are so accustomed to seeing every thing done by the State that they can form no conception of its being done in any other way. All they propose is a State in which the people (that is, a majority of the people) shall hold the places now held by the usurping few. That English-speaking workmen should seek to wholly replace themselves under the yoke of a tyranny from which they have taken ages to partially escape, is only to be explained by the vagueness of the forms in which this paradise is usually pictured, and by that lack of power of bringing before the mind's eye word-painted pictures.

Again, in Germany—and it is that with which we are more nearly concerned today—it is said that scientific men under the protection of the government do better work than other men who are not under the protection of their governments. That this apparently flourishing condition of science under the patronage of the German government is no more real than was the condition of literature under Louis XIV, and that it cannot continue, I think a little examination will enable us to see. As Leslie Stephen has demonstrated, to suppress one truth is to suppress all truth, for truth is a coherent whole. You may by force suppress a falsehood, and prevent its ever again rising to the surface; but, when you attempt to suppress a truth, you can only do so by suppressing all truth, for, with investigation untrammeled, some one else is bound in time to come to the same point again. Do you think that a country, one of whose most distinguished professors, Virchow, is afraid of giving voice to the doctrine of evolution, because he sees that it inevitably leads to Socialism (and Socialism the government has decided is wrong, and must be crushed out), is in the way of long maintaining its supremacy as a scientific light, when the question which its scientific men are called upon to decide is not what is true, but what the government will allow to be said? I say nothing for or against the doctrine of evolution; I say nothing for or against its leading to Socialism; but I do say that the society whose scientific men owe devotion, not to truth, but to the Hohenzollerns, is not in a progressive state. As Buckle has shown, the patronage of Louis XIV killed French literature. Not a single man rose to European fame under his patronage, and those whose fame was the cause of their obtaining the monarch's favor sank under its baneful influence to mere mediocrity.

It seems to be generally forgotten by those who favor State aid to science that aid so given is not and cannot be aid to science, but to particular doctrines or dogmas, and that, where this aid is given, it requires almost a revolution to introduce a new idea. With the ordinary conservatism of mankind, every new idea which comes forward meets with sufficient questioning as to its truth, utility, etc.; but, when we have added to this natural conservatism, which is sufficient to protect society against the introduction of new error, the whole force of an army of paid officials whose interest it is to resist any idea which would deprive, or tend to deprive, them of their salaries, you will readily see that, of the two forces which tend to keep society in equilibrium, the conservative and the progressive, the conservative will be very much strengthened at the expense of the progressive, and that the society is doomed to decay. Of the tendency which State-aided institutions have shown up to the present to resist progress, excellent evidence is furnished by one, at least, of those very men, Huxley, who now clamors so loudly for State aid to science. When we consider that we have now reached but the very outposts of science; that all our energies are required for storming its citadel; that human nature, if placed in the same conditions, is apt to be very much the same; that those persons who have the power and the positions will endeavor to maintain them,—do you think it wise to put into the hands of any set of men the power of staying our onward movements? That which we feel pretty sure of being true today may contain, and in all probability does contain, a great deal of error, and it is our duty to truth to cultivate the spirit which questions all things, which spirit would be destroyed by our having high-priests of science. Hear Huxley in testimony thereof in his article on the "Scientific Aspects of Positivism":

"All the great steps in the advancement of science have been made just by those men who have not hesitated to doubt the 'principles established in the science by competent persons,' and the great teaching of science, the great use of it as an instrument of mental discipline, is its constant inculcation of the maxim that the sole ground on which any statement has a right to be believed is the impossibility of refuting it."

Is the State, then, to reward all those who oppose a statement as well as all those who support it, or is it only to reward certain of the questioners, and, if so, which, and who is to decide what statements have not been refuted? Are some persons to be aided in bringing their opinions, with their reasons for holding them, before the world, and others to be denied this privilege? Are the scientific men to be placed in power so different in nature from all those who have preceded them that they will be willing to cede the places and the salaries to those who show more reason than they? Here is Huxley's testimony in regard to the manner in which the State-aided classical schools promoted the introduction of physical science into those schools:

"From the time that the first suggestion to introduce physical science was timidly whispered until now, the advocates of scientific education have met with opposition of two kinds. On the one hand they have been pooh-poohed by the men of business, who pride themselves on being the representatives of practicality; while on the other hand they have been excommunicated by the classical scholars, in their capacity of Levites in charge of the arts of culture and monopolists of liberal education."

Science and Culture

And again, the State, or the State-aided institutions have never been able, even with the most Chinese system of civil-service examinations, to sift the worthy from the unworthy with half the efficiency which private individuals or corporations have done. But let us hear Huxley upon this subject:

"Great schemes for the endowment of research have been proposed. It has been suggested that laboratories for all branches of physical science, provided with every apparatus needed by the investigator, shall be established by the State; and shall be accessible under due conditions and regulations to all properly qualified persons. I see no objection to the principle of such a proposal. If it be legitimate to spend great sums of money upon public collections of painting and sculpture, in aid of the man of letters, or the artist, or for the mere sake of affording pleasure to the general public, I apprehend that it cannot be illegitimate to do as much for the promotion of scientific investigation. To take the lowest ground as a mere investment of money the latter is likely to be much more immediately profitable. To my mind the difficulty in the way of such a scheme is not theoretical, but practical. Given the laboratories, how are the investigators to be maintained? What career is open to those who have been encouraged to leave bread-winning pursuits? If they are to be provided for by endowment, we come back to the College Fellowship System, the results of which for literature have not been so brilliant that one would wish to see it extended to science, unless some much better securities than at present exist can be taken that it will foster real work. You know that among the bees it depends upon the kind of a cell in which the egg is deposited, and the quantity and quality of food which is supplied to the grub, whether it shall turn out a busy little worker or a big idle queen. And in the human hive the cells of the endowed larvae are always tending to enlarge, and their food to improve, until we get queens beautiful to behold, but which gather no honey and build no court."

Universities, Actual and Ideal

One of my chief objections to State-aid to anything is that it tends to develop a great many big idle queens at the expense of the workers. There is no longer any direct responsibility on the part of those employed to those who employ them, as there is where private contract enters into play. In fact, the agents determine how and for what the principals shall spend their money, and they usually decide in favor of their own pockets. I cannot furnish you with a better illustration than that supplied by my own experience. Before I studied medicine I taught school for a couple of years in an almshouse. The waste there was perfectly enormous. The officials, when remonstrated with, made answer: "It was all on the county." The freeholders came once a week, and ate sumptuous dinners—at the expense of the county. At the close of my college course it was my good fortune to enter the Infirmary, where I saw everything ordered with the economy of a private household. No waste there! Those who furnished the funds were directly interested in seeing that they were used as economically as possible. I never heard of the trustees of the Infirmary proposing to have a dinner at the expense of the Infirmary.

Even were the government perfectly honest, which it is practically impossible for it ever to be (being divorced from all the conditions which promote honesty), not bearing the cost, it is always inclined to make experiments on too large a scale, even when those experiments are in the right direction. When we bear the expenses ourselves, we are apt to make our experiments slowly and cautiously, to invest very little until we see some hope of return (by return I do not mean necessarily a material return), but when we can draw upon an inexhaustible treasury-farewell to prudence!

Of course, I do not mean to deny that under any state of society, until men and women are perfect, there always will be persons who are inclined to become big idle queens, but what I do object to is that we ourselves should voluntarily make the conditions which favor the development of these queens "who gather no honey and build no court."

Of the tendency of governments to crystallize and fossilize any institutions or ideas upon which they lay their protecting hands no better example can be furnished than that of the effect of the English government on the village communities of India, as reported by Maine ("Village Communities"). Where the institutions were undergoing a natural decay, the English government stepped in and, by its official recognition of them in some quarters, gave them, says Maine, a fixedness which they never before possessed.

There is another point to which I wish to draw the attention of those of our brethren who clamor for State aid. Who is to decide what ideas are to be aided? The majority of the people? or a select few? The majority of the people have never in any age been the party of progress; and, if it were put to a popular vote tomorrow as to which should be aided,— Anna Kingsford in her anti-vivisection crusade, or Mary Putnam Jacobi in her physiological investigational, I am perfectly sure that the populace would decide in favor of Anna Kingsford. Carlyle says:

"If, of ten men, nine are fools, which is a common calculation, how in the name of wonder will you ever get a ballot-box to grind you out a wisdom from the votes of these ten men?... I tell you a million blockheads looking authoritatively into one man of what you call genius, or noble sense, will make nothing but nonsense out of him and his qualities, and his virtues and defects, if they look till the end of time."

If, of ten men, nine are believers in the old, I say, how can you in the name of wonder get a ballot-box to grind you out support of the new from the votes of these ten men? They will support the old and established, and the outcome of your aid to science is that you or I, who may be in favor of the new, and willing to contribute our mite towards its propagation, are forced by majority rule to give up that mite to support that which already has only too many supporters. But perhaps you will say that not the populace, but the select few, are to decide what scientific investigations are to be rewarded. Which select few, and how are they to be selected? Of all the minorities which separate themselves from the current of public opinion, who is to decide which minority has the truth? And, allowing that it is possible to determine which minority has the truth on a special occasion, have you any means by which to prove that this minority will be in favor of the next new truth? Is there not danger that, having accomplished its ends, it in turn will become conservative, and wish to prevent further advance? A priesthood of science would differ in no manner from any other priesthood the world has yet seen, and the evil effect which such a priesthood would have upon science no one has more clearly seen or more clearly demonstrated than Huxley in his "Scientific Aspects of Positivism." Again, admitting that great men endowed with supreme power could remain impartial, we still have no evidence on record to prove that great men are endowed with more than the ordinary share of common sense, which is so necessary in conducting the ordinary affairs of life. Indeed, if the gossip of history is to be in any way trusted, great men have usually obtained less than the ordinary share of this commodity. Frederick the Great is reported to have said that, if he wished to ruin one of his provinces, he would hand its government over to the philosophers. Is it into the hands of a Bacon, who had no more sense than to expose himself (for the sake of a little experiment which could have been made just as well without the exposure), a Newton who ordered the grate to be removed when the fire became too hot for him, a Clifford, who worked himself to death, that the direction of the affairs of a people is to be given, with the assurance that they will be carried on better than now?

Without multiplying evidence further, I think I have given sufficient to prove to you that there is no means by which State aid can be given to science, without causing the death of science, that we can make no patent machine for selecting the worthiest and the wisest; and I now desire to show you that, even if it were possible to select the worthiest and the wisest, and to aid none but the deserving, still aid so given would be immoral, and opposed to the best interests of society at large.

Of course I take it for granted that I am appealing to a civilized people, who recognize that there are certain rights which we are bound to respect, and certain duties which we in society owe to one another. We have passed that stage, or, at least, we do not often wish to acknowledge to ourselves that we have not passed it, in which "he may take who has the power, and he may keep who can." Next to the right to life (and indeed as part of that same right) the most sacred right is the right to property, the right of each to hold inviolable all that he earns. Now, to tax a man to support something that he does not wish for is to invade his right to property, and to that extent to curtail his life, is to take away from him his power of obtaining what he desires, in order to supply him with something which he does not desire. If we once admit that the State, the majority, the minority (be it ever so wise), has a right to do this in the smallest degree, no limit can be set to its interference, and we may have every action, aye, every thought, of a man's arranged for him from on high. Where shall we draw the line as to how much the State is to spend for him, and how much he is to spend for himself? Are grown men to be again put into swaddling clothes? You may say that you desire to increase his happiness, his knowledge, etc., but I maintain that you have no right to decide what is happiness or knowledge for him, any more than you have to decide what religion he must give adherence to. You have no right to take away a single cent's worth of his property without his consent. Woe to the nation that would strive to increase knowledge or happiness at the expense of justice. It will end by not having morality, or happiness, or knowledge. Do you think that the citizens of a State, who constantly see their rights violated by that State, who constantly see their property confiscated without their ever being consulted, are very likely to entertain a very high respect for their neighbors' rights of property or of person, do you think that they are very likely to be very moral in any way, any more than children, whose rights are constantly invaded by their parents, are likely to show an appreciation of one another's rights? To suppose that public life may be conducted in one way, and private life in another, is to ignore all the teaching of history, which shows that these lives are always interlaced.

The first step in immorality taken, the State having confiscated the property of its citizens, preventing them from expending it in the way they desire, to spend it for them in a way they do not desire, ends by starving their bodies and cramping their minds. Witness the case of modern Germany. Again the testimony is not mine. I always wish the advocates of Statism to furnish the evidence that kills them. Some little time since,—probably our new alumnae will remember the circumstance,—one of our professors who never wearies of telling us of the glories of German science, while speaking of the sebaceous horns which appear on the faces of German peasants, and describing a case which once came to his clinic, incidentally remarked of this case: "You understand he had never seen the growth himself, as these peasants have no looking-glasses." The thought at once occurred to me: "Is this what Germany gives to its people, to the vast majority of its population, on whom it lays its enormous burden of taxation?" Is not the advance of science of great importance to the German peasant who never sees a looking-glass? Would it be any wonder that in wild rage he should sometimes seek to destroy this whole German science and culture which end only by crushing him still farther into the earth? Of what use is science unless it increase the happiness and the comfort of the people? Is it a new fetich [sic] upon whose altar millions must be sacrificed? No, the science which would seek to entrench itself upon class-domination is a false one, and inevitably doomed to perish. Have we, the outcome of English civilization, determined to lower the standard raised by Bacon, that the object of the "new philosophy is to increase human happiness and diminish human suffering"? Are we willing to assist in dividing the people of this country into two classes, one of which is to have all the luxuries which science and art can afford, and the other to have no looking-glasses? Now is the time for us to decide.

How then is science to be advanced, you may inquire, if the majority cannot decide that which is true, and the select few also cannot decide? In the way in which up to the present it has been advanced,—by individuals contributing their small shares; and with ever increasing force will it advance, as the general culture becomes greater and broader. It will advance by having no opinion protected from discussion and agitation, by having the greatest possible freedom of thought, of speech, and of the press. That the unaided efforts of a people are capable of causing advance belongs fortunately no longer to the domain of opinion, but of fact. They have already caused all the progress that has been made, not only without the aid of the State, but in opposition to the State and the Church, and all the other conservative and retrogressive forces in society. They have already, as Spencer says, evolved a language greater in complexity and beauty than could be conceived of in any other way. They have, as Whatley says, succeeded in supplying large cities with food with scarcely any apparent waste or friction, while no government in the world, with all the machinery at its command, has ever yet succeeded in properly supplying an army.

Yes, freedom, hampered as it has been, has done and is doing all these things, and all that it is capable of doing in the future none but the prophets may see.

> We have the morning star,
> O foolish people! O kings!
> With us the day-springs are,
> Even all the fresh day-springs.
> For us, and with us, all the multitudes of things.

✱ ✱ ✱ ✱

"The Root of Prostitution"
September 12, 1885

> What slurs our cruel streets from end to end
>   With eighty thousand women in one smile
>   who only smile at night beneath the gas?

Do the working-people realize that it is their daughters, and theirs only, that are being sacrificed by the thousand every year to the money lords in the manner that has been recently exposed by the *Pall Mall Gazette*? Do they realize that the capitalistic system, after extorting the last cent from the working-women, forces them into the street to re-earn by prostitution a part of the wages that have been stolen from them? Do they realize that both directly and indirectly the present unjust distribution of the products of labor is the *sole* cause of prostitution? Some may assert that the viciousness of men is the cause, of, at least, *a* cause. To these we make answer that, if the people did not furnish to these men the time and means to support their viciousness, it could not exist. Of all the societies, White Cross, Social Purity, etc., which have arisen to combat the "social evil" not one has struck a single blow at its root. No society that we have ever heard of, no government, has ever proposed to pay women sufficiently well for their work, so that they would not be forced to eke out by prostitution their miserable wages. In the published governmental and society reports we often find admissions that destitution is the chief cause of prostitution, but, when we come to examine the remedies proposed, we find not a word on the subject of paying women, not justly (this we could scarcely expect), but even of making their wages equal to those of a man for the same work. We find all sorts of schemes for making men moral and women religious, but no scheme which proposes to give woman the fruits of her labor.

For fear some of my readers may be inclined to think I am making too broad a statement in attributing prostitution entirely to the unjust distribution of wealth, we will quote a few of the more prominent writers in this subject, those who cannot be accused of being rabid socialists.

> The result of my researches—and they have been numerous—is that needlework is insufficient to furnish to the larger part of those that work at it that which is strictly necessary to lodge, feed, and clothe them; that we must attribute to this insufficiency the immorality of a great number, and consequently the necessity in which they find themselves of delivering themselves into prostitution.
>
> Parent Duchatelet, *Prostitution de Paris*

In the work just quoted Duchatelet gives some very valuable tables, showing that the recruitment of the prostitutes is almost entirely from the artisan class.

> Paul Leroy Beaulieu has calculated that there are at least fifteen thousand women in Paris who cannot, by unremitting toil, obtain more than from twenty to thirty cents a day. Mms. de Barau, who has made a social study of the subject, is convinced that the average wages paid for female labor do not exceed forty-nine cents, and M. d'Haussonville arrives at the same conclusion. We cannot, then, avoid the inference that the mass of Paris working girls are *inexorably* compelled to seek assistance from the other sex by their sheer inability to support themselves.... It is undeniable that much of the sexual immorality which prevails in Paris is

directly traceable to the frequent failure of the most conscientious efforts on the part of the working-women to earn an honest livelihood.

New York Sun, June 3, 1883, on Statistics of M. d'Haussonville published in *Revue des Deux Mondes*

Needlework is so badly paid for in London that young persons who follow this employment with difficulty earn from three to five shillings a week, through working sixteen to eighteen hours daily. The wages of an embroiderer for a long day are from six to nine pence, shirt makers six pence a shirt. Nothing can be more frightful than the lives of these girls. They rise to work at four or five in the morning in every season, and work unceasingly to midnight, and light. Is it to be wondered at that some, alarmed at finding the path of virtue so rough, should have recourse to prostitution.

London Times, April 20, 1857

Now here there is a real speculation to engage in, supported on the one hand by gilded libertinage, and the other by youth and beauty without bread and without social protection.

M. Ryan, M.D., *Prostitution in London*

Considered as a class, the fate of the needlewomen has not changed. They remain exposed to the same distress, having always in perspective, as a term of this fatal struggle, suicide, prostitution, or theft.

Leon Faucher

But when trade falls off and work decreases, a number of these girls repair to Edinburgh to find means of subsistence. These they seek in prostitution; most of them, indeed, would find it difficult to make their living any other way.

The Greatest of the Social Evils by A. Physician

Innumerable cases of prostitution through want solely and absolutely are constantly occurring.

Mayhew, *London Laborers and the London Poor*

No belief is more false than that woman prostitutes herself to satisfy her own sexual desires. But, as we shall see presently, she is wholly dependent upon man for the means of subsistence, and is obliged to barter her virtue for a livelihood.

Ward, *Dynamic Sociology*

We might multiply these quotations, but sufficient have been made to show the unanimity of opinion on this subject.

The close quarters in which the working classes are compelled to live favor prostitution eventually by removing from the daughters of the poor every incentive to decency and morality. This we could also prove by quotations from numberless accepted respectable authorities, but a few must suffice.

> Few girls can grow up to maturity in such dens as exist in the First, Sixth, Eleventh, and Seventeenth Wards, and be virtuous.... If a female child be born and brought up in a room in one of these tenement-houses, she loses very early the modesty which is the great shield of virtue.
>
> C. L. Brace, *The Dangerous Classes of New York*

> The illicit intercourse and general licentiousness of the sexes result from the conditions in which they are placed.
>
> Wade, *Working Classes*

> In one single block in the Eleventh Ward, there are 52 tenement-houses, occupied by 586 families,—in all, by 2356 inmates.
>
> *New York Tribune*, July 1883

> Glasgow has 35,000 houses of one room each, 52,600 of two rooms each. There is a population of 10,000 persons in 1853 apartments, or more than five to a room.
>
> *Report of Bret Harte to Department of State*, 1883

Of 5375 laborers' cottages in England, Dr. Hunter found that 2195 had only one sleeping-room, which was often also the living room, 2390 only two rooms, and 280 more than two.

According to the census of 1851, 346,000 houses in the agricultural districts of France have no other opening than the door, while 1,817,535 have but a *single* window.

Any one desiring to know further how the poor live, and how much morality is to be expected under these conditions, has only to consult the reports of the English and United States Boards of Health, the reports of the Bureaus of Labor Statistics, etc.

Lastly, the money with which the daughters of the people are purchased is supplied by the people themselves, men, women and children, working in the mines and factories, thus making complete the chain of slavery.

> Our fathers are praying for pauper's pay,
> Our mothers with death's kiss are white,
> Our sons are the rich man's serfs by day,
>   Our daughters his slaves by night.

****

"The Inconsistency of Governmentalists"

March 26, 1887

The fact that persons of more than ordinary intelligence and honesty are deluded into the acceptance of governmental remedies for social evils is often at first sight very disheartening to the Anarchist, but on further reflection he may find in it some solace, for, if the principles of liberty are true, they must ultimately triumph, and no permanent injury can be done them by the most earnest and honest advocacy of their opposites. As Mill says, there is no keener intellectual enjoyment than the holding of certain opinions as true, after we are sure that we have seen and examined all the arguments that may be brought to bear against them. This enjoyment is one that is wholly lost by all those who would wish to set any limit whatsoever to free discussion. Another fact, and one of great practical importance, is that errors being upheld by persons both honest and intelligent are more likely to be carried to their logical consequences, and hence made more easily demonstrable that they are errors, thus leading in the end to the gain of the cause of truth.

I was led into these reflections recently by reading Annie Besant's report of the Fabian Conference. She says:

"It is a most extraordinary thing that people who are in favor of the nationalisation [sic] of the raw material should be against the nationalisation of the means of production. Men who are Socialist in their aspect to the one remain Individualistic in their aspect to the other. They illogically refuse to apply to capital the arguments which they hold valid as against private property in land; and I notice a curious tendency among Radicals who are strongly in favor of the nationalisation of land to lose their tempers when they are pressed with their own argument applied to capital, and to take refuge in denunciation and the free use of uncomplimentary epithets, instead of relying on reason and sound logic."

Mrs. Besant is perfectly right as to the state of inconsistency in which the minds of most people are. They see no reason why we should not have liberty to settle this question, and authority to settle that, according as it may suit the whim of the moment. They have no idea of a deep underlying principle to which they are bound to conform all their acts. There are unfortunately very few of those "slaves to an idea" whom Tak Kak [*Liberty* contributor James L. Walker] so much despises (though I notice that he himself is a slave to the idea that he must not be slave to an idea). But Mrs. Besant herself is not quite consistent. Why should we draw the line at the nationalization of the means of production any more than at that of the land? Why exempt the manufactured articles? This line Kropotkine, being still more logical than Mr. Besant, refuses to draw. In the series of articles on "Expropriation" now running through "Le Revolte," he argues logically and fairly that it is nonsense to confine the idea of capital to raw material and the means of production, but that expropriation must begin with the manufactured articles; that houses, and clothing, and food, are as much a necessary part of the laborer's capital as the raw material upon which to work; and that his need of them implies his right to use them. Are you prepared to go that length, Mrs. Besant? If you are not, you are only a very little more logical than your Radical friends.

Kropotkine must get the prize for consistency so far, but even he will not stand a very severe test. He has a wholesome fear of the State, as he well ought, from his experience in France and Russia, but he has no conception of justice without some State arrangement to carry it out. He will have the citizens go down into the street and divide up the expropriated good after the revolution. What these indefinite citizens are (I suppose some ghostly affair, like Communistic Anarchy), how they will differ from a State, and who is to decide what are the "needs" of the different people, I have not yet been able to make out.

It is very curious that a man of Kropotkine's ability fails to see that there is no necessity for this expropriation which he contemplates; that all that is necessary is to cease to support the present system, which will then die for lack of nourishment; that what is called capital, even the most solid portions of it, could not exist a year, unless it were constantly renewed and revivified by labor; that expropriation, however just it may be, would "not pay."

One of the most frequent charges brought against Anarchists is that they have no conception of the unity and solidarity of the human race; that each one wishes to act as if he alone existed in the world; that they entirely deny that we are our brothers' keepers. Rather a strange charge to be brought by those who are constantly making and dreaming of artificial devices [e.g., state laws] for keeping men and women from devouring each other, while we are so convinced that the interests of all human beings are so bound together that no artificial bond is needed, that all artificial restraints tend to push them apart (by dividing their interest) instead of keeping them together. We, and we alone, are true believers in the unity of the human race, and it is for this reason, as Proudhon says, that we look not to an organization of society, but to an organization of the economic forces for the establishment of peace upon earth.

Notes

Introduction

1. Although the American tradition draws heavily upon British classical liberalism—especially the work of British feminist Mary Wollstonecraft—American women organized around issues that were uniquely their own, such as Puritanism, the American Revolution, and the American experience of slavery.

2. For a bibliographic essay on the history of individualist feminism in America, see Wendy McElroy, "A Brief Bibliographic Essay," in *Sexual Correctness: The Gender-Feminist Attack on Women* (Jefferson, N.C.: McFarland, 1996), 169–79.

3. As quoted in Wendy McElroy, ed., *Freedom, Feminism, and the State*, 2nd ed. (New York: Holmes and Meier, 1991), 31.

4. Recent books addressing this reversal of gender justice and its negative impact are: Daphne Patai, *Heterophobia: Sexual Harassment and the Future of Feminism* (New York: Rowman & Littlefield, 1998); Cathy Young, *Ceasefire: Why Women and Men Must Join Forces to Achieve True Equality* (New York: Free Press, 1999); and J. Edward Pawlick, *Freedom Will Conquer Racism (and Sexism)* (Wellesley, Mass.: Mustard Seeds, Inc., 1998).

5. As an illustration of this theory, consider a universe which is parallel to our own but which runs along different metaphysical rules. The inhabitants of this alternate universe fill their needs simply by wishing for goods or other forms of satisfaction. Food magically appears in their hands, clothes miraculously drape their limbs, and a bed pops into existence under their tired bodies. In such a society, it is unlikely that the concept of money would evolve, simply because that peculiarly human concept arose as a means to solve the problems of transferring and storing wealth—problems that exist in our universe, but not in the parallel one.

6. "The Attitude of Anarchism toward Industrial Combination," in *Liberty* XIV (December 1902): 3.

7. Equally, the National Organization for Women (N.O.W.), American feminism—in the mainstream—has tended to define "equality" as equal treatment for men and women under existing laws and equal representation within existing institutions. Certainly, mainstream feminists have called and do call for the reform of laws and the overhauling of institutions, such as the court system.

8. Margaret S. Marsh, *Anarchist Women 1870-1920* (Philadelphia: Temple University Press, 1981), 46.

9. Adrienne Rich, *Of Woman Born: Motherhood as Experience and Institution* (London: Virago, 1977), 57.

10. Catharine A. MacKinnon, *Toward a Feminist Theory of the State* (Cambridge, Mass.: Harvard University Press, 1989), 114.

11. Andrea Dworkin, *Our Blood: Prophecies and Discourses on Sexual Politics* (New York: Harper and Row, 1976), 48.

12. For an individualist theory of class, see Franz Oppenheimer, *The State* (Toronto: University of Toronto Press, 1940), or Ludwig von Mises, *Human Action: A Treatise on Economics* (San Francisco, Calif.: Fox & Wilkes, 1997).

13. The nineteenth century parallel to the twentieth century rebellion against "white male culture" is to be found in the social purity crusades that characterized the last decades of the 1800s. The purity crusades revolved around various issues such as pure food, prostitution, and temperance.

14. Marsh, *Anarchist Women 1870-1920*, 45.

15. The situation is further confused by the fact that individualists sometimes called the social arrangements they favored "socialism." The term, as they used it, had a different meaning than is currently ascribed to it. For example, an advertisement for a pamphlet entitled "Socialism!" in *The Word* included free trade and the issuance of private currency (free money) as expression of socialism. (*The Word* VIII [January 1880]: 4).

16. The article, "The Root of Prostitution," is reprinted in chapter 6 of this book.

17. The article is reprinted in chapter 6 of this book.

18. "The Wages of Sin is Death," in *Liberty* 81 (May 22, 1886): 5.

19. Ibid.

20. Twentieth-century individualist feminists generally express a different view of economics than their nineteenth-century counterparts. Nineteenth-century individualists accepted a labor theory of value. Although they championed the free market, they opposed capitalism as a distortion of the marketplace. By contrast, twentieth-century individualist feminism abandoned the labor theory of value and generally incorporated an advocacy of laissez-faire capitalism.

21. Moses Harman as quoted in *Lucifer* (May 8, 1885): 2.

22. *The Word* has been misidentified as a socialist periodical, yet its editor, Ezra H. Heywood, and the contents of its pages fall clearly and solidly within the individualist framework.

23. Ezra Heywood, ed., *Declaration of Sentiments and Constitution of the New England Reform League* (Boston, 1869), p. 6, Article 2.

24. For background information see Lewis Perry, *Radical Abolitionism: Anarchy and the Government of God in Anti-Slavery Thought* (Ithaca, N.Y.: Cornell University Press, 1973); and Blanche Glassman Hersh, *The Slavery of Sex: Feminist Abolitionists in America* (Chicago: University of Illinois Press, 1978). For an overview of women's participation in the American Revolution, see Linda Kerber, *Women of the Republic: Intellect and Ideology in Revolutionary America* (Chapel Hill, N.C.: University of North Carolina Press, 1980).

25. Aileen S. Kraditor, ed. *Up from the Pedestal: Selected Writings in the History of American Feminism*. (Chicago: Quadrangle Books, 1968), 13–14.

26. Ed. William Lloyd Garrison, available on microfilm from the Massachusetts Historical Society.

27. Hal D. Sears. *The Sex Radicals: Free Love in High Victorian America* (Lawrence, Kans.: Regents Press, 1977), p. 20.

28. The best source for women in freethought is George A. MacDonald's two-volume *50 Years of Freethought* (New York: Truth Seeker, 1929, 1931), which centered around the periodical *The Truth Seeker* (1873–present). Raymond Lee Muncey's *Sex and Marriage in Utopian Communities: 19th Century America* (Bloomington: Indiana University Press, 1973) provides a good general overview of feminism within utopian communities.

29. *Lucifer* succeeded the *Valley Falls Liberal* (1880) which began with no formal editors; it was, in turn, succeeded by *The American Journal of Eugenics* (1907–1910), ed. by Moses Harman.

30. More accurately stated, the first persecution galvanized radicals. When Heywood continued to flaunt the Comstock law, many fellow travelers began to blame the Heywoods for so flagrantly flaunting the law and, thus, bringing legal problems down upon themselves.

Chapter 1

1. The full title of this pamphlet is *Cupid's Yokes. The Binding Forces of Conjugal Life: An Essay to Consider Some Moral and Physiological Phases of Love and Marriage, Wherein Is Asserted the Natural Right and Necessity of Sexual Self-Government.* Estimates of its distribution range from tens of thousands to hundreds of thousands, and it was instrumental in the arrest of several prominent radicals, including D. M. Bennett, editor of *The Truth Seeker.* For an excellent discussion of the drama surrounding *Cupid's Yokes,* see *The Sex Radicals: Free Love in High Victorian America* (Lawrence, Kans.: Regents Press, 1977) by Hal D. Sears.

2. The full title is *Uncivil Liberty: An Essay to Show the True Basis of Property and the Causes of Its Inequitable Distribution* (Princeton, Mass., 1873).

3. *The Word* (September 1892): 2.

4. *The Word* (April 1881): 3.

5. "Tourist" as quoted in *The Word* (November 1881): 2–3.

6. Angela claimed to have psychic powers and embraced the spiritualism that characterized much of late nineteenth-century radicalism.

7. The full names of the children were: Vesta Vernon, Hermes Sidney Ezra, Psyche Ceres, and Angelo Tilton.

8. *The Word* (June 1890): 1.

9. For more on Lucy Tilton, see listing in Biographical Dictionary of the Women of *The Word* in chapter 2 of this book.

10. *The Word* (July 1873): 1.

11. No. 130, Vol. XI, #10, February Y.L. 11, p. 2. This quote and the personal details rendered in the preceding biographical sketch come from Angela's self-portrait in *The Word.*

12. Ibid.

13. Angela was a constant presence, often serving as an officer, at such organizations as the Union Reform League, the Anti-Tax League, and the Anti-Death League.

14. *The Word* (December 1873): 4

15. Ibid.

16. *The Word* (February 1874): 3

17. Ibid.

18. *The Word* (September 1874): 2. *The Word* (July 1879): 4 advertised, "Mountain Home … Will receive guests on and after July 1st. A quiet healthy summer resort centrally located: large, airy rooms, good fare, clear, invigorating atmosphere, a wide prospect, terms reasonable. Address: Mrs. A. T. Heywood, Princeton, Mass."

19. For more on J. Flora and Josephine Tilton, see listing in the Biographical Dictionary of the Women of *The Word* in chapter 2 of this book. It is not clear whether Anna Newell, another of Angela's sisters, was involved in the Lady Agents network.

20. *The Word* (May 1875): 2.

21. The free-love movement had nothing whatsoever to do with licentious behavior. Indeed, it aimed at the opposite. It demanded individuals take full responsibility for their actions and their consequences. Its political theme was: All sexual choices must be left to conscience of the adult parties involved, rather than be subjected to the State or to any other coercive influence.

22. *The Word* (May 1876): 2.

23. Angela's theories of sexual energy were deeply influenced by her belief in spiritualism—a belief common in radical circles of the day. Her specific form of spiritualism seemed to verge on reincarnation, as she remarked upon having lived three or four hundred years in all. The Sears book provides a particularly good overview of the impact and extent of spiritualist belief within the free love movement.

24. *The Word* (December 1876): 2. To his credit, Tucker resumed an editorship role of the periodical when Ezra was imprisoned for the first time under the Comstock law. His act cost him dearly: Tucker had been publishing an excellent freethought quarterly, *The Radical Review*, which he terminated in order to help his old friend.

25. *The Word* (July 1877): 3.

26. For an explanation of what nineteenth-century libertarians meant by the term "socialism," see introduction of this book.

27. *The Word* (April 1878): 2.

28. *The Word* (May 1878): 2.

29. *The Word* (July 1878): 2.

30. *The Word* (November 1879): 3.

31. Not everyone shared this opinion. One reader was critical of Ezra instead, and wrote, "… Mrs. Heywood [is] a real angel, but that Mr. Heywood is a clumsy fool, or an imposter.…" Ezra's critic went on to state a belief that Mrs. H. wrote *Cupid's Yokes* and "if only Mrs. Heywood wrote for *The Word* with her large heart and pure soul, sensible philanthropy, free love would spread and increase.…" *The Word* (December 1881): 2.

32. *The Word* (December 1879): 2.

33. *The Word* (October 1881): 3.

34. *The Word* (September 1889): 3.

35. For overviews of Ezra's several arrests, see Sears, *The Sex Radicals* and James J. Martin's *Men Against the State: The Expositors of Individualist Anarchism in America, 1827–1908* (Colorado Springs: Ralph Myles Publisher, Inc., 1970).

36. Because this essay is an introduction to Angela's articles, which follow, I am not pursuing many of interesting details and dramas of her life. One of them was the persecution she suffered at the hands of her brother-in-law Samuel R. Heywood. Ezra described Angela's ordeal, "Samuel R. Heywood … foreclosed a mortgage & put my family into the street, when, imprisoned for my faith, I was powerless to aid them.…" *The Word* (February 1883): 1.

37. *The Word* (March 1883): 2.

38. Jesse H. Jones, in *Foote's Health Monthly*, Sept. 1892, as quoted in *The Word* (October 1892): 2. An earlier arrest, in 1883, had been for the specific offense of giving away a pamphlet in which Angela's article "A Woman's View of It—No. 1" was reprinted. The article is reprinted later in this chapter.

39. As quoted in *The Word* (August 1883): 1.

40. Stephen Pearl Andrews quoted from *The Truth Seeker*, in *The Word* (October 1883): 1.

41. Ezra Heywood No. 190, Vol. XVII, No. 10, April Y.L. 17, p. 2. "History.—The second U.S. case ended Apr. 12, '83, in my acquittal, before Judge Nelson in Boston; but clandestine bigots had, on the sly, entered a third complaint, Feb 1st in Worcester; May 23 Dep. Sheriff Hair took me suddenly from home on a Bench Warrant, and I was held for trial in $1,000 bonds, H.H. Bigelow, surety. Below is the obscene matter indicted, one of a series of five articles which originally appeared in *The Word*, Jan.—May, '83."

Chapter 2

1. *The Word* (November 1877): 3.
2. This policy, conducted largely by Angela T. Heywood, insisted upon using biologically correct language to discuss sexual matters.
3. The Free Love Bureau (FLB) was a match-making service conducted through *TW*.
4. Of the FLB, *TW* wrote (November 1882, p. 2) "Flooded with letters & appeals for our opinions & advice relative to Sexuality, which, for lack of time & money, we cannot possibly give, we have opened the Free Love Bureau noted on 4th page; in Plato's phrase Lovers are persons in whose favor 'the gods have intervened'; we are glad to quicken Divine Life on *earth* everywise possible; A.T.H., ourself & near friends of both sexes will give personal attention to all cases submitted to the Bureau; courtship, marriage, divorces—the joining, sundering, ecstasy, tragedy, bliss, fears now vexing Altar & Courts will be considered, & Life, Liberty & Happiness encouraged without leave of priest or magistrate."
5. See chapter 4 of this book for more information.

Chapter 3

1. The best reference work on Moses Harman and the *Lucifer* circle is Hal D. Sears' *The Sex Radicals: Free Love in High Victorian America* (Lawrence, Kans.: Regents Press, 1977.) Some of Harman's papers are maintained by the Labadie Collection, University of Michigan, Ann Arbor. A complete run of *Lucifer* is available from the Kansas State Historical Society, Topeka.
2. For an overview of the circulation of birth control information in mid-to-late nineteenth century America, please see Janet Brodie *Contraception and Abortion in Nineteenth Century America* (Ithaca, N.Y.: Cornell Univ. Press, 1994).
3. Sears' *The Sex Radicals*, pp. 264–265. For more on Shaw's reaction see *Lucifer* (October 12, 1905), p. 392; (November 23, 1905), pp. 413–414; (January 4, 1906), pp. 437–438.
4. *Lucifer* (April 7, 1897), p. 106.
5. *Lucifer*, August 31, 1901, p. 264. The article offers an in-depth description of *Lucifer's* evolution and a rare glimpse of biographical material on Harman.
6. The National Liberal League was founded in 1876, largely due to the unifying efforts of Francis Abbot's periodical *The Index*. The history of the League is presented in Samuel P. Putnam's *Four Hundred Years of Freethought* (New York: Truth Seeker, 1894), pp. 528–34. Its early membership included Elizabeth Cady Stanton.
7. *Lucifer* (August 31, 1901), pp. 264–267.
8. This form of liberalism is often called "classical liberalism" and reflects the tradition of such thinkers as Locke and Cobden. It stresses individual rights and freedom as opposed to State interference.
9. Ibid.
10. The full title of this pamphlet is, "Motherhood in Freedom: A Short Essay or Sermon upon the Rights, Duties and Responsibilities of Motherhood, from the Standpoint of Equal Freedom for All and Special Privileges for None."
11. *Lucifer* (March 10, 1897), pp. 79–80.
12. Sears, p. 73.
13. For more on the Walker-Harman challenge to State marriage laws and the sex slavery of women, see pp. 125–132 of this book.

14. As quoted in *The Word* (March 1890), p. 2.
15. As quoted in *The Word* (April 1890), p. 2.
16. Sears, p. 115.
17. *Lucifer* (May 24, 1906), p. 517.
18. Letter dated Feb. 27, 1906.
19. *Lucifer* (June 7, 1906), p. 526.
20. In her article "Was My Life Worth Living?" published in *Harper's Monthly Magazine*, Vol. CLXX, December 1934, Goldman described Harman as "the pioneer of woman's emancipation from sexual bondage."

Chapter 4

1. Space restrictions do not allow me to publish a lengthy commentary on Edwin C. Walker and Lillian Harman, nor to include reprints of their work in this chapter. For more information, please see Sears' *The Sex Radicals*.

Chapter 5

1. See Holmes' listing in Biographical Dictionary of the Women of *The Word* in chapter 2 of this book.
2. An electronic version of this work is available at http://www.geocities.com/Wellesley/Gazebo/3073/.
3. *Liberty* (February 25, 1888): 5.
4. *Liberty* (May 26, 1888): 1.
5. *Liberty* (May 1899): 8.
6. *Liberty* (May 12, 1888): 6.
7. Ibid., 7.
8. *Liberty* (May 26, 1888): 6–7.
9. *Liberty* (June 23, 1888): 7.
10. "The Problem Which the Child Presents," in *Liberty* (September 1, 1888): 7.
11. *Liberty* (September 15, 1888): 7–8. Tucker's commentary on Victor's "Individualism, Communism, and Love."
12. *Liberty* (September 29, 1888): 7–8.
13. Her argument foreshadowed the debate that would erupt some hundred issues thereafter—among the men, not the women.
14. *Liberty* (September 3, 1892): 3.
15. "Children Under Anarchy," ibid., 2.
16. The circle around *Lucifer, the Light Bearer*—which included Lillian Harman—generally took a different tack on children's rights, preferring to acknowledge the soveriegnty of the child. Lillie White, who edited the periodical for a short period said: "...There is no person living more competent to decide the matter of association than the child itself. A fair acquaintance with both parents, freedom of choice, liberty to come and go, to visit or stay, will always be found, most convenient and effective in adjusting these relations."
17. "Ideal Marriage," in *Liberty* (January 19, 1889): 7.

Chapter 6

1. *Liberty* (March 6, 1886): p. 4.
2. "Proudhon and the Woman Question," in *Liberty* (March 12, 1887): 8. In making this statement, Kelly was reaffirming a strain of feminism that insists that women be accorded precisely the same treatment as men under just law, because both

are human beings with the same natural rights. This feminism aims to remove all legal obstacles and privileges that are based upon gender.

3. Ibid.

4. Ibid.

5. *Liberty* (September 12, 1885): 5.

6. "A Woman's Warning to Reformers," in *Liberty* (January 23, 1886): 7.

7. Ibid.

8. "The Unconscious Evolution of Mutual Banking," in *Liberty* (February 12, 1887): 7.

9. "The Wages of Sin is Death," in *Liberty* (May 22, 1886): 5.

10. Ibid.

11. Her two brothers—John F. Kelly and Alan Kelly—apparently agreed. See Wm. Gary Kline, *The Individualist Anarchists: A Critique of Liberalism* (Lanham, Md.: University Press of America, 1987), 63. The two brothers were also contributors to *Liberty*.

12. *Liberty* (June 19, 1886): 8.

13. As reported in Paul Avrich's *An American Anarchist: The Life of Voltairine de Cleyre* (Princeton, N.J.: Princeton University, 1978), 49–50.

14. *Living My Life*, vol. 1 (New York: Dover, 1970), 10.

15. *Liberty* (September 18, 1886): 5.

16. *Liberty* (September 10, 1887): pp. 6–8. Speech reprinted later in this chapter.

17. Ibid.

18. Ibid.

Select Bibliography

Paul Avrich, *An American Anarchist: The Life of Voltairine de Cleyre.* Princeton, N.J.; Princeton University, 1978.

Janet Brodie, *Contraception and Abortion in Nineteenth Century America.* Ithaca, N.Y.: Cornell University Press, 1994.

Ellen Carol Dubois. *Feminism and Suffrage.* Ithaca, New York: Cornell University Press, 1980.

Andrea Dworkin. *Our Blood: Prophecies and Discourses on Sexual Politics.* New York: Harper and Row, 1976.

Emma Goldman. *Living My Life.* 2 vols. New York: Dover, 1930.

Blanche Glassman Hersh. *The Slavery of Sex: Feminist Abolitionists in America.* Chicago: University of Illinois Press, 1978.

Ezra H. Heywood. *Cupid's Yokes.* Princeton, Mass., 1879.

_____, ed. *Declaration of Sentiments and Constitution of the New England Reform League.* Boston, 1869.

Linda Kerber. *Women of the Republic: Intellect and Ideology in Revolutionary America.* Chapel Hill, N.C.: University of North Carolina Press, 1980.

Wm. Gary Kline. *The Individualist Anarchists: A Critique of Liberalism.* Lanham, Md.: University Press of America, 1987.

Aileen S. Kraditor, ed. *Up from the Pedestal: Selected Writings in the History of American Feminism.* Chicago: Quadrangle Books, 1968.

George A. MacDonald. *50 Years of Freethought.* 2 vols. New York: Truth Seeker, 1929, 1931.

Catharine A. MacKinnon. *Toward a Feminist Theory of the State.* Cambridge, Mass.: Harvard University Press, 1989.

Margaret S. Marsh. *Anarchist Women 1870–1920.* Philadelphia: Temple University Press, 1981.

James J. Martin. *Men Against the State: The Expositors of Individualist Anarchism in America, 1827–1908.* Colorado Springs: Ralph Myles Publisher, Inc., 1970.

Wendy McElroy, ed. *Freedom, Feminism, and the State,* 2nd ed. New York: Holmes & Meier, 1991.

_____. *Sexual Correctness: The Gender-Feminist Attack on Women.* Jefferson, North Carolina: McFarland, 1996.

Ludwig von Mises. *Human Action: A Treatise on Economics.* San Francisco, Calif.: Fox & Wilkes, 1997.

Raymond Lee Muncey. *Sex and Marriage in Utopian Communities: 19th Century America.* Bloomington: Indiana University Press, 1973.

Franz Oppenheimer. *The State.* Toronto: University of Toronto Press, 1940.

Daphne Patai. *Heterophobia: Sexual Harassment and the Future of Feminism.* New York: Rowman & Littlefield, 1998.

J. Edward Pawlick. *Freedom Will Conquer Racism (and Sexism)*. Wellesley, Mass.: Mustard Seeds, Inc., 1998.

Lewis Perry. *Radical Abolitionism: Anarchy and the Government of God in Antislavery Thought*. Ithaca, N.Y.: Cornell University Press, 1973.

Samuel P. Putnam. *Four Hundred Years of Freethought*. New York: Truth Seeker, 1894.

Adrienne Rich. *Of Woman Born: Motherhood as Experience and Institution*. London: Virago, 1977.

Hal D. Sears. *The Sex Radicals: Free Love in High Victorian America*. Lawrence, Kans.: Regents Press, 1977.

Cathy Young. *Ceasefire: Why Women and Men Must Join Forces to Achieve True Equality*. New York: Free Press, 1999.

Index

Abbott, Lyman 171–172
abolitionism 11
Adams, Lizzie 49
Advance Thought 69
Advertisers' Guide 115
Ady, Mr. 120, 122
Alarm 169
Albertson, Mary E.B. 49
Allen, Sarah S. 49
Allyn, C. Fannie 49
Alumnae Association of the Women's
  Medical College of the New York
  Infirmary for Women and Children
  168, 175
American Free Dress League 72, 76, 82
American Journal of Eugenics 97
American Labor Reform League
  (ALRL) 17, 48, 51, 52, 56, 59, 60, 61,
  66, 67, 68, 69, 74, 75, 78, 79, 81, 82
American Woman Suffrage Association
  95
American Woman's Emancipation
  Society 23, 50, 56, 62, 63, 64, 66,
  67, 68, 69, 71, 76, 79
Ames, Lucia True 49
Anarchist Women 4, 8
Andrews, Mary D. 49
Andrews, Stephen Pearl 29–32, 50,
  81–82, 140, 151
Anthony, Susan B. 11
Anti-Death League (ADL) 48, 49, 51,
  53, 55, 56, 58, 62, 65, 67, 70, 74,
  75
Anti-Tax League (ATL) 49, 57, 69, 70,
  74, 75, 76, 78, 81, 85, 86
Anti-Usury Society (AUS) 49, 55
Appleton, Henry (Honorius) 166
Association of Libertarian Feminists
  v

Atwell, Mrs. 49
Bacon, Francis 182, 183
Bailey, Sadie 49–50
Bakounine [Bakunin], Michael 136
Ballot Box 85
Ballou, Addie L. 50
Barry, James H. 97
Barter, H.L. 60, 73
Bax, E. Belford 143, 144
Beaman, P.A. 50
Beaulieu, Paul Leroy 185
Beckwith, E.M. 50
Beecher (scandal) 85
Bell, W.S. 80
Bennett, D.M. 61, 64, 75, 78, 80, 82,
  86, 119
Besant, Annie 51, 188–189
Birney, Catherine H. 51
birth control 20, 32–34, 44–47
Blackstone, Lydia Eve 51
Blackwell, Alice Stone 95
Bolles, Ellen M. 51
Bolton, Mary 51
Boston Advertiser 61
Boston Herald 52
Boston Investigator 20, 57
Bowdrie, Annie W. 51
Brace, C.L. 187
Bradford, S.B. (Attorney General)
  129
Brigham, Nahum (Mrs.) 51
Brinkerhoff, Mrs. 51
Brown, John 60
Bullock, Etta 51
Butler, Gen. 43
Buxton, Maria L. 51, 83

Caird, Mona (Mrs.) 52, 141
Caldwell (Judge) 121, 122

201

Cambridge Press 24
Campbell, A.F. (Mrs.) 52
Campbell, Rachel 52–53
Campbell, Sara Crist 96
capitalism 8–9, 144, 165–166 *see*
  Woman's Labor
Carlyle, Thomas 172, 181
Center for Libertarian Studies v
Chandler, Lucinda B. 53
Channing, Dr. Wm. F. 36
Chapman, H. Dean (Mrs.) 53
Chappelle, S.L. (Mrs.) 53
Charlotte Cushman, Reminiscences of her
  Earth Life with Some of her Spirit
  Experiences 84
Chase, Josephine 53–54
Chase, Sarah B. (Dr.) 54
Cheney, A.C. (Etta) 54–55
Cheney, Cordelia (Mrs.) 55
Chernyshevsky, N.G. 143–144, 148
Chicago Radical Review 71
children *see* family
Christian Science Monitor 69
Christian Union 171
church and state *see* marriage
Civil War 11, 90
Claflin, Tennie (Tennessee) 55
class 4–6
Clemens, G.C. 129
Collins, Jennie 55
Collins, W.W. 51
Colman, Lucy N. 55
Comstock, Anthony (Law) 12, 19, 20,
  26–29, 43–47, 50, 54, 55, 57, 65, 66,
  71, 73, 78, 81, 87, 90, 92, 115, 138
Constitution (U.S.) 11, 101
Cook, Rev. Joseph 26, 29
Co-operative Publishing Company 24,
  50, 78, 79
Corson, Miss 167
Coughlin, Michael v
Cowles, Julia 56
Crane, Jonathan Mayo 95
Crosby, Ernest Howard 112
"'Culture' and Thought" 170–173
Cupid's Yokes (CY) 19, 26, 43–44, 49,
  50, 51, 52, 60, 64, 70, 73, 75, 78,
  79–81, 82, 83
Cushman, Charlotte 64
Cutler, Mary A. 56
Cutter, Abbie E. (Dr.) 56

Daily Journal (Chicago) 124
Daily Tribune (Chicago) 124
The Dangerous Classes of New York
  187
Daniels, E.L. (Mrs.) 56
Darrow, Clarence 97
Davidson, Clara Dixon 12, 140
Day, Sarah M. 56
Day, Stanley 115
de Barau, Mms. 185
Debs, Eugene 97
Decalogue 102
de Cleyre, Voltairine 57, 167–168
Denton, Elizabeth M.F. 57–58
DePuy, Alvira 58
DePuy, Etta 58
Dexter, Fannie C. 58
d'Haussonville, M. 185–186
Diana 73
Dickenson, Anna E. 58
Dietrick, Ellen Battelle 12
Dike, Abbie C. (Mrs.) 58
Dike, Mary S. 58
Dike, Mattie 58
Dillard (Marshall) 119
Dillingham, Mrs. 58
Dingwell, Mary (Mrs.) 58
Doane (Monsignor) 171
Doane, Jennie A. (Mrs.) 59, 78
A Double Wedding: or, How She Was
  Won 84
Duchatelet, Parent 185
Dworkin, Andrea 5
Dynamic Sociology 186

Eaton, Amie (Mrs.) 59
Egli, Minnie Maria (Mrs.) 59
Eldridge, Laura C. 19–20
Emerson, Ralph Waldo 11, 22
L'Enfant Terrible 140
equality 3–4, 6, 144–146
"The Ethics of Sexuality" 39–43
Everybody's 124

Fair Play 62
Fairbanks, Fanny 59
Fales, Anna 55
family 105–111, 137–141, 147, 149–154,
  158–163
Faucher, Leon 186
Field, Kate 12, 59

Financial Problems 71
Fisher, Marie C. 60
Fletcher, Susan Willis 59
Follett, Maria L. 60–61
Foote's Health Monthly 29, 54
Foster, Abbie K. 61
Foster, Judge 118, 119, 120, 121, 122
Foster, Stephen S. 61
Foundation Principles 83
Fowler, Charles 49, 50
Frederick the Great 182
free love 11–12, 40–42, 50, 90, 97–105,
    105–108; *see* Moses Harman
Free Love Bureau (FLB) 49, 55, 58,
    59
"A Free Man's Creed" 97–105
"Free Unions and Parental Responsi-
    bility" 105–111
Freedom 51
Freethought 59, 102
Frick, Mr. 61
Fruits of Philosophy 78

Gage, Matilda Joslyn 104
Gambetta, Léon 133
Gardner, Helen H. 61
Garrison, William Lloyd 22, 65, 100,
    112, 115
George, Henry 176
Giles, A.E. (Esq.) 26
Gilluly, W.F. 129
Gilman, Charlotte Perkins 138
Goldman, Emma 13, 61, 97, 168
Gould, Jay 172
government *see* political system
Gramont, duc de 141
The Greatest of the Social Evils 186
Green, H.L. 80, 99, 102
Greene, Anne Shaw 61
Greene, Bessie 61
Greene, Wm. B. 56, 61
Gregg, Ida (Mrs.) 61
Gregg, Ken v
Grimke, Angelina 1–2
The Grimke Sisters 51

Hale, Rev. Edward Everett 170,
    172–173
Hall, S. Mira 61
Hammond, Orpha 61–62
Hammond, Rev. Ranter 71

Harman, Ellen Beard (Dr.) 62
Harman, George 91, 93, 115, 117, 125
Harman, Lillian 12, 13–14, 62, 71, 91,
    93, 112, 123–124, 125–131
Harman, Moses 12, 13, 62, 83, 84;
    biography 89–97; reprints 97–124,
    125, 126, 127
Harte, Bret 187
Harvard University Press 10
Hayes, President 65
Haymarket Incident 167–168
Heinzen, Karl 71
Henck, Mary H. 62
Henrietta (pseudonym) 136, 141
Henry, Patrick 34
Herald (Newburyport) 79
Heroines of Freethought 82
Hewes, Eliza 62–63
Heywood, Angela Fiducia Tilton
    12–13, 58, 62, 63, 73, 75, 78, 79, 80,
    83, 85; biography 19–32; reprints
    32–47
Heywood, Angelo 21
Heywood, Ezra H. 12–13, 17, 19–22,
    23–31, 43–47, 50, 51, 53, 54, 55, 56,
    57, 59, 62, 63, 64, 65, 66, 71, 72, 73,
    75, 78, 79, 80, 82, 84, 85
Heywood, Hermes 21
Heywood, Psyche 21
Heywood, Samuel R. 29
Heywood, Vesta 21, 63
Higby, Annie E. 63
High, Jack v
History of Woman Suffrage 11
History of the Woman's Costume Reform
    77
Hoar, Dorcas Roper (Mrs.) 63
Hoffman, Clara (Mrs.) 63
Holmes, Lizzie M. 64, 97
Holmes, Sarah Elizabeth 14, 63; biog-
    raphy 135–141; reprints 141–142,
    149–158, 158–163
Honorius (pseudonym) *see* Appleton,
    Henry
Hooker, Beecher (Mrs.) 51
Housch, E.T. (Mrs.) 63
housework 22
Hughes, Elizabeth 63
Hull, Elvira 64
Hull, Mary Florence 64
Hull, Mattie *see* Mattie Sawyer

Hull, Moses 23–24, 64, 70
Hull, Sawyer & Co. 71
Hull's Crucible 23–24, 59, 64, 70, 79
The Humanitarian 86
Hunt, C.F. 64
Hunt, Hannah, J. 64
Hunt, Helen 64
Hunt, S.A. 64
Hutchinson, Anne 10
Hutchinson, Lydia (Mrs.) 64
Huxley, T.H. 178–179, 181

"The Inconsistency of Governmental-
   ists" 188–189
Independent 64
individualist feminism 1–3, 4–12
Ingalls, Olive H.F. (Mrs.) 64
Ingersoll, Robert G. (Col.) 71, 104,
   109, 110
International Working People's Associ-
   ation of Boston 61
Ireland 136
Irene, or the Road to Freedom 50,
   118
Irish Women's Council 170
Irish World 166

Jackson, Josephine 64
Jacobi, Mary Putnam 181
Jesus 36, 68, 115
Johnes, Rev. Jesse H. 26
Joslin, L.K. (Mrs.) 64–65
Joslyn, Abbie 65
Joyce, A.P. (Mrs.) 65
justice 6–7

Kansas Liberal 91
Kelly, Gertrude B. 7, 8–10, 12, 14–15,
   136; biography 164–170; reprints
   170–189
Kendrick, Laura 65
Kimball (Mrs.) 65
Kingets Health Journal 54
Kingman, Martha C. 65
Kingsford, Anna 181
Knapp, Abbie (Dr.) 65
Knights of Labor 58
Koontz, Alan v
Kraditor, Aileen S. 11
Kropotkine [Kropotkin], P.A. 189
Kropotkin, Sophie 136

Lady Agents 24–25 *see* Tilton, J.
   Flora; Tilton, Josie S.
La Guardia, Fiorello 170
Laissez Faire Books v
Lake, H.S. (Mrs.) 65
Lant, Anna M. 65
Lant, John 65
Law of Population 51
L'Enfant Terrible 140
League of Women Voters 4
Lee, Ann 65
Leland, Mary A. (Mrs.) 65
Lenont, S.J. (Mrs.) 66
Leonard, Cynthia (Mrs.) 66
Lesigne, Ernest 136
Lewis, Helen M. 66
Leys, Jennie 66
The Liberal 81
Liberal League 8, 62 *see* National
   Liberal League
The Liberator 11, 79
Libertas 71
Liberty v, 8, 12, 14, 15, 95, 135, 138,
   139, 140, 164, 166, 169, 188; prospec-
   tus 133–134; reprints 141–164,
   170–189
"Liberty for Man, Woman and Child"
   104
*Libra Dawn, or Dawn of Liberty, A
   Sequel to* Cupid's Yokes 60, 72
Lincoln, Elmer (Mrs.) 66
Lindsay, Eleanor L. 66
The Little Freethinker 73
Little Lessons for Little Folks 73
Livermore, Mary C. (Mrs.) 66
Living My Life 13, 168
Lloyd J. William 139, 147, 160
Locke, Angela 22
Lohman, Ann 66
London Laborers and the London Peer 186
London Times 186
Longley, J.S. (Mrs.) 66
Louis XIV 177
love 32–43, 141–163 *see* free love
"Love and Labor" 37–39
Love and Theology 85
Love and Transition 77
Lucifer, the Light Bearer 10, 12, 13, 14,
   62, 84, 89, 91–97, 125; prospectus 87;
   reprints 97–124
Lum, Dyer D. 28, 169

Macdonald, A.C. (Mrs.) 66
MacDonald, George 59, 95
Mackinley, Frances Rose 66
MacKinnon, Catharine 5
Malthus 147
Man and Superman 89
Markland letter 92, 94, 117–119, 121–123
marriage 14, 20, 35–37, 40, 99–105, 105–108, 113–114, 125–131, 137–141, 141–149, 149–158
Marriage As It Was, As It Is 51
Marsh, Margaret S. 4, 8
Martin, James J. v
Martineau, Harriet 66
Marvin, Bertha 12
Marx, Karl 133, 176
Mayflower (Halifax) 79
Mayhew 186
McCarty, Josephine 66
McGee, Mrs. 55
Melvin, Dolly A. (Mrs.) 67
Memoirs of a Millionaire 49
The Memory Hole v
Men Against the State v
"Men's Laws and Love's Laws" 35–37
Meriwether, E.A. (Mrs.) 67
Merton, Minnie (Mrs.) 67
Michel, Louise 31, 67
Middlebrook, Anna M. (Mrs.) 67–68
Mill, John Stuart 167, 188
Miller, Leo 76
"Miller-Strickland Defense" 76
Miller-Strickland, Edwin 76
Mitchell, Seward 53
morality 7
Mott, Lucretia 43
Mulliken, Lula (Mrs.) 68

Nash, Helen 68
National American Woman's Suffrage Association 4
National Defense Association (NDA) 49, 65, 70, 78
National Liberal League (NLL) 49, 55, 71, 76, 91
natural law 2–3, 11
Nemesis 169
Newark Bureau of Association Charities 170
Newark Liberal League 164

New England Free Love League (NEFLL) 25, 26, 49, 51, 52, 53, 55, 56, 57, 58, 59, 60, 65, 67, 69, 70, 74, 75, 76, 78, 79, 82, 83, 84, 85
New England Labor Reform League (NELRL) 10, 17, 22, 23, 49, 51, 53, 55, 56, 57, 58, 59, 61, 64, 65, 68, 69, 70, 74, 75, 78, 79, 81, 82, 83, 84
New York Sun 55, 67, 186
New York Times 73, 89
New York Tribune 187
New York Women's Medical College 8–9
Newton, Emma A. 68
Newton, Isaac 182
Notable American Women 10

Of Woman Born 5
O'Neill, Dr. 94
O'Neill letter 83, 84, 94, 119, 120, 121–123
Our Age 83
Our Blood 5
Overmeyer (Attorney) 120, 129
Overton, Mary 68

Pall Mall Gazette 184
Palmer, E.L. (Mrs.) 68
Parmelee, Fanny H. 68
Parsons, Albert 55, 68
Parsons, Lucy 55, 68
Patterson, L.M. (Mrs.) 68–69
Paul (the Apostle) 114
Paul, Ellen Frankel v
Peden, Joseph v
"The Penis Trust" 28
Pentecost 54
Perry (District Attorney) 122
Peterson, M. 69
Philbrooke, Eliza W. 69
Phillips (Judge) 121, 122
Phillips, Wendell 22, 65, 79
Physician, A. 186
Pickering, J.F. 44–45
Pilot (Le Claire, Iowa) 60
Pinney, Lucien V. 20–22
Plays Pleasant and Unpleasant 124
Plunkett, M.H. (Mrs.) 69
Poems (Tillotson) 77
political system 4, 8–10

"The Political Theory of Mazzini and the International" 136
Polley, Chappel (Mrs.) 69
Pomeroy, Brick 69
Poole, L.M.R. (Mrs.) 69–70
Post, Louis F. 97
poverty *see* women and labor
Prescott, Emeline A. 70
Principles of Sociology 175–176
"The Problem Which the Child Presents" 158–163
property 3
prostitution 23–24, 25, 33–34, 184–187
Prostitution de Paris 185
Prostitution in London 186
Proudhon, Pierre-Joseph 143
Public 97, 124

radical feminism 4–7
Radical Review 79
Ramsden, Lucy A. (Mrs.) 70
Reclaiming the Mainstream v
Record-Herald 124
Replogle, Georgia 70
"Reply to Victor" 136, 138–139, 149–158
Restell, Madam *see* Ann Lohman
"Review of Prosecution in Kansas" 115–123
Revue des Deux Mondes 186
Rice, Sadie (Mrs.) 70
Rich, Adrienne 5
Rich, Andrea Millen v
The Rights of Women and the Sexual Relations 71
Robert Elsmere 84
Robinson, Olive N. 70
Rodriguez, Bradford vi
Roosevelt, Alice 113
"The Root of Prostitution" 164–165, 184–187
Rothbard, Murray N. v
Royal, Grace 70
Russell, M.A. (Mrs.) 70
Ryan, M. 186

San Francisco Star 97
Sanger, Margaret 13
Sargent, J.T. (Mrs.) 70
Saunders, M. (Mrs.) 70
Sauton, George 136

Savonarola 172
Sawyer, Mattie E.B. (Mattie Hull) 70–71
Scheuck, Susan 90
Schreiner, Olive 71, 136
Schumm, Emma 12
Schumm, Georgia 71
Science of Life Club 66
The Science of Society 140, 151
Sears, Hal D. 11
Seaver, Horace 71
Seneca Falls Conference 135
Servetus, Michael 60
Severance, Juliet 12, 71–72
sex/sexuality 43–47, 147
The Sex Radicals 11
Sexual Science Association 56, 59, 69, 70
Shakespeare, William 99
"Shall Woman Beg for Liberty?" 136, 141–142
Shaw, George Bernard 89, 97, 124
Shepard, Olivia F. 74
Shull, Belle C. 72
Sims, Dr. 54, 55
Slenker, Elmina 70, 73–74
Smith, Charlotte 74
Smith, E.D. (Mrs.) 74
Smith, Isabella (Miss) 74
Smith, K.R. (Mrs.) 74
Smith, L.E. 74
Smith, Laura Cuppy 74
Spencer, Eliza F. 75
Spencer, Herbert 167, 175–176
"The Socialistic Letter" 136
Stanton, Elizabeth Cady 43, 75
Stanton, Kate 75
"State Aid to Science" 8, 168–169, 175–184
"State v. Walker and another" 125–131
Steinmetz, L.G. (Mrs.) 75
Stetson, Charlotte Perkins 12
Steward, Mary B. 75
Still, Emma (Dr.) 75
Stone, Josephine R. 75
The Story of an African Farm 71
Strickland, Mattie 75–76
Stuart, Frances A. (Mrs.) 76
Sumner, Charles 51
Swain, J.H. 27

Taming of the Shrew 103–104
Taylor, Joan Kennedy v
Tchernychewsky [Chernyshevsky],
  N.G. 143–144, 148
Tell, William 115
Templeton, M. (Mrs.) 76
Thoreau, Henry David 11
Three Dreams in a Desert 136
Tibbals, Sarah L. 76
Tillotson, Mary E. (Mrs.) 76–78
Tilton, Daniel 22
Tilton, J. Flora 24, 78
Tilton, Josephine 12, 24, 79–81
Tilton, Lucy M. (Mrs.) 22, 23, 37, 81–82
Titus, Francis W. (Mrs.) 82
"To *Lucifer*'s Friends: Greeting and
  Farewell" 111–115
Tomorrow Magazine 124
Toward a Feminist Theory of the State 5
Townsend, M.S. (Mrs.) 82
transcendentalism 11
Truth, Sojourner 82
The Truth Seeker 55, 60, 71, 72, 73, 74,
  81, 95
Tucker, Benjamin R. v, 3, 12, 25, 26, 71,
  72, 79, 95, 133–134, 135, 136, 139-141
Tufts, Helen 12
Twiss, H.V. 68
"The Two Socialisms: Governmental
  and Anarchistic" 136

Uncivil Liberty 19, 51, 78
Underwood, Sara A. 82
Union Reform League (URL) 49, 51,
  52, 53, 55, 57, 58, 59, 61, 62, 63, 65,
  66, 67, 69, 70, 71, 74, 75, 76, 78, 81,
  82, 85
Up from the Pedestal 11

Valley Falls Liberal 91
Valley Falls Liberal League 91
Van Benthuysen, Geo. C. 75
Vance, Virginia E. 82
Vibbert, S. Alice (Dr.) 82
Virchow 177
"A Visit to the Prisoner" 123–124
Voltaire 133
The Voluntaryist v

Wade 187
Wainwright, Deputy Marshall 111, 114

Waisbrooker, Lois (Mrs.) 12, 82–83,
  84, 120
Waite, Mr. 27
Wales, Cordelia (Mrs.) 83
Walker, Dr. (Mrs.) 84
Walker, Edwin Cox 13–14, 62, 71, 93,
  115, 117, 125–131
Walker, James L. 188
Walton, Helen M. 84
Ward 186
Ward, Humphrey (Mrs.) 84
Warfield, C.A. (Mrs.) 84
Warner, Lydia M. 84
Warren, A. 138, 160
Warren, Josiah 61, 165
Watner, Carl v
Westminister Review 52
Whatley 184
What's To Be Done? 148, 157–158
Wheeler, A.D. 58
Whipple, Hope (Mrs.) 84
White, Lillie D. 64, 84
Whitehead, Celia B. (Mrs.) 59, 84, 94,
  117, 118–119, 121
Whitman, John L. (Warden) 112
Whitney, M.J. (Mrs.) 84
The Wife of Number 4,237 136
Williams, Martha (Dr.) 85
Williams, Sarah R.L. 85
Wilmans, Helen 85
Wilson (United States Commissioner)
  115
Wilson, Rev. Dr. 171
Winslow, Mary A. 85
Winsted Press 20, 73, 74, 86
Wolley, Celia Parker 85
Woman, Church and State 104
"The Woman Question" 136–137,
  143–149
Woman's Journal 95, 96
woman's labor 22–23, 33, 37–39,
  52–53, 164–165, 170–173; *see also*
  prostitution
"Woman's Love: Its Relations to Man
  and Society" 32–34
Woman's National Labor Conven-
  tion 49, 58, 61, 66, 68, 84,
  85
Woman's Suffrage Society 51
"The Woman's View of It—No. 1
  through No. 5" 43–47

"A Woman's Warning to Reformers"
   173–175
The Woman's World 85
Women and Economics 138
Women at Work 63
Woodhull, Maud 86
Woodhull, Victoria C. 62, 68–69, 85–86
Woodhull and Beecher scandal 85
Woodhull and Claflin Weekly (*W&CW*)
   49, 55, 72, 85
Worcester Telegram 59
The Word v, 10, 12, 13, 14, 19–20,
   24–32, 48, 49–86; prospectus, 17;
   reprints 32–47

Working Classes 187
The Working Woman 74
The World's Friend 72
Wright, Francis 10

Yarros, Victor 14, 136–141; reprints
   143–149, 149–158
Yerrinton, Mr. 79
Young, S.E. (Mrs. Dr.) 86
Yours or Mine 79

Zelm *see* Holmes, Sarah Elizabeth
Zube, John v